How to Manage
a Successful Software Project

How to Manage a Successful Software Project

Methodologies, Techniques, Tools

Sanjiv Purba
David Sawh
Bharat Shah

A Wiley–QED Publication
John Wiley & Sons, Inc.
New York • Chichester • Brisbane • Toronto • Singapore

Publisher: Katherine Schowalter
Editor: Robert Elliott
Managing Editor: Maureen B. Drexel
Text Design & Composition: Publishers' Design and Production Services, Inc.

ISBN 0-471-04401-6

Printed in the United States of America

10 9 8 7 6 5 4 3 2 1

Contents

Preface

OVERVIEW

As companies discover new ways to become more efficient, customer friendly, and competitive, responsibility for actual implementation continues to fall on information systems (IS) managers and staff. This will continue well into the next century.

The last few years have seen a surge in business philosophies, such as restructuring, downsizing, rightsizing, and re-engineering, all aimed at helping businesses survive and grow in an intensely competitive business environment. All of these philosophies also have at least one other characteristic in common. At some point, an IS project manager is generally empowered to deliver a computer application to support the business decisions.

The last decade has also seen a surge in the variety of computer technology available (e.g., database servers, languages, operating systems, network software, GUIs, pen-based computing, and voice automation). A broad range of architectures (e.g., open systems, client/server, distributed) allow many of these products to be connected in innovative ways for a variety of applications. Here too, an IS project manager is asked to step in, regardless of the nature of the technical solution.

The project manager's role appears to be secure in the future; however, one additional thing is clear. With the momentum of business changes, coupled with a continuing technological revolution, the management discipline is becoming more complicated and critical than before.

PURPOSE OF THIS BOOK

This book is about management at the project level. It is intended to provide information to project managers, or aspiring project managers, to allow them to deliver IS projects successfully. Guidelines and techniques presented in this book are based on the actual work experiences of the authors, and supported by advice provided by over 50 managers who were interviewed or surveyed for this book.

This book provides a framework for introducing projects in a planned, cohesive, and coordinated manner, so that they are driven by demonstrated business needs. The book can be used as a handbook to initiate, develop, and implement projects on time and within budget. A new methodology, iterative project development methodology (IPDM), is introduced in this book. IPDM has been successfully used on a broad range of projects, including client/server architecture, mainframe applications, and open systems.

The authors have written this book with the hope that it will stimulate critical thinking and provide an opportunity to analyze business needs and objectives, assess risks and benefits, and understand the total lifecycle costs of a project before it is actually undertaken.

Within this framework, this book demonstrates how typical problems associated with information technology projects—such as changing business requirements and specifications, cost overruns, projects behind schedule, and poor product quality—can be significantly minimized.

PROJECT MANAGEMENT SURVEY

Over 50 Information Systems managers were surveyed and interviewed on a variety of management-oriented questions to provide empirical evidence that supports key conclusions presented in this book. Some interesting discoveries were made or confirmed through the survey:

❑ A departure from traditional project planning has been effective in delivering value to clients. Projects that are structured for implementation within five to eight months typically enjoy high customer satisfaction.

❑ Project development methodologies must be flexible and not merely follow a recipe-like set of activities.

❑ Responsibility for delivering projects is shared equally between Information Systems and business users.

❑ There is strong consensus among managers that common, quantifiable factors derail projects, such as bad planning, changing requirements, and poor communication.

AUDIENCE

The audience of this book includes a broad cross-section of readers who are interested in the project management discipline. The book is aimed at systems developers, project managers, users of systems, managers, executives who pay for the development and implementation of projects, computer software and hardware vendors, information technology planners, business and systems analysts, and university students.

The book can be used by individuals working on small or large projects. The project management approach discussed in this book can be applied to any phase of the systems development lifecycle, either to in-house projects or projects that are contracted out to vendors.

ORGANIZATION OF THE BOOK

The approach to project management in this book is based on understanding the fundamental building blocks shown in Figure i.1.

These building blocks show that the management of typical IS projects involves the following steps:

1. Receive executive approval to initiate a project.
2. Examine past experiences in building a project plan.
3. Select a suitable project development methodology and update the project plan accordingly.

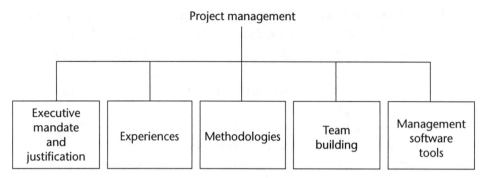

FIGURE i.1 Building blocks of project management.

4. Build a suitable project team.
5. Manage the project using suitable software or other tools and techniques.

The chapters in this book are divided using these categories.

Basic Project Management and Definitions

Chapter 1   The Role of a Project Manager

Chapter 4   Project Planning and Scheduling

Block 1. Executive Mandate and Justification

Chapter 2   Project Management Concepts

Chapter 3   Project Initiation and Justification

Block 2. Experiences

Chapter 5   Why Projects Fail

Chapter 6   Why Projects Succeed—Case Studies

Block 3. Methodologies

Chapter 7   Iterative Project Development Methodology (IPDM)

Chapter 9   Outsourcing of Information Technology Projects

Block 4. Team Building

Block 5. Management Software Tools

The appendices provide information that supplements the chapters.

ACKNOWLEDGMENTS

We wish to thank over 50 practicing project managers who generously volunteered their time to discuss their project management experiences with us and also responded to the management survey conducted for this book: Tony Alderson, Diane Ali, J. Agsalog, William Bixby, Steve Brandt, Karen Burnside, Bob Carter, Dennis Choptiany, Ian Clarke, Gillian Coulter, Barry Darbey, D. Dattani, Selim El Raheb, Peter Fernie, Mike Flynn, V. Gibson, Dora Gugliotta, Sharad Goel, Bob Habkirk, Joanne Hiscock, Stan Hodge, Bill Houston, R. Hunt, R. Jahagirdar, Ron Kawchuk, J. Lee, Danny Leung, G. Lewis, B. McCaan, Robin McNeil, H. McVea, D. Middleton, John Miniaci, Stellios Missirlis, M. Honeth, R. Pierce, Glen Pleshko, Frances Renaud, Gerald Roddau, Mary Ann Romaniw, George Ross, John Rylarsdam, W.R. Patrick, John Shelley, Mike Shields, J. Simonetti, Stewart Slassford, Eric Steinberg, Graham

Talbot, Ashok Tandon, Mike Tkachuk, R. Tanjuakio, Kim Toffoli, F. Yagi, H. Vakharia, Ronald A. Wencer, Richard Woodrow, Tanya Zablishinsky.

Thanks also to James Fehrenbach, Christine Stevens, Christine Burnett, Fayek Bastowros, and Vena Sawh. Special thanks to Peter Fernie.

Special thanks to Bill Houston (Senior Management Consultant and Project Manager) and Ron Wencer (Senior Management Consultant and Project Manager) for reviewing this book.

DEDICATION

This book is dedicated to our family and friends.

How to Manage
a Successful Software Project

The Role of a Project Manager

1

OVERVIEW

In this chapter a reader will learn about:

- An approach for managing projects
- The management pyramid
- The flow of management authority
- The role of the hands-on manager
- Project lifecycle

THE NEW HANDS-ON MANAGER: RETURNING TO THE FRONT LINES

This book is concerned with managers at the base of the pyramid who are directly responsible for the delivery of information systems (IS) projects from inception to implementation. These managers have multiple levels of authority, including the ability to hire, fire, and promote. More importantly, they are close to the front lines on a daily basis. These are managers of projects, rather than managers of multiple departments. The issues that confront hands-on managers are very different from the ones confronting managers closer to the top of the management pyramid.

The hands-on manager may delegate responsibility to other managers, project leaders, architects, or analysts for key activities in a project, but he or she must stay closely involved in pulling all the pieces of the project together. The manager must still assume full responsibility for the ultimate implementation of the project. Figure 1.1 shows a typical management pyramid.

In order to understand how the management pyramid functions, let us briefly look at the levels above the hands-on manager. Authority flows down from the top of the pyramid, beginning with the board of directors, shareholders, or owners of the company. The top level of the pyramid is concerned with issues such as stock prices, corporate expenditures, and profitability. The board generally empowers other officers of the company to control the corporate direction and operations.

The next level in the pyramid is executive management. Executive management is concerned with acquisitions, corporate profitability, sales, stock prices, hostile takeovers, and corporate costs. Their involvement in IS projects tends to be restricted to receiving the information that an infrastructure is in place for a corporate initiative when it is needed.

Senior management, the third level from the top of the pyramid, generally holds responsibility for a group of departments and projects.

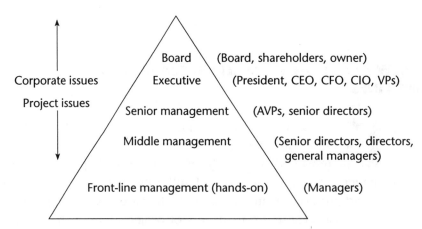

FIGURE 1.1   Management pyramid.

In many organizations, senior management officials set direction, allocate a budget to a project, empower a manager, bring in outside assistance (e.g., auditors) and attend steering committee meetings. They also get involved in extending additional funding, removing impediments to a project, and in some cases, terminating a project.

Although this group is impacted by the success or failure of a project, these managers are not close enough to directly influence projects on a daily basis. Their presence at steering committee meetings gives them an intermittent opportunity to react to what is happening on a project and makes them accountable if they do not take appropriate action in response to the information they receive. It is important to recognize that lower levels of management generally provide this information and that many of the details of a project may be lost through filtration to the upper levels.

The lower levels of the pyramid shown in Figure 1.1 consist of middle and front-line management. There can be a certain amount of overlap between these groups, as some directors and general managers sometimes become directly involved in project delivery. However, this is not the norm. In most cases, middle management is involved in attending steering committee meetings and providing guidance or problem resolution. Their responsibilities also span multiple projects, so although they are closer to projects than the management groups already discussed, and they do have some direct influence on projects, they are still too far away to know precise details (e.g., few senior directors will need to know what version of C is being used on a project).

Front-line (or hands-on) management, which includes information systems (IS) project managers, is involved directly in the delivery of projects. Project managers are empowered to control and deliver a project for an organization—and they are fully accountable for its success or failure. We focus on this level of management throughout the book.

FLOW OF MANAGEMENT AUTHORITY

Project managers occupy a middle ground within organizations; they manage others, but they, in turn, are managed themselves. This relationship is shown in Figure 1.2.

FIGURE 1.2 Flow of management authority.

Project managers receive a mandate from higher levels of management to deliver one or more projects successfully. In order to achieve
this, they are empowered with a budget and a broad range of authority. (Some managers have total control over a budget, while others
have access to a budget but no flexibility in how it is spent. Managers
in the latter group generally do not feel as strong as those in the former.) Project managers are also responsible for the direct management
of staff such as developers, analysts, and project leaders. Managers can
often purchase and implement technology such as computer platforms,
network devices, and software packages. They also control physical
resources such as office space, telephones, and other miscellaneous
items.

In addition to the controls placed on them by executive management, project managers are managed from several other sources. External constraints, such as laws and regulations, limit what the manager
can do within a project. For example, employment laws in some places
limit how many hours an employee can be made to work and establish
guidelines for physical working conditions. Business clients, also called
users, typically determine the business requirements and, consequently, the details of a project solution. Other policies in the organization place various constraints on a manager. One of these is the need

to maintain consistent technology or software standards across an organization. Another constraint is the frequent competition between projects for relevant but limited resources within a company.

By virtue of the middle ground that project managers occupy, they have significant influence over their business clients and the executive management of the company. In the former case, managers are expected to work cooperatively with their business clients to fulfill a requirement identified by someone in higher management. In practical terms, the manager must build a relationship that allows the business clients to contribute their relevant expertise to the project. Managers sometimes have to lay down a law for their clients to follow (this should be done with tact—see Chapter 6, "Why Projects Succeed— Case Studies"). In order to make a project a success, managers sometimes are required to discreetly manage their own bosses.

Managers also have a great deal of influence over executive management through a regular reporting process and in steering committee meetings. Project managers serve as the most common pipeline through which information flows from a project upwards and is filtered into the management pyramid's upper layers. Through this information, executive management can be influenced to increase budgets, allocate additional resources, shift deadlines, change standards, and remove obstacles.

Managers can also influence other projects within the company, either through executive management or through their personal contacts with other managers. The likelihood of success depends on the importance of their project and/or their ability to persuade others to their own way of thinking.

A MANAGER'S ROLE AND RESPONSIBILITIES ON IS PROJECTS

Managers are fully responsible for the success or failure of an IS project. If the project succeeds, the manager should willingly share credit for its success with other members of the project team. Their future cooperation will increase the manager's chances of success on new projects. Professionals who want greater job satisfaction, the possibility of exceptional income, and authority will find management positions more attractive. Those who want job security may need to look elsewhere. (Current job trends place a high emphasis on people with solid technical skills. Job security may mean learning a range of IS tools—client/server, object oriented (OO), UNIX, or open systems.)

Figure 1.3 shows the multiple roles and multiple responsibilities that the typical manager holds on a project. These are listed in order of decreasing importance (e.g., vision is the most important). It can be argued that managers are responsible for assuming any roles that are required to make a project a success. (Project success is defined in Chapter 5, Why Projects Fail.) This makes them the most important person on the project team.

The responsibilities identified in Figure 1.3 are described in further detail in this section.

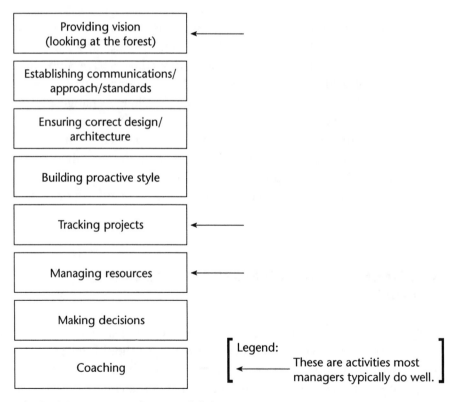

FIGURE 1.3 A manager's responsibilities.

Providing Vision

The most important role a manager can play on a project is that of visionary. A manager must have an intrinsic understanding of the importance of a project to the organization. This vision must remain consistent for the duration of the project, and it must be shared with others in the company—especially the project team.

A manager must also have a global vision of the project. Typical projects are like living organisms that can contain thousands or millions of tiny, dynamic details, each of which requires anywhere from an hour to years of person days of effort for completion. The manager is in a position to view these details in context, ensure that each piece fits the master puzzle called the project, and make appropriate adjustments to protect the integrity of the vision.

Establishing Communications/Approach/Standards

Because so many people are involved on a project, a manager must ensure that relevant groups communicate appropriate information to each other. This involves establishing guidelines on information communication and documentation development and distribution. Managers must also ensure that information is not guarded or withheld. This is very important to the success of projects, especially those with long durations. Techniques for doing this are discussed in Chapter 4, Project Planning and Scheduling.

A manager is also responsible for defining an acceptable approach for conducting a project. This can include regular status meetings, training programs, billing methods, working hours, and others. This approach must be communicated to the project team, and the manager must ensure that it is correctly interpreted and followed.

Standards should be defined for the items shown in the following list to make their integration and maintenance easier.

□ The methods used for writing programming code
□ Software packages (e.g., WordPerfect for documentation, Microsoft Project for Project Management, Lotus for spreadsheets, and Microsoft Access for quick database retrieval. This should not be

confused with the technology infrastructure or standards that are established during the technical design phase.)

□ Style of documentation

Ensuring Correct Design/Architecture

Managers may not have the skills to design the architecture for a program solution, but they are responsible for getting it done properly. This is not as easy as it sounds. On many projects, one of two things happens: The application is so complex that no one wants to tackle the design work, or everyone on the team wants to take credit for completing the design work.

The first event occurs because there are usually so many things happening on a project that most people naturally prefer to spend their time doing the easy things first. As long as his or her staff is busy, a manager sometimes does not insist that the more difficult activities be completed. This situation could go on for years.

The second event occurs when those who are clearly unqualified to do the work compete to assume responsibilities for which they are unprepared. These persons can hinder qualified individuals from doing the real work. The potential for more insidious repercussions also exists. A project can degenerate due to all sorts of internal problems. (See Chapter 5, Why Projects Fail.)

Managers should not tolerate either of these two situations, which have derailed many straightforward projects. Instead, they should hire capable, experienced professionals (staff or consultants) to do this extremely important work correctly. Managers should also rely on skills transfer to train staff who have the ability, but lack the experience, to do the kind of work needed. It is important to be clear and direct with the design team regarding who is really leading and who is following under these circumstances.

Managers should invest the time to understand and agree with the design and architecture of a project solution. This should not be a quick review of a design document, but should be a detailed review of the system design and architecture with the design team. Questions should be asked during the review process to ensure that the manager can track the remainder of the project against this design.

Building Proactive Style

Proactive resolution occurs when managers anticipate and resolve problems before they actually happen. Failure to do this can cause a manager to become reactionary instead, so that he or she is continually trying to catch up. The end result is that the project is never under control.

Some managers succeed in building a proactive style of management. They are the ones who move from one successful project to the next. They are also the managers parachuted into problematic projects, which they will be able to turn around and deliver successfully.

Proactive managers tend to stand out in meetings. They are the ones who ask questions that lead the project team toward actual deliverables (e.g., producing the measurable objectives of a project). They use their experience, judgment, and intelligence to stay a few steps ahead of the project team. While their staff is working on a problem, the proactive manager ensures that resolution occurs, avoids procrastination, and plans the next few steps in detail. Proactive managers have a canny knack for staying on top of important issues. They also fit all the pieces of the project together and retain a global view. Proactive managers tend to retain the respect and esteem of their team and ultimately encourage others to be proactive.

Tracking Projects

This can become an administrative management role in which a manager compares estimates on project activities to actual time spent by project team members. Project tracking should be a value-added activity that resolves conflicts and problems. There is a risk, however, that it can become a thankless job involving reading numbers off a timesheet and entering them into a spreadsheet or a project management tool.

Managers tend to spend a great deal of time in this role. They should ensure that they are receiving value for their efforts. Project tracking should be used to monitor the progress of a project at regular intervals, allowing enough time for adjustment and correction. It should not be used simply as a procedure, as this adds no value to the bottom line of a project.

Managing Resources

This involves managing all types of resources, with an emphasis on human resources. Managers are responsible for hiring, firing, promoting, and training their staff. Since individuals who tend to gravitate toward management enjoy working with people in some capacity, managers tend to spend a great deal of time in this role as well.

Making Decisions

Managers have the final say on their projects, unless they lose the confidence of higher levels of management. They are frequently called on to make decisions, such as the following examples:

□ Who to hire or fire
□ Who is right or wrong?
□ Can Jorge take Friday off?
□ Should another $5,000 be spent upgrading PC software?
□ Should Amanda be promoted?
□ Should Tony be given a raise?

Coaching

A manager can also serve as a mentor or coach to keep team members happy, productive, and successful. This may be a value-added activity for the current project, as contented team members tend to stay around longer and work more productively. Managers should be careful to strike a balance and ensure that this role does not get in the way of project completion.

MATRIX OF ROLES/RESPONSIBILITIES

Table 1.1 contrasts the manager roles and responsibilities with how well they are generally performed on various projects.

Based on the information in this table, managers should concentrate on developing skills in at least the following areas: communica-

TABLE 1.1 Manager Roles and Responsibilities

Role/Responsibility	Attempted	Successfully Completed
1. Providing vision (looking at the forest)	Yes	Sometimes
2. Establishing communications/approach/standards	Not always	Not always
3. Ensuring correct design/architecture	Yes	Sometimes
4. Building proactive style	Yes	Not always
5. Tracking projects	Yes	Usually
6. Managing resources	Yes	Usually
7. Making decisions	Yes	Not always
8. Coaching	Not always	Not always

tions/approach/standards, proactive resolution, decision making, and coaching. This can be done using the following techniques:

☐ Reading management books and journals
☐ Receiving constructive criticism from knowledgable sources (e.g., colleagues, mentors)
☐ Attending management seminars
☐ Discussions with colleagues
☐ Personal reflection and goal setting
☐ Attending courses at universities and colleges

EMPOWERED TEAMS

A project manager is the most important person on a team by virtue of his or her authority and responsibility; conversely, the other members of a project team are the most important people to the manager. A project manager cannot deliver any sizable project without the efforts of talented team members. A symbiotic relationship between these groups is desirable.

The traditional hierarchical approach to project management is giving way to a new approach known as team empowerment. Just as project managers are empowered by their superiors to deliver a project, project managers empower various members of their project team to deliver parts of a project. Figure 1.4 shows that in return for being empowered, members of a project team must return meaningful information to the project manager. If this information is not forthcoming, project managers themselves must get involved and become more proactive in getting things done. Clearly, the level of empowerment will change with the success or lack thereof achieved by the project team. At no time should a project manager simply empower (or delegate) and forget to monitor.

Managers must deal with people in the real world. Some people take well to being empowered, others do not. It is the manager's responsibility to ensure that empowerment is used effectively so as not to threaten the success of the project.

Some managers are ineffective because they refuse to empower their staff, choosing instead to stay directly involved in even the smallest details of a process. These managers find themselves chronically short of time and unable to meet deadlines. They also find that their most talented employees are constantly moving on to other opportunities. At the other extreme, some managers never get a project under control because they empower ineffective staff. They then compound the error by not correcting their earlier lack of judgment.

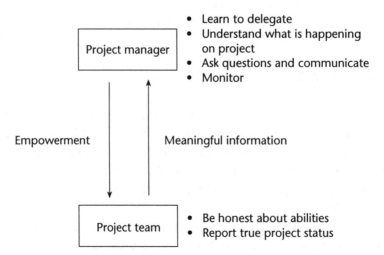

FIGURE 1.4 Team empowerment.

STRUCTURE OF PROJECT TEAMS

The composition of project teams is naturally diverse. Project managers generally have a great deal of control over the skill sets of their teams. They should ensure that there is a broad mix of skills and enough overlap to buffer staff turnover. Another consideration is striking a balance between leaders and workers. There will always be the need for short-term skills or expertise. This can be obtained through training current staff or bringing in contract or consulting personnel for the duration. Project managers also have the option of tapping into outsourcing firms, or contracting out components of a project, as discussed in Chapter 9, "Outsourcing of Information Technology Projects."

Figure 1.5 shows a recommended generic composition for a project team. The project manager can draw on short-term expertise through architects, consultants, and experts. Consultants can be those with special short-term skills, such as facilitators, auditors, data modelers, and network specialists. Many of these skills are available in full-time staff, however, due to a spike in demand for resources or specific expertise, consultants can be used on an as-needed basis. Some man-

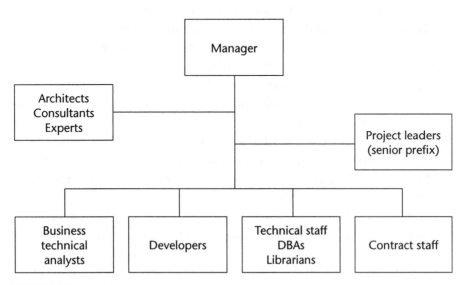

FIGURE 1.5 A typical project team.

agement responsibility can be delegated to project leaders or other team members with the "senior" prefix in their job titles—for example, senior systems analyst or senior business analyst. Business and technical requirements are supported by business/technical analysts. Developers are required for a range of software products (e.g., database, programming, network software, operating systems) that are used on the project. Projects also require specialized roles such as database administrators (DBAs) for database control, network administrators for backup/recovery and security, and librarians for standards. Contract staff can provide any skills that are in short-term supply. They offer the advantage of being temporary expense items that will automatically disappear at the end of the project. These roles are discussed further in Chapter 8, Project Resourcing—Roles, Responsibilities, and Monitoring.

SUMMARY

This chapter focused on the roles that managers play within the management pyramid and within the general organization of a company. A distinction was made between front-line functional project managers and their superiors. It was discovered that the former were empowered with budgets and authority for the singular purpose of successfully completing projects. Those above the front-line managers are too far removed from the everyday details of a project to remain as effective as the project manager in influencing projects.

This chapter defined projects as living organisms with many details that must be integrated and monitored. In this context, the project manager was deemed to be the most important person on a project team because of his or her authority and close proximity to the project. Project managers must enter into a symbiotic relationship with their staff in order to successfully deliver IS projects.

Project managers have a broad range of roles and responsibilities on a project. These include providing vision, establishing communications/approach/standards, ensuring correct design/architecture, building proactive style, tracking projects, managing resources, making decisions, and coaching. Other roles and responsibilities can be added to this list as the need arises. Essentially, the project manager is responsible for the successful delivery of a project, and will consequently assume the roles that are necessary to ensure that this occurs.

Empowered teams—where managers delegate their authority to key individuals with the provision that they are provided with information—were also discussed in this chapter. This information allows project managers to react to events on a project.

Project Management Concepts

2

OVERVIEW

In this chapter a reader will learn about:

- Project management concepts
- The project management process
- Project fundamentals
- Project definition
- Project stakeholders
- Project methodology
- The strategic planning process
- Tactical and operational plans

This chapter provides an overview of project management concepts. It includes commonly used project management terminology, the relationships between these terms, and their significance in undertaking and completing projects. Although project management concepts and methodology can be applied to any type of project, emphasis is placed on information technology projects in a business environment.

The computer industry continues to evolve, delivering newer products and solutions at a lower cost and improved performance.

With every new hardware or software product, there is usually a project team of developers, engineers, and marketers who are committed to providing improved functionality and are also responsible for successfully bringing these products to the marketplace. These rapid changes in the industry are due to a number of factors, as depicted in Figure 2.1.

These developments are causing larger investments, both from the consumer and business communities, to capitalize on the benefits of newer technology and to achieve improved productivity. To translate these investments in computer technology, projects are typically undertaken to achieve the desired objectives. These projects translate the business and investment opportunities into actionable items and provide tangible and intangible benefits to the organization.

Like any business investment, resources committed to a project should undergo scrutiny to ensure that there are benefits derived from them. An organization should address some of the issues concerning project initiation by evaluating how this project would help to achieve business goals.

Here are some typical questions about project initiation and the ultimate results of the project:

Time

Potential of realizing value-added solutions through the use of computer technology

Computers becoming more pervasive in society—use of computers in everyday living such as kitchen appliances, watches, home security systems, and automobiles

Rapid obsolescence of hardware and software

Push by computer vendors to offer nonproprietary products with enhanced functionality at a lower cost

Increasing sophistication of end-users and expectations from the computer industry

Pressures on business to stay competitive and improve their profitability

FIGURE 2.1 Evolution of the computer industry.

❑ Who is paying for the project and what is the rationale for supporting it?

❑ How will the project be monitored and reported so that there are virtually no surprises?

❑ What management tools are required so that the expected benefits are realized?

❑ What management skills are necessary to complete projects on time and within budget?

❑ What essential attributes are required of project team members to ensure that they are working together toward a common goal?

❑ What are the risks of project failure?

❑ Were these project risks addressed with the client?

❑ Will the project have the right combination of technology and people resources?

❑ What mechanisms will be in place to ensure that project requirements are understood, communicated, and accepted by the client?

The preceding are some typical questions that will be addressed throughout the book. This chapter focuses on developing an understanding of the project management process by describing the project planning phase and the process of initiating projects in a business. It goes on to describe project fundamentals such as project definition, an overview of the activities and tasks of a project and the relationship between them, and the different types of projects that can be undertaken by a consumer or a business to achieve its objectives.

PROJECT DEFINITION

In a broad context, a project can be defined as a unit of work. This unit has clearly defined objectives, scope, expectation of results, and deliverables. To produce the deliverables, a project typically involves a project plan, project tasks, responsibilities to achieve the tasks, resources to complete the tasks, and timeframes to complete them. A number of related tasks or a group of activities constitute a project. A project is a way of organizing related tasks in order to achieve a defined objective. Projects are not ongoing—they have start and end dates to accomplish the objectives set out by the project sponsor. Figure 2.2 depicts the key project attributes.

A project can be applied to any business function of an organization—manufacturing, purchasing, marketing, sales, and so on. In each of these areas, there is an opportunity to benefit from initiating projects so that specific related tasks can be completed. Each project involves a project sponsor who has requested that the project be initiated and a project manager who has the responsibility to ensure that tasks are completed and delivered to the project sponsor. The relationship between the project and the sponsor is depicted in Figure 2.3.

Projects can be applied to various facets of business and family life. For instance, let us examine a project to purchase a new automobile for the Smith family. Let us assume that Mrs. Smith is the client because she needs the new automobile to replace the current seven-year-old car. She has asked Mr. Smith to be responsible for a project to acquire a new automobile. She has also specified the following parameters to help Mr. Smith in ensuring that the project meets its objectives.

Project Objective: Acquire a new and reliable automobile. (This is the reason for initiating a project.)

Project Scope: The automobile should be new and must not be a first-time model, that is, it must have a proven track record of a minimum of three years. (The project scope imposes constraints within which the project will operate.)

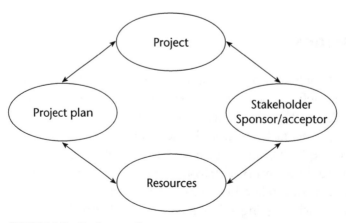

FIGURE 2.2 Project attributes.

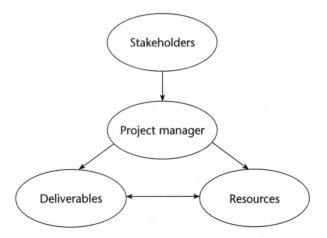

FIGURE 2.3 Relationship between a project and a sponsor.

Project Sponsor: This is Mrs. Smith. (The project sponsor has an ultimate stake in the outcome of the project and usually provides resources to complete the project.)

Project Costs: Not to exceed $23,000, inclusive of all taxes and freight. (Project costs are part of the resources required to complete the project. Cost is an important constraint—typically, a project ends when project funds have been expended.)

Project Completion: The project should be completed in three months from the start date. (The time required to complete the project is another important constraint. If a project is not completed on time, it is conceivable that it has lost the relevance and the need to achieve the project objectives.)

To complete this project, Mr. Smith has decided to start with a project plan. His project plan is described in the next section.

PROJECT ACTIVITIES FOR SMITH FAMILY

The key activities to achieve the result are as follows:

☐ Determine initial requirements that must be met by the features in a new automobile (i.e., a mid-size four-door sedan from a North American manufacturer with air conditioning, antilock braking system, dual air bags, standard transmission, and within the designated price range)

☐ Review requirements for a new automobile with Mrs. Smith including features, cost, availability, and warranty

☐ Document these requirements for initial acceptance by Mrs. Smith

☐ Conduct research regarding different automobiles that meet Mrs. Smith's requirements, for example, review consumer reports and magazines regarding features, performance, reliability, and customer satisfaction data pertaining to new cars in the price range

☐ Compile a short list of three automobiles that meet the requirements

☐ Obtain comparative prices from three dealers

☐ Take Mrs. Smith for test drives to experience car performance, handling, and other features

☐ Narrow the selection to two cars based on a number of factors, including cost, comfort, performance, reliability, warranty and service levels, the number of "extras" provided at no additional cost and perceived to be of value by Mrs. Smith, and track record of the automobile as determined by consumer reports

☐ Recommend the most cost-effective automobile to Mrs. Smith

The following additional parameters are now considered:

Project Deliverables: Purchase/lease the new automobile

Project Review: Assess if the project deliverables meet the requirements identified by the project sponsor

The preceding activities are one example of applying project management to the acquisition of a new automobile. Other personal or family-related project examples include buying a house, going on a vacation, renovating a kitchen, or preparing a retirement plan. These examples illustrate how project management concepts can be applied to get the job done in a timely manner, within budget, and with minimal or no surprises.

To complete the Smith family automobile acquisition project, no sophisticated tools were required. The project was completed using a piece of paper, a calculator, and a pen. As the number of activities and size of the project team increases, project management becomes more complex and requires automated tools to monitor activities and resources. For instance, developing and implementing a computerized order processing system for a large retailer servicing 200 locations in North America would require using a more sophisticated project management tool.

PROJECT STAKEHOLDERS

A project stakeholder is a person or a group of persons who have a stake in the outcome of the project. Depending on the size and complexity of the project, stakeholders could include a number of players including project sponsor and/or the person funding the project, the ultimate user(s) of the project, and persons impacted by the project.

The key stakeholders who are an integral part of this evolving process are the consumer as a user of cost-effective computer technology; businesses as users of technology to remain competitive; computer hardware and software vendors; and computer services vendors who integrate the different components and make them work.

The project manager is a catalyst of change and is responsible for ensuring that results are achieved in a timely manner, within budget. Typically, the project manager's role begins when the project has been defined and its rationale understood by the stakeholders. The project manager is appointed to execute the project as per the objectives set out by the stakeholders, consistent with the objectives of the organization. The consumer as a project manager is responsible for determining requirements, exploring alternatives, and acquiring the right technology to meet objectives.

PROJECT MANAGEMENT METHODOLOGY

Project management requires a methodology to successfully undertake and complete projects on time and within budget. The project management methodology is like a recipe—it provides a checklist of activities, a sequencing of these activities, roles and responsibilities of the project team, and designated resources. However, there is no guarantee that the project will be a success, even when following a project management methodology. Furthermore, by following a methodology too closely, there is a risk of being overwhelmed when unexpected problems arise.

What happens if you set out to deliver projects without following a project management methodology or tools? Typically, for smaller projects—less than three person-months in duration—chances are that there will be minimal impact on the outcome if a formal methodology is not followed. In such instances, the project manager has a plan of action, but the plan is not documented—it resides in the project manager's head.

As the project becomes more complex, it is increasingly difficult to deliver it successfully without a project methodology and the associated tools. For instance, buying an automobile for the Smith family could have been accomplished without following a project methodology, but using one helped the Smith family achieve their objectives.

The project management methodology can be supplemented with the use of a software tool that allows the project manager to document the tasks and their relationships and understand the various constraints on a project. The software tool can be a spreadsheet showing activities and planned completion dates, or it can be project management software, such as Microsoft Project.

A project manager who is charged with the responsibility of delivering the project should have several skills to increase the chances of success. These skills include, but are not limited to, the following:

☐ Leadership skills to motivate and direct the project team and ensure that they remain focused on results
☐ Organizational skills to enable timely reporting of progress and delivery of project objectives
☐ Selection of the right team with the required technical and interpersonal skills so that their efforts and project goals are in alignment
☐ Right level of technical skills to understand when the project team may be off course and direct them appropriately
☐ Delegation skills so that tasks are assigned to the most suitable team member
☐ Communication skills to report on project progress including problems
☐ Political skills to manage the expectations of the stakeholders

PROJECT DIVERSITY

Project management can be applied to a variety of situations to achieve an end result. As a simple example, we reviewed the Smith family's planning to purchase/lease a new automobile. Examples of projects that can benefit from understanding a methodology and using tools to help in monitoring its progress include:

- Setting up a recordkeeping system
- Developing an advertising strategy
- Developing a human resource plan for a department, including hiring staff, completing performance appraisal of staff, and other functions
- Building a house
- Planning a vacation
- Starting a business
- Developing a computer application
- Planning a construction project, such as building an office tower or a road
- Planning an engineering project, such as building a factory or designing a power plant

The preceding projects are different in scope and require different skill sets and resource requirements, but they have one thing in common— these projects follow a standard project management process to achieve the desired results, hopefully in a timely manner and within budget.

INFORMATION TECHNOLOGY PROJECTS

A project is undertaken to address specific organizational goals and objectives. It requires commitment from stakeholders to provide direction and the required resources to make it happen. It is important that the project team understands this stakeholder commitment and related project constraints in order to successfully complete the deliverables and meet stakeholder expectations. Figure 2.4 illustrates the relationship between the project manager and the expected deliverables.

FIGURE 2.4   Relationship between a project manager and expected deliverables.

An information technology project can be defined as the use of computer technology to automate business processes and practices of an organization. An information technology project is initiated to respond to a set of demonstrated business needs. The solution to a business problem is driven by a set of objectives, including the need to lower costs, to provide faster turnaround for services, to restructure how a product or service is provided, or a combination of all of these reasons. The nature of a business problem might be:

☐ The financial system is not current and does not produce reports that are readily usable for decision making.
☐ The payroll system is not flexible enough to allow for payments based on different staff classifications.
☐ Sales data is not helpful in launching new products and services.
☐ Billing information does not capture relevant information to inform the customers.
☐ It takes a long time to process customer orders.

Information technology projects include a variety of initiatives, such as systems development and maintenance projects, infrastructure projects, information technology planning projects, hardware and software acquisition projects, and user support projects. Some examples of applying project management principles to information technology projects are:

☐ Acquiring a database management system
☐ Developing a new financial management system to replace the legacy system
☐ Outsourcing data center services
☐ Developing a wide area network
☐ Establishing hardware, software, and communications standards
☐ Updating the company's information technology strategic plan

When a project is initiated, it generates expectations from the stakeholders. It is important to have a consistent understanding among stakeholders regarding project deliverables and the use of required resources.

In most organizations, project management is neither practiced nor accepted as essential. Typically, project management is taken seriously when problems arise—behind schedule, over budget, experiencing difficulties between the project personnel and sponsors or with some of the project team members. Introducing project management discipline only when a project is in trouble is usually indicative of throwing resources at a problem and magically expecting results, since intervention comes too late. Conducting project management by default is bound to fail.

A project management methodology is desirable to establish a consistent way of handling different projects in an organization. But how does a project management methodology help in delivering successful projects? A project management methodology helps a project manager and the project team to ensure that they are following the right steps to monitor project progress and successful delivery. To define a project methodology, the following questions may be helpful:

☐ Are the project goals and objectives clearly understood by the stakeholders?
☐ Who is responsible for approving the project deliverables?
☐ How frequently are you required to report on the status of the project?

☐ Are the expectations of the stakeholders clearly defined and understood by the project team?

☐ What is the culture of the project team (e.g., requires minimal supervision)?

☐ Are all projects required to follow a project management methodology?

The notion of projects is well suited to the information technology disciplines because there is an expectation by the client that results will be provided within a fixed time period. Information technology groups are typically viewed as providing leadership in introducing new tools and techniques and as having the ability to translate business goals into practical solutions. When a project is undertaken, it is aiming to bring about a change in a business process and thus becomes a catalyst.

A project manager sets the tempo of the project and provides direction to the team and makes daily decisions based on prior experience in managing projects. The ultimate success of the project depends on how strongly the project management principles are practiced by the entire project team, how well the team delivers the results, and how well the change necessitated by the project impacts the productivity of the business.

Project commitment is hard to define but relatively easy to spot. A committed project team works together to achieve the results in a timely manner and is also synergistic and supportive of team members' efforts. A committed team looks for solutions. Without a committed project team the project is bound to fail, even though the individual team members have the required skills.

THE PROJECT MANAGEMENT PROCESS

In the Smith family example, the elements of a project were applied to realize the deliverables. Building on that example, the project management process can be described as follows:

1. *Identify project objective.* Involves a clear definition of the project and the rationale for undertaking the project.

2. *Define project scope.* Includes the areas impacted by the project. Project scope can be as limited as a department in an organization or as broad as an international cartel; project size can be based on a certain dollar amount; project timeframe can be as short as weeks or months or as long as years.

3. *Introduce project sponsor.* The person responsible for identifying an opportunity, initiating the project, and having the responsibility for financial resources.

4. *Identify stakeholders.* Include all persons who have an investment in the development and outcome of the project. For instance, for a systems development project, stakeholders might include users, user managers, customers, and systems staff.

5. *Establish project costs.* Include the total lifecycle costs for the project, fixed and variable, as well as required resources. Project resources include staffing of project team with the required skill sets; financial resources for supplies, hardware, software, and travel; and administrative support personnel.

6. *Define project benefits.* Include the benefits derived from implementing the project—hard-dollar, soft-dollar, and value-added benefits.

7. *Outline key project activities.* Include the tasks required to complete the project. This is discussed in Chapter 4 in greater detail.

8. *Specify project deliverables*—the tangible results of completing a project. A deliverable could be a report, a presentation, a business system, an information technology strategic or operational plan, or a feasibility study, for example.

9. *Set up project schedule*—an integral part of the project plan. Shows the relationship among activities over the life of the project.

10. *Define milestones*—important targets to be achieved during the life of a project. For instance, a milestone could be to complete the design for a system.

PLANNING AND PROJECT MANAGEMENT

Planning is deciding what to do and why it needs to be done before you actually start work. It enables the right things to be done in the right order so that scarce resources are effectively utilized to achieve organizational objectives. The plan should include the overall business direction, the strategies to ensure that this direction will be achieved, and projects to realize the strategies. Planning provides an opportunity for senior management to discuss priorities at an organizational level instead of allocating resources on suboptimal projects that may benefit one part of the business to the detriment of another part.

Information technology plans are typically initiated to ensure that investments in information technology are coordinated and introduced in a cost-effective manner, consistent with the business plans of the organization.

The information technology plan is initiated at a senior management level. Normally, in large organizations the development of the information technology plan rests with the chief information officer. The information technology plan must be viewed from within the framework of the corporate vision, management's view of information systems, and the stage of information system maturity within the organization. The plan describes the current environment and framework used by an organization to direct information systems development, the current and planned business and information technology environments, and the strategies and policy directions governing the organization's development and management of its information technology for the future. The plan also describes the framework the organization will use to direct information systems development over the long term and the infrastructure for developing, maintaining, and supporting information systems in the organization, including new functions necessary to ensure that future systems development is, in fact, shaped and directed by the plan.

The information technology plan provides a framework to guide the organization's investment in and management of information over several years. The plan also outlines the specific initiatives required to translate the strategies into results and the cost and benefits of these initiatives.

THE STRATEGIC PLANNING PROCESS

Projects are initiated because there is a specific business need in an organization. For instance, a project may be initiated because the accounting department wants to keep track of all movable and fixed assets in the company. The controller may decide to initiate a project to automate the recordkeeping of all assets in the company. It is conceivable that the controller may end up with an excellent assets management system, but the hardware and software used may not be compatible with other computer applications in the organization. How do you prevent an "islands of technology" syndrome?

The information technology planning process is one effective way to ensure that individual requirements are not considered in isolation. The planning process enables the organization to identify its "basket of requirements" over a three-to-five year planning period, and determine the most cost-effective and integrated ways of delivering those requirements.

Planning Practices

Strategic planning practices call for an appraisal of the current environment, identification of the issues and trends that must be addressed, and a depiction of the proposed future or target environment. From this picture, goals and objectives can be set out and broad strategies for accomplishing them can be developed.

Since information and technology are themselves becoming major resources used by more and more organizations to further their strategic objectives, it has become clear that planning for them must be done in the context of a strategic business plan. However, the interactions between business plans and information management plans are becoming increasingly complex.

The information technology strategic plan must serve the business strategy by defining the data, applications, and technology required to support the organization's products and services efficiently and effectively; setting out the principles by which these can be developed, implemented, used, and maintained in a manner consistent with an organization's management culture and the rate of change for priorities; and ensuring adequate consideration of those areas where technology itself may be an underlying change agent.

As a starting point, the strategies in the plan should be developed by reviewing trends and issues with the organization's managers and outlining several future business scenarios where management of information technology will be an issue.

To ensure that strategic plans remain current and are representative of the realities of the business, they should be periodically reviewed. Typically, an annual review of a strategic plan is desirable because it enables organizations to review business and information technology objectives and update them where necessary.

In general, changes to the types and numbers of clients, products, and services provided and the types of new value-added services provided all have an impact on how information technology is deployed in the organization.

Figure 2.5 shows the key elements of an information strategic plan and how they are interrelated.

The key objectives of developing an information strategic plan are

☐ to provide a single focus of responsibility and authority for deploying information and systems strategically in the organization
☐ to provide an information technology structure that is responsive to client needs and provides a competitive weapon
☐ to provide an appropriate information technology platform for the delivery of applications in a timely, reliable, and cost-effective manner
☐ to develop flexible systems that can be quickly built and changed to meet the changing nature and requirements of the business

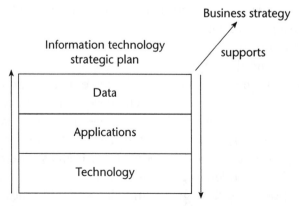

FIGURE 2.5 Elements of an information technology strategic plan.

☐ to develop corporate or common applications in a coordinated manner to ensure better alignment of information technology with the organization's goals

☐ to develop an applications portfolio that is responsive to business needs and that has a demonstrated payback.

Operational Plans

To translate the strategic plan, operational and tactical plans are developed for implementing a variety of projects over the planning period. The operational plan is a primary tool for highlighting projects planned for implementation, and the associated costs, benefits, and risks of achieving the objectives. Operational plans typically extend to one fiscal year, while the tactical plans cover about a three-year period.

The operational plan should include a description of the project, project scope, key stakeholders, and a broad assessment of costs and benefits. Figure 2.6 shows the relationship between strategic, tactical, and operational plans.

FIGURE 2.6 Relationship between strategic and operational plans.

Elements

The following elements are essential in the development of a strategic plan:

1. Establish the steering committee. In many organizations, steering committees are set up to provide direction and guidance to the project. The steering committee's membership is typically five to seven members, chaired by the chief information officer, and representing departments impacted by the project. Membership could be as follows: one representative from senior management; three representatives from departmental management; and two representatives from the systems department. The committee reviews the project progress and provides feedback regarding prioritization of various departmental and corporate initiatives.
2. Refer to the business plan of the organization. The information technology plan should be consistent with the goals and objectives of the organization as described in its business plan.
3. Initiate the project to develop a technology plan. Define purpose and scope of the study, including deliverables to be produced. Review the planning schedule and ensure that the deliverables are realistic and attainable.
4. Identify resources and skill sets required for the project team.
5. Assess the business and technology environment. Include critical success factors, changes to the business environment, and new products and services.
6. Identify business needs and priorities. Include business processes, current problems, and proposed opportunities.
7. Formulate an information technology strategic direction.
8. Translate the strategies into concrete initiatives, such as a listing of applications and projects that need to be undertaken for specific improvement of departments or processes.
9. Justify the overall portfolio of projects and prioritize these initiatives so that results are obtained over a four-to-five-year planning horizon.
10. Monitor and update the plan on an annual basis to reflect changes in priorities and business direction.

SUMMARY

This chapter has reviewed the basic tenets of project management. It has addressed some different types of projects that can be initiated and can benefit from a project management methodology. There is no guarantee that using a project management methodology will ensure project success. However, as depicted in Figure 2.7, the use of a methodology with appropriate software tools and an experienced project team can help in monitoring the progress of the project and in reducing the risk of project failure.

The chapter also reviewed the strategic planning process as one way of introducing projects in an organization in an integrated, coordinated, and cost-effective manner.

Project management is a discipline requiring a commitment from stakeholders, a results-oriented attitude to get the job done, trained staff, effective tools to monitor the project, and a good understanding of the limits and potential of technology and its impact on the organization. Good project management requires proper planning and a commitment to implement the deliverables as outlined in the project plan.

The project manager is a key player in delivering projects on time and within budget. Like a quarterback on a football team, the project manager provides leadership, direction, delegation, and the support needed to enhance the chances of project success.

FIGURE 2.7 Project management elements to enhance project success.

Project Initiation and Justification

3

OVERVIEW

In this chapter the reader will learn about:

- Reasons for project initiation
- How projects are justified
- The project portfolio
- Business cases
- Launching projects
- Tracking benefits

This chapter deals with how projects are initiated and justified in organizations. As discussed briefly in Chapter 2, projects can be initiated for a variety of reasons. An immediate business problem can motivate a stakeholder to launch a project, or the strategic planning process can be to build a prioritized list that allows project selections to be made in a coordinated and integrated manner.

Project initiation and justification are initially addressed in the information technology plan where the project portfolio is developed, prioritized, and approved based on the goals and objectives of the organization. The project portfolio indicates which designated projects should be implemented, subject to the acceptance of a detailed business case.

Project justification is based on the value of the project to the organization. A project translates an idea or a concept to an actionable result. The value of a project is assessed in terms of monetary and nonmonetary benefits to the organization versus the costs and potential risks.

At the completion of this chapter, the reader will have a good understanding of how projects are initiated, how they are prioritized and justified, and the rationale behind the project approval process.

Reasons for Project Initiation

Projects can be initiated from any part of the organization where there is a demonstrated need to address a business problem. A project can be initiated by many different individuals in an organization—a plant manager, director of marketing, vice president of finance, supervisor in the human resources department, or an individual staff member in an organization who believes that there is a better way of doing business. Projects are driven by the necessity of providing products or services more effectively. The project initiation process is depicted in Figure 3.1.

There are a variety of reasons for initiating projects, as shown in Table 3.1.

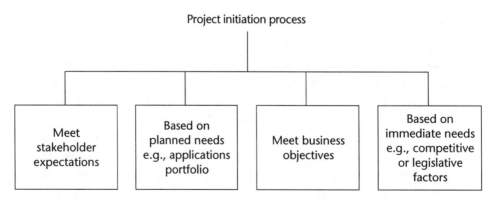

FIGURE 3.1 Project initiation process.

TABLE 3.1 Reasons for project initiation

Reason	Rationale
Providing timely and more responsible service	Client service is an important business indicator—e.g., a retail store providing prompt customer service regarding product availability, price, warranty, and service.
Marketing in-house computer applications to other businesses	This initiative would be aimed at increasing the revenues of the organization by developing a market for their in-house applications.
Reducing cost of a product or service	This is a typical reason to undertake an information technology project. Cost reduction includes streamlining a business process, thereby reducing the time and resources required. For example, in the case of a bank, reducing the time required to process a loan application.
Providing newer products or services	Based on customer spending patterns, this initiative provides a more focused way of selling products and services to customers.
Building partnerships with suppliers	This initiative uses information technology to reduce inventory and carrying costs through "just-in-time" techniques.
Fostering better coordination between departments	This initiative will lower the overall cost of manufacturing a product or providing a service by ensuring that the information is better coordinated and more integrated between departments.
Providing improved decision support systems	This initiative provides managers and executives with information to support their decisions—for example, information about competition, market share, and price sensitivity to their products.
Utilizing extra money in the budget	"Unspent" monies in the budget can be used to initiate projects
Satisfying political considerations	This initiative responds to the need to, for instance, justify reorganization of a department or influence a decision.
Complying with legislative factors	This initiative responds to the need to initiate or enhance an information system to provide reports based on legislative requirements or support other legislative requirements (e.g., a new tax).

PROJECT INITIATION

Project Portfolio Approach

As described in Chapter 2, projects can be initiated within the context of an information technology strategic plan to ensure that requirements are addressed in a cohesive and integrated manner. At a high level, this project portfolio describes a list of initiatives that should be undertaken over a three-to-five-year period. The project portfolio includes a brief description of each project, the resources required to complete the project, and the skill sets of a project team to complete the project.

The projects in the applications portfolio will be implemented over a one-to-five-year span, depending on the priorities established in the strategic plan. Subject to budgetary pressures and resource availability, it is likely that the higher priority projects will be implemented first.

Typically, before a project is implemented, there will be a detailed assessment to ensure that the project is still relevant and addresses the designated business problems. However, for each project included in the applications portfolio, the following items should be included:

☐ Project overview, briefly describing the project and the business objectives addressed
☐ Key project stakeholders
☐ Project scope
☐ An overview of preliminary costs and benefits
☐ Timeframe for project completion

It is interesting to note that not all organizations follow the formal process of developing an applications portfolio. In some organizations, projects are developed in a reactive manner based on a designated need at a specific time.

Figure 3.2 illustrates how an applications portfolio is developed.

Immediate Needs Approach

Sometimes a project is required to address sudden competitive needs or to address a business need necessitated by a change in legislation. These projects may fall outside the realm of the planning process and

Strategic and tactical plans

Identification of business opportunities

Identification of applications

Priority of applications to be implemented   ⟶   Applications portfolio

Timeframes for projects' completion

Estimated total cost for implementation

FIGURE 3.2 Applications portfolio.

may not be included in the applications portfolio. Furthermore, some of these projects may require immediate attention to comply with deadlines. Typically, these projects have a sponsor with a direct stake in the outcome of the project. The project sponsor is also interested in ensuring that the project is carefully planned and executed by a competent project team.

Before starting a project, there will be a variety of ideas and opinions about the purpose and scope of the project, what the final product of the project will be, and how the project will be implemented. Stakeholders with a vested interest in the outcome of the project are typically the source of these ideas. It is quite likely that these ideas may be diverse and incongruent in many areas.

The project initiation phase deals with taking these diverse ideas and developing them into a more focused project with formal provisions for resources and timelines to make it happen. Before projects are initiated, they must follow a rigorous process to ensure that the investment in a project is supported by demonstrable benefits and that the project is providing a value to the enterprise. The vehicle used to initiate and justify a project is referred to as a business case.

PROJECT JUSTIFICATION

Using a Business Case

The business case provides a mechanism for funding a project and providing resources. The business case will identify the projected benefits of the project, and balance these against the costs and risks associated with these benefits. The business case can be used to monitor the estimated benefits with the actual benefits if the project is approved and implemented.

As indicated in Figure 3.3, the business case analysis may actually reduce the number of projects being implemented, either because some of the projects may not be cost effective or because they are not meeting the business objectives. The business case analysis also may alter project scope and the priority of projects to be implemented.

For consistent preparation and evaluation of business cases and in seeking approvals, the template of a business case described in this section should be used as a guideline. The details required in preparing a business case should be contingent on the actual size of the project and type of business. For instance, a project estimated to cost $25,000 will require less supporting documentation than a project with a budget of $1 million.

The business case can also be used for audit purposes—to compare projected results against actual results in order to assess the ultimate success of the project, and to apply any good experiences to other projects.

After it is completed, the business case should be reviewed and approved by the project sponsor, who is typically responsible for ensuring that resources are available to complete the project. The approval process is required to obtain financial commitment to the pro-

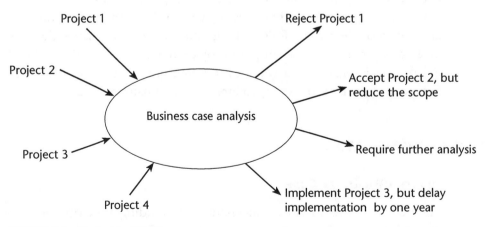

FIGURE 3.3 Project justification.

ject, and also to affirm that the project will achieve the objectives and benefits identified in the business case.

Template for Preparing a Business Case

I. Identifying Information

Business case for the acquisition of xxxxxx.

Department:

Contact name:

Total cost of acquisition:

Account code to charge:

II. Objectives

The project should clearly define what the project is intended to achieve and the level of interest in the project. Explain business problems to be resolved, or opportunities to be realized.

The system objectives—such as improving response time, increasing throughput, providing a friendlier user interface, and migrating to a client server processing environment—should also be addressed.

III. Project Scope

The project scope deals with the boundaries within which the project will operate. It includes the specific business units and functions that will be impacted (e.g., marketing and accounting departments), the key stakeholders who will be affected, and any constraints or limitations of the project. An example of a project scope would be that the project will be implemented only in one geographical location using a dedicated workstation.

IV. Business Requirements

This section of the business case will assess the current business functions and processes and identify any weaknesses and potential opportunities for improvement. It will also describe the organization of work groups where the requirements exist, and the level of automation utilized.

The business requirements should be documented by addressing the following items and providing a rationale for the proposed project:

☐ Business tasks and activities requiring automation

☐ Methods currently being used to accomplish/perform these activities

☐ Use of proposed information technology to accomplish or perform these activities

V. Alternatives

Identify the alternatives considered to address the business requirements along with costs, benefits, risks, and reasons for rejection. Alternatives include:

☐ Status quo

☐ Other technology solutions

VI. Costs and Benefits

A. Costs: Provide the following costs:

☐ One-time costs of hardware, software, planning, and implementing the product/service

☐ Ongoing costs of operating, upgrading, and maintaining the product/service (e.g., service, training)

B. Benefits

1. Provide quantifiable monetary benefits that can include:

☐ One-time cost savings

☐ Annual cost savings such as eliminating the services provided on an annual basis by an external agency, reductions in staffing, and deferred hires

2. Quantifiable nonmonetary benefits that are improvements in performance directly attributable to the implementation of information technology. Quantifiable nonmonetary benefits can include:

☐ Measurable increases in the number of clients serviced

☐ Measurable increases in the number of requests serviced

☐ Measurable improvements in response to service requests

☐ Staff time savings redeployed to other quantifiable activities

☐ Increased confidence in the decision due to the availability of more relevant information

☐ Increased understanding of customer demographics

    ☐ Improved coordination between organization units, thereby decreasing time needed to make decisions

C. Summary of Costs and Benefits: Prepare a summary table of costs and benefits.

Wherever possible, value-added benefits should be quantified and shown under nonmonetary (quantifiable) benefits. Where it is not possible to quantify benefits, a brief description of these benefits should also be provided.

Summary Table of Costs and Benefits for Project XYZ

Costs	Year 1	Year 2	Year 3	Total
One-time costs				
Ongoing costs				
Other costs				
Total costs				
Benefits	*Year 1*	*Year 2*	*Year 3*	*Total*
One-time savings				
Annual savings				
Nonmonetary benefits (quantifiable)				
Other benefits				
Total benefits				
Net benefits				
Cumulative benefits				

VII. Payback

Payback is defined as the number of years it takes to recover the investment. Typically, the total monetary benefits should at least offset total estimated costs within a three-year period from the date of implementation.

VIII. Summary of the Business Case

Include implications if the business case is not approved.

IX. Risks

Identify any risks that might arise as a consequence of the project and indicate ways for these risks to be minimized or avoided altogether.

X. Approvals

Obtain approvals from the project sponsor. If the project sponsor is not authorized to allocate funds, obtain approval from the person authorized to allocate funds. After receiving approval, projects can be formally initiated and completed in accordance with the objectives set out in the business case.

Results from the Management Survey

Based on our management survey, we found the following characteristics regarding project justification and initiation:

☐ Most respondents use a business case as a means to justify and initiate projects. The level of detail covered depends on the size and complexity of the project. The supporting documentation for a business case varied from a brief memorandum outlining the reasons for initiating a project with departmental management approval to comprehensive documentation requiring cost and benefit justification and risk assessment.

☐ Most respondents agreed that a business case provided an opportunity to document the business requirements, prioritize project requirements, and communicate them to the stakeholders.

☐ Most respondents agreed that project risks are better understood in the context of a business case, especially when alternatives are described and their implications are understood. Respondents also indicated that a benefit tracking process would finetune the business case process and provide more accountability to the project management process.

☐ Most respondents also were in favor of developing a project portfolio, especially where larger projects were involved, because it encourages approval of higher priority initiatives that maximize the value to the organization. The project portfolio also provided a picture of various initiatives over time thereby enhancing the relationship between projects.

After the business case is prepared and approved, the project can be formally launched.

PROJECT LAUNCHING

After the project has been approved, the project manager is selected and assigned a series of tasks to start the project, including:

1. Prepare a project plan and obtain approval from the project sponsor and/or the steering committee. The project plan should include key tasks, milestones, responsibilities, deliverables, and corresponding completion dates to achieve them (see Chapter 4, Project Planning and Scheduling).
2. Identify the staff resources and skill sets of the project team.
3. Identify the funding requirements for the project, including hardware, software, office space, and administrative support.
4. Select the project team members. This could be a combination of in-house personnel and consultants, depending on the specific requirements of the project.
5. Identify key project review points with stakeholders.

TRACKING BENEFITS

When several competing projects require attention, project prioritization becomes important so that higher priority projects with greater payback are initiated first, followed by other projects in a descending order of importance and value. However, projects necessitated by legislative requirements or projects that belong to the infrastructure category may be considered as higher priority projects by the senior management of an organization.

One of the primary reasons for justifying a project is the value of benefits provided to the organization. Consequently, benefits tracking and reporting are essential to the project justification process. The benefits tracking process should include how benefits will be reported and the accountability for realizing them after the project has been successfully implemented.

A key focus of tracking benefits is to ensure that managers are accountable for identifying, capturing, monitoring, and reporting on quantifiable technology benefit measures resulting from the proposed investment. Tracking and reporting of benefits is fundamental to ensuring that a rigorous process was followed in the acquisition process with appropriate accountability for those acquisitions.

As part of the benefits measurement and reporting process, the following benefit management principles should be observed:

☐ Every investment in information technology must be clearly directed to meeting the business needs of the organization.
☐ Every investment in information technology must be justified by an approved business case prior to any acquisition.
☐ Benefits realized through the use of information technology will be captured and reported back to senior management of the organization.
☐ Wherever possible, information technology resources should be optimized to ensure that resources can be shared or otherwise redeployed to meet the organization's business needs.

To track benefits, a benefits tracking form can be used for a better understanding of planned versus actual benefits and the reasons for variances, if appropriate. Figure 3.4 shows a sample benefits tracking form to capture and monitor benefits and encourage management accountability.

SUMMARY

This chapter dealt with how projects are justified and initiated in an organization. Projects can be initiated by addressing a business need

Benefits Tracking Form

Name of Department:			
Project Name	*Year 1*	*Year 2*	*Year 3*
	Planned Actual Variance	Planned Actual Variance	Planned Actual Variance
Project 1			
Project 2			
Project 3			
Project 4			
Project 5			
. . . .			
. . . .			
Totals			
Brief Explanation of Variances by Project:			

FIGURE 3.4 Benefits tracking form.

identified by a stakeholder to resolve a business problem. Projects can also be initiated in a more coordinated and integrated manner as part of the corporation's strategic planning process. Since a project is an investment, it should be subjected to a review where alternative projects and associated costs and benefits are assessed.

The chapter discussed how projects are initiated and justified as part of the technology planning process and how projects are prioritized and approved based on the goals and objectives of the organization. The technology planning process can be used to develop a project portfolio describing which projects should be undertaken and when they should be implemented.

A standardized template was provided as a way of preparing and evaluating the business case. The proposed business case could be applied to a variety of projects and initiatives, such as developing new computer applications, acquiring hardware and software, implementing computer networks, and even outsourcing projects.

A benefits tracking form was developed to study planned versus actual benefits and thereby encourage accountability as part of the project management process. Depending on the size of the project, the details of the business case may be adjusted—for instance, project lifecycle costs of less than $10,000 may not be as comprehensive as those for projects over $100,000.

It is critical that the project initiation and justification phase of a project lifecycle is done thoroughly and is supported by the stakeholders.

Project Planning and Scheduling

OVERVIEW

In this chapter the reader will learn about:

- The project planning process
- Building project plans
- Facilitating work sessions
- Planning tools
- Definitions of project planning terms
- Introduction to project estimating

STARTING THE PROJECT

A project manager is usually assigned or parachuted into a project after it is initiated. When a project manager leaves a project prematurely, another manager is assigned to the project ("parachuted"). The new manager has a tough job to quickly learn the ropes, tackle and resolve the problems that affected the previous project manager, while winning the project team's loyalty.

One of the first steps that is typically undertaken is planning. This is an integral component of project management, and the extent to which this is done effectively determines the level of success that a project ultimately enjoys. The project management survey conducted for this book identified a lack of effective project planning as a serious contributor to the failure of projects (as discussed in Chapter 5—Why Projects Fail).

The project planning process generates a formal project plan (or schedule) that identifies all the steps needed to satisfy a project's requirements at a specific point in time and within specific resource constraints.

The planning process commences immediately after a project mission statement is issued but prior to project execution. This is illustrated in Figure 4.1. This chapter discusses the project planning process and associated tools and techniques.

THE PROJECT PLANNING PROCESS

A project manager, or in some cases, a group of management level personnel, generally conduct the project planning process, which consists of the stages shown in Figure 4.2.

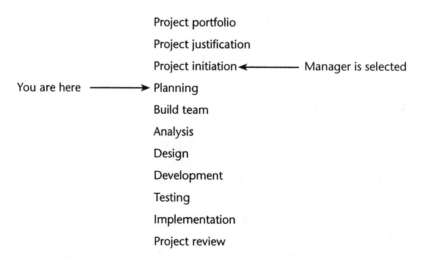

FIGURE 4.1 Placement of the project planning process.

Confirm executive approval

Understand project requirements

Reflect on issues

Identify milestones

Identify phases

Identify activities within phases

Identify tasks within activities

FIGURE 4.2 Breaking down the planning process.

Confirm Executive Approval

A manager must identify all sources of power and influence that could impact a project. It is important to verify that a prospective project has executive support and an executive sponsor, who in turn has executive support. A steering committee should be established as soon as possible to resolve the inevitable issues that will arise. This information can be used to build a standard escalation process.

It is also important to identify the key users of the project and how the project will ultimately be accepted or rejected. It may be necessary to develop more than one steering committee and staff them differently. A common practice is to have a tactical steering committee staffed with business and technical users to deal with day-to-day issues on the project. A second, executive, steering committee is staffed with senior management, and focuses more on budgeting and strategic issues.

A manager should also understand the nature and importance of a prospective project. Is the project mission-critical to the organization? What is the relative priority of the project compared to others? What is the level of risk? Answers to these questions will allow a manager to understand the pecking order of active projects within the organization. The more important the project, the more visible it will be within the organization. This will make it easier to get resources. On the other hand, the increased visibility also places a manager under greater pressure to deliver.

Understand Project Requirements

A manager cannot plan without understanding the requirements of a project. In order to do this at this early stage, several factors must be balanced. Generally, at the time of planning, project requirements are not well understood. In practical terms, the requirements tend to be vision statements or strategic directions. Detailed business requirements are developed in activities specified in the project plan. The manager is faced with the challenge of building a project plan without having the benefit of fully understanding the business requirements. This problem becomes acute when the project plan is used to estimate project costs and deadlines. Many managers are able to balance these problems and plan successfully through a combination of experience, intellect, hard work, and intuition. Another helpful personality trait is the ability to accept a lack of precision and the unknown.

Design meetings can be used to great advantage in trying to understand requirements. A manager can either run the meetings personally, or hire an architect-level resource to do much of the work. Prior to calling design meetings, a manager should learn as much as possible about the project's objectives and requirements. These should be documented in easy-to-follow dataflow diagrams, data models, flowcharts, and entity relationship diagrams (see Chapter 7, Iterative Project Development Methodology, for details). These should be presented in the design meetings with the words: "This is what I think we're doing—correct me where I'm wrong." Attendance at the design meetings should be open to anyone the manager feels can assist in getting a better understanding of what a project is trying to achieve. The only obligation here is that key users must be in attendance.

As an example, consider the requirements for a payroll system for contract staff at a medium sized business. These are described in the following paragraph and shown in Figure 4.3.

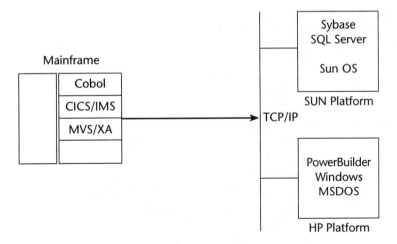

FIGURE 4.3 Payroll project.

Migrate a mainframe-based Cobol application supported by a CICS interface and IMS files to a client/server-based architecture using Sybase SQL Server and Powerbuilder on a LAN/WAN by Jan 4 of the following year.

The contract staff payroll system must interface with the payroll system for the rest of the company. There are some differences, especially in the approval process. The total payroll system feeds the corporate general ledger.

The contract staff payroll application consists of a series of user screens, some of which are shown in Table 4.1.

Reflect on Issues

The project manager is the most important single entity on a project. As the person who is ultimately responsible for the fate of a project, the manager is empowered to interview any resource and ask any question, no matter how silly it seems. Indeed, the manager is obligated to exhaust all possibilities before committing to a plan. Some initial items to consider can be divided into the following functional groups.

TABLE 4.1 Payroll project user screens

Screen Name	Purpose	User Group
Timesheet	All company staff use this screen to enter the hours they worked during the week into a computer system.	Employees
TimeApproval	Timesheets entered by staff are examined and approved online by their immediate managers.	Administration
PayApproval	Payroll staff accept invoices from contract staff and do a line item consolidation with the hours reported on the timesheets and those approved on the system. Payroll staff also access daily rates and any other pertinent information to approve the invoice. The invoice is accepted or rejected online.	Payroll
Corrections	The system allows corrections to items based on a security table. Staff members are allocated clearance to specific items and functions. Values that are not posted to production can be modified by staff having the appropriate clearance. After posting, the items are protected against changes, but can still be browsed.	Employees
History	Browse pay checks for up to one year after generation.	Payroll

Strategic Items

Strategic items focus on the long-term viability of a project.

- ☐ Does the project have a true purpose?
- ☐ Does the project have a mandate?
- ☐ Does the project have management backing?
- ☐ Does the project have an adequate budget?
- ☐ Does the project have adequate time for delivery?
- ☐ Who is the champion of the project?
- ☐ Who is the sponsor of the project?
- ☐ Is the technology infrastructure in place, or will it be considered as part of the project?
- ☐ What is the relative pecking order of the project in the resource pool?

Tactical Items

Tactical items focus on the day-to-day operations of a project.

☐ Does the project require custom development?
☐ Does the project require a commercial software package(s)? Does the project require a combination of a package solution as well as development (e.g., interfacing to legacy systems)?
☐ Who are the key users?
☐ What factors can cause the project to fail?

Resourcing Items

Resourcing items focus on human, technology, space, and other physical resources.

☐ What is the technology architecture (hardware and software)?
☐ Are staff resources adequate to deliver the project?
☐ Should one or more pieces be outsourced to consultants?
☐ Is outside (i.e., agency) assistance required to recruit adequate resources for the project?
☐ Managers should ask themselves the following candid question: "Am I able to properly manage the project, or should another architect or manager be involved?" If the answer is yes, the manager could either resign from the project (not suggested) or plan to hire the required expertise on a contract basis, as needed. This will also allow the manager to develop skills for the next project.
☐ Should day-to-day operations be given to a facilities management firm?
☐ How much working space is needed for the project team?

Background Information

Background information refers to anything that is already known or documented about the project.

☐ Is there a data model?
☐ Is there a process model?
☐ Are there other written requirements or documents?
☐ Were there previous attempts to do this project? What happened?
☐ Were any feasibility studies or benchmarking tests done?

Acceptance Criteria

As functionality of the project is delivered, it is important to have evaluation criteria to assess the value of deliverables as per the requirements.

☐ What are the acceptance criteria?
☐ Who will ultimately make the decision to accept the project?
☐ What are the acceptance metrics for the various deliverables on the project?
☐ Who can develop test plans for the various types of testing?

Answering yes to each of these items is insufficient. A manager must be able to articulate substantial details as well. For example, if the budget is adequate, there are still more questions to answer. What is the total amount allocated for the project? Who is paying for the project? How does the budget break down by phase or activity? How closely should the budget be monitored? Is it possible to get an increase in the budget?

Identify Milestones

Every project has clearly defined events, called milestones, that have significant importance between the time the project starts and ends. By definition, a milestone should be something that leads toward the success of a project. A milestone is typically accompanied by something called a deliverable, which can be defined, measured, and demonstrated. A deliverable is not always a milestone—it may just be the measurable product of expended effort on a project.

For the payroll system, possible milestones are a pilot project, mapping of the legacy data and functions to a client/server system, development of screens in Powerbuilder, physical database development, data conversion from the legacy system, and report development.

Identify Phases

Project phases allow large projects to be divided into manageable pieces based on a prioritized list of user requirements. Phases are generally constructed to implement project deliverables in an order that provides users with important functions first, with a minimum of risk to the business unit. A project phase can produce multiple deliverables.

Another benefit of dividing a project into phases is to facilitate control over the budgeting process. A project need not be funded in its entirety. This allows continuous refinement of a project plan and its budget as issues develop. Since important functions can be completed in earlier phases, it becomes possible to delay subsequent phases (that have less important functionality) without affecting an application's core functionality.

A common consensus among managers who were surveyed for this book is that large projects should be divided into phases of six to eight months' duration, as a standard. For reasons discussed in Chapter 7, Iterative Project Development Methodology, this appears to optimize application development, testing, and implementation.

The payroll system can be divided into two basic phases. Phase 1 involves mapping, user interface design and development, physical database, and data conversion activities. Phase 2 involves building control reports and administrative functions (that previously required batch scripts and operational support to satisfy).

Each phase can be divided into start/end dates, resourcing requirements, budget allocation, and deliverables.

Identify Activities within Phases

A phase should be divided into activities so that each activity produces a single deliverable. An activity is defined by a start date and time, an end date and time, with resources allocated to it.

The following activities can be defined for each phase of the payroll system:

Phase 1 (Deliverables: Mapping, user interface, physical database, data conversions)
> *Activity 1 (Deliverable: Mapping)*
> *Activity 2 (Deliverable: Build user interface)*
> *Activity 3 (Deliverable: Build physical database)*
> *Activity 4 (Deliverable: Data conversions)*
> *Activity 5 (Deliverable: System testing approval)*

Phase 2
>   *Activity 1 (Deliverable: Build control reports)*
>   *Activity 2 (Deliverable: Build administrative functions)*

Identify Tasks within Activities

Complex activities can be divided into a series of tasks. A task is defined by a start date and time, an end date and time, and resources.

A task list can be developed for each activity of the payroll system, as follows:

Phase 1
>   *Activity 1 (Mapping)*
>>   *Task a (Gather existing documentation and programs)*
>>   *Task b (Develop data dictionary list for existing system)*
>>   *Task c (Develop data dictionary list for new system)*
>   *Activity 2 (Build user interface)*
>>   *Task a (Gather all forms and reports)*
>>   *Task b (Gather CICS screen prints: Enter employee hours, maintain employee history, browse checks, support corrections, reprint checks, consolidate, feed general ledger, initiate batch program)*
>>   *Task c (Develop prototype of Powerbuilder user interface)*
>>   *Task d (Demonstrate prototype to users)*
>>   *Task e (Fix prototype based on user comments)*
>>   *Task f (Analyze "enter employee hours" function)*
>>   *Task g (Build "enter employee hours")*
>>   *Task h (Test "enter employee hours")*
>>   *Task i (Analyze "maintain employee history")*
>>   *Task j (Build "maintain employee history")*
>>   *Task k (Test "maintain employee history")*
>>   *Task l (Analyze "browse checks")*
>>   *Task m (Build "browse checks")*
>>   *Task n (Test "browse checks")*
>>   *Task o (Analyze "support corrections")*
>>   *Task p (Build "support corrections")*
>>   *Task q (Test "support corrections")*
>>   *Task r (Analyze "reprint checks")*
>>   *Task s (Build "reprint checks")*
>>   *Task t (Test "reprint checks")*
>>   *Task u (Analyze "consolidate")*

> *Task v (Build "consolidate")*
> *Task w (Test "consolidate")*
> *Task x (Analyze "feed general ledger")*
> *Task y (Build "feed general ledger")*
> *Task z (Test "feed general ledger")*
> *Task aa (Analyze "initiate batch program")*
> *Task ab (Build "initiate batch program")*
> *Task ac (Test "initiate batch program")*
> *Activity 3 (and so on)*

These names, of course, are not cast in stone. A phase could be called a process, which means that activities could be referred to as phases, and so on. Further levels of breakdown are also possible, in that tasks can be divided into subtasks, and so on. The important element being presented here is the division of a project into several implementation schedules, each of which satisfies one or more project requirements. It is also necessary to define a method of reaching each measurable. These relationships are shown in Figure 4.4.

Figure 4.4 shows that a collection of subtasks makes up a task; a collection of tasks makes up an activity; a collection of activities makes up a phase; a collection of phases makes up a project.

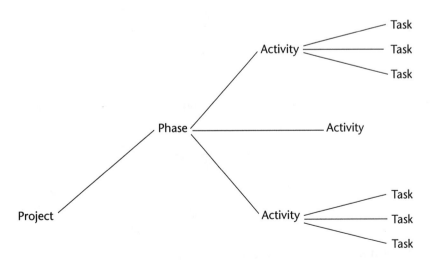

FIGURE 4.4 Dividing a project into time periods.

PROJECT PLANNING CONSTRAINTS

Constraints are applied at various stages in the life of a project. A constraint is a limiting factor on a project (e.g., budget, delivery date). A collection of constraints applicable to most projects is shown in Figure 4.5, and discussed in more detail in this section.

Budget

An overall budget is usually assigned to a project during the project justification stage. Depending on the sophistication and frequency of measurement, the budget can include human skills, equipment, space, time-sharing, fixed costs (e.g., telephone, stationery), and lunches. Budgetary limitations are also applied at other levels of a project: They are fairly common at the phase level, but not so common for activities or tasks. Shifting budget amounts proportionately between phases is commonly done to shift project priorities.

Budget expenditures are tracked on an ongoing basis for management reporting. A common frequency is to consolidate budget expenditure reports monthly for senior management meetings.

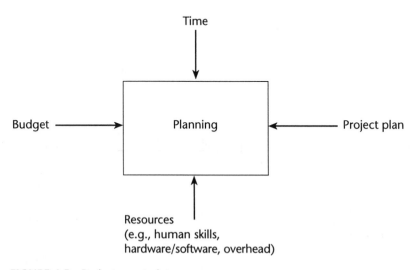

FIGURE 4.5 Project constraints.

Time

A project starts and ends on specific target dates. The duration of the project is iteratively divided into shorter periods, often called phases, activities, tasks, and subtasks. Dates for the phase and activity levels are usually related to measurable deliverables.

Sometimes start and end target dates for the project are flexible. In such instances, a manager can use the sum of the individual lower levels to determine the total duration of the project, and thus the start and end dates.

The day-to-day progress of a project is usually tracked in terms of time spent.

Resources

Multiple types of resources are applied to a project. A project manager generally tracks these at various times during a project. Some types of resources are required only at specific times (e.g., skills to build a network), while other resources are required on an ongoing basis (e.g., the services of a developer). Project resources are divided into the following categories:

Human Skills Human skills are often the only project resource that many managers consider when planning their projects. Managers should determine which skill sets are required on a project at an aggregate level and then divide them across a task or activity level. Required skills can sometimes be provided by the same human resource. For the purpose of allocation on the project plan, each resource should be identified as follows:

Resource title, resource name, % of time on project, rate, start date, end date

Suppose that Neil Sector is an architect on the project. He can be used half time; his hourly rate is $200. He is only available between January 3 and July 20 of any given year. This information translates into the following example:

Architect, Neil Sector, 50%, $200/hr, January 3, 19xx, July 20, 19xx

IS Hardware/Software In client/server and open systems environments, it is increasingly important to plan for the availability of technology at the time it is needed on a project. For example, in most client/server applications, many different hardware and software components are required, but not always at the same time. Development can begin on a small UNIX-based machine with limited capacity, but testing of the application should be done on a larger machine. This means that the larger machine should be budgeted and delivered in time for testing to begin. Getting the machine too soon may result in needless expenditures; getting the machine too late will delay the project.

The authors have seen examples on client/server projects with tight deadlines where the development software was available, the hardware platforms were leased and available, the development team was hired and trained, the business requirements were signed off, but meaningful work could not begin because the operating system on the hardware platform was inconsistent with the database server. This stopped meaningful development from beginning for several weeks on a 12-week project. Although other work could be done in the meantime, there is no question that this sort of delay was costly and harmful to the success of the project.

Managers must be careful to ensure that the correct hardware/software combinations (with the proper add-ons) have been selected for the project and ordered when required. They must also ensure that it is technically possible to do what is planned.

Overhead Requirements This involves planning for resources such as office space, telephone lines, and furniture. Demand for these resources can fluctuate dramatically (e.g., hiring twelve testers during testing). Optimization of these resources can save significant amounts of money on the project. For example, use of office space can be combined with the needs of other departments to share available space. Other methods include short-term leases of office space, flexible working hours, and work-at-home strategies.

PITFALLS IN PLANNING

Project planning is not an exact science, thus it is rare that the plans of any two projects are the same. Every project has unique aspects that make the planning process unique and problematic. For managers who are looking to duplicate the same management approach from one project to another, there is significant jeopardy to their success. Following a generic recipe is not possible and should not be done. Furthermore, the problems this approach causes may not become visible until it is too late to save the project.

Human nature is another key pitfall in the planning process. Given difficult and easy tasks, many managers (who, of course, are human beings) have the tendency to do the easy ones instead of focusing on the new challenges of the current project. Add to this that bad planning does not become evident for many months, or years, and it becomes apparent that lazy or sloppy planning is easy to get away with. This is not to say that managers want to follow this route deliberately, just that they may be doing so without realizing it.

Chapter 5, Why Projects Fail, describes many factors that contribute to project failure. Some of these are particularly applicable during the planning process, and include the following:

□ Lack of a project plan
□ Requirements not understood by the project team
□ Insufficient funding
□ Unrealistic expectations of stakeholders
□ Lack of project management and leadership skills

Managers who do not have the ability to plan effectively should be prepared to hire resources to assist them in avoiding the pitfalls mentioned in this section. This can be done painlessly by hiring contract architects or project leaders for assistance, with the clear mandate for skills transfer. These contractors do not become permanent expense items, nor do they compete with the project manager.

Another insidious pitfall in the planning process occurs when managers, uncomfortable with their ability to deliver the project successfully, resist putting a proper project plan together to avoid being held to a particular schedule. Managers sometimes use this technique to delay a project until they can get themselves safely out of the picture. In other cases, the manager is comfortable with the technique with no plans to change. Completion dates of such projects usually slide and slide until executive management either cancels the project or motivates the manager to commit to a plan and deliver the product . . . or else.

Project managers can improve their management ability by learning the objectives and tools of planning, understanding the guidelines, and attending management courses.

PLANNING TOOLS

This chapter has discussed project planning at a conceptual level—generally a weak area for many managers, who tend to spend more time at the execution and administrative levels. Effective planning requires the ability to analyze a project and build a series of steps that allows its successful completion with incomplete information. Creating the proper plan is a mental exercise, while putting it into a format that can be communicated and monitored requires physical tools.

A project plan can be started by simply writing it down on a piece of paper or typing it into a word processing file. In fact, this is a useful method of beginning the planning process, as the manager is free to reflect and plan without the distraction of using the complex editing facilities that are offered by most planning tools. At this stage, speed of thought and typing is important, as the plan is constantly changing. Once the skeleton of the project plan is in a reasonable state, it can be imported or entered into a project management tool and subsequently refined.

To gain an understanding of a project and to be able to communicate it to others, a manager can start investigating at either the activity or the task level. This requires an understanding of the following information:

☐ Activity number and name or task number and name
☐ Title
☐ Resources
☐ Start Date
☐ Target Date
☐ Deliverables
☐ Dependency

□ Duration
□ Person Days
□ Description

The authors have found it convenient to use a word processing package like WordPerfect or Microsoft Word to enter this information for each activity into a file. The file is then printed and iteratively validated until a good understanding of the project activities and deliverables is attained. This is shown in the following example:

> *Filename: payplan.1 Summary of Findings for Phase 1*
>   *Activity No: 1   Mapping*
>   *Title: Gather existing documentation and programs*
>   *Resources: Neil Sector, Rohit Jaiswal*
>   *Start Date: Jan 5, 95*
>   *Target Date: Jan 20, 95*
>   *Deliverables: Data dictionary, function list*
>   *Depends on: nothing*
>   *Duration: 10 days*
>   *Person Days: 20*
>   *Description: Use current documentation and application as a*
>   *source. Technology is CICS, IMS, VSAM, Cobol, and PL/1.*
>   *Activity No: 2   Build User Interface*
>   *Title: Develop user interface in Powerbuilder.*
>   *Resources: Darryl Coombs*
>   *Start Date: Jan 5, 95*
>   *Target Date: Feb 1, 95*
>   *Deliverables: The following screens: Timesheet, TimeApproval,*
>   *PayApproval, Corrections, History.*
>   *Depends on: nothing*
>   *Duration: 10 days*
>   *Person Days: 10*
>   *Description: Migrate current CICS screens.*
>   *Activity No: 3   Build Physical Database*
>   *Title: Build an optimized physical database for the payroll application for Sybase SQL Server.*
>   *Resources: Amarjit Singh*
>   *Start Date: Jan 22, 95*
>   *Target Date: Feb 15, 95*

> *Deliverables: Database creation script, data script.*
> *Depends on: Activity 1*
> *Duration: 8 days*
> *Person Days: 20*
> *Description: Build a logical data model and convert it to a physical data model for optimized implementation under Sybase SQL Server System 10.*

The preceding file should be expanded for the remaining activities previously defined in this chapter. After receiving confirmation for the activities, the file can be modified to include details for the tasks. During the process of seeking confirmation, a manager should be open to making changes to the plan. Clearly, this is a time-consuming and complex process. But this is the nature of planning. Time spent doing this properly will benefit the project greatly.

Several iterative cycles later, when the file has been fixed and validated, it can be typed into a project management tool and archived (it probably will not be required again). The version of the plan in the project management tool is subsequently used. Some popular tools on the market for this purpose are Microsoft Project and Project Workbench. Project plans are commonly built in the form of Gantt charts. A sample Gantt chart is shown in Figure 4.6. Gantt charts are a pictorial representation of a project plan with the following elements:

□ Task Name: This is the user-defined name of a phase, activity, task, subtask, or other line item.

□ Duration: This is the length of time required for the line item defined under task name (generally in days).

□ Start Date: Start date of the line item defined under task name.

□ End Date: Expected end date of the line item defined under task name.

□ Resources: One or more resources can be allocated to the line item under task name. These resources can be selected from a pool of resources that are either allocated to the project or a group of projects.

The reader is referred to Chapter 10 of this book for a tutorial on Microsoft Project.

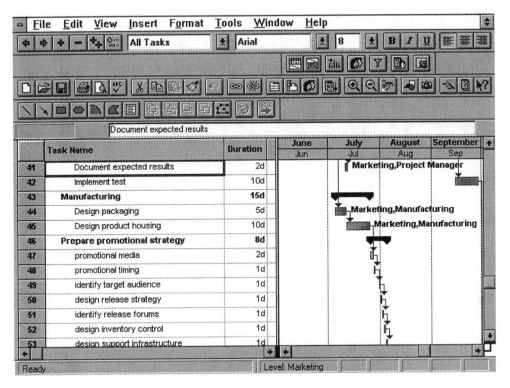

FIGURE 4.6 A sample Gantt chart.

OTHER PICTORIAL TOOLS

In addition to Gantt charts, several other pictorial tools are available to assist in the project planning effort. Although the Gantt chart is, in the opinion of the authors, the most useful, the following tools serve a useful purpose as well:

Critical Path Method (CPM)

This graphical technique identifies critical tasks in a project plan. A CPM network shows the minimum amount of time required to deliver the project. Changing any of the tasks on the critical path will change the time required to complete the project. CPM also shows dependencies between tasks and priorities between tasks. A sample CPM network is shown in Figure 4.7.

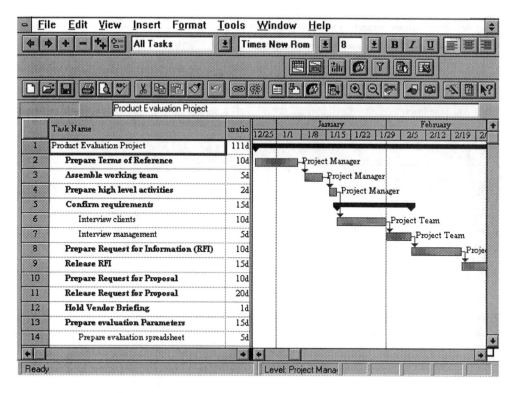

FIGURE 4.7 Sample CPM network.

Program Evaluation and Review Technique (PERT)

This graphical tool is essentially used to identify dependencies between tasks. A sample PERT screen is shown in Figure 4.8.

PROJECT DEVELOPMENT METHODOLOGIES AND THE PROJECT LIFECYCLE

Project development methodologies have become common in most organizations where the question is not "Is there a development methodology in this organization?" but rather, "How many methodologies does this organization have, and which one is being used in this department at the current time?" Methodologies have become a selling feature for many consulting organizations who offer their services,

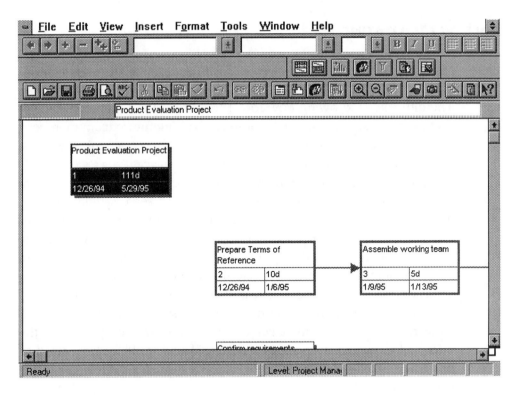

FIGURE 4.8 Sample PERT screen.

along with a proprietary methodology that was developed with the support of several large clients. All of these methodologies have some success stories.

The planning stages discussed in this chapter are standard in a broad range of methodologies. A project manager can designate the remaining unused processes defined in the methodology as activities in the project plan. The specific details, such as the duration or cost for a process, depend on several factors, beginning with the methodology being used and, of course, the specifics of the project. Chapter 7 of this book defines a methodology called the Iterative Project Development Methodology that has been used successfully in projects ranging in size from $25,000 to several million dollars. This methodology is a refinement on Rapid Application Development (RAD), which has been popular in the last couple of years.

ROLE OF FACILITATING

Many project managers may be sincere in wanting to develop a meaningful project plan by conducting a comprehensive planning process. The difficulty is knowing how to get the information that is needed to do this, and also how to reach consensus among future team members. Documentation will only get you so far, and in most organizations this is either absent, out of date, or only a starting place.

Properly conducted Joint Application Design (JAD) sessions consisting of two or more members can be used to serve a dual purpose. A manager should do a fair bit of learning in private and endeavor to build a series of pictorial views of a project, including a data model, process model, flow of the application, and a rudimentary project plan at a minimum. This information should be checked with key users in a series of one-on-one meetings (call them JADs, but they are just effective meetings). This information should be used to improve the documentation. When the manager is satisfied with the quality of the information obtained about the project, JADs should be organized to bring key people within the organization together to review the documented information.

JAD attendees should include key business users, architects, designers, project leaders, and anyone else who has an interest or influence in the project. The manager should be careful to limit attendance to a dozen people at most. When numbers go beyond this limit, different groups of JADs should be a organized to maintain effectiveness of the process.

The JAD sessions will allow key members of the organization to become involved in the process, provide input, confirm the proposed solution, and get to know each other. The importance of these factors on the success of the project cannot be underestimated. In most cases, the JAD sessions will also generate changes to a manager's documentation. This is good, because the end product will be a better plan than at the start of the process.

There are several potential pitfalls to the JAD process. Some people in the organization may not see value in attending them, or object to the amount of time they consume. The manager should attempt to overcome these objections by drawing on success stories. If this does not work, a manager can promise to limit the amount of time a particular member needs to actually spend in the meeting, or provide a written summary if attendance is impossible. As a final resort, it may be necessary to force an invitation and cooperation by involving a higher authority in the company. This has also been known to work.

Another potential pitfall in the JAD process is insufficient planning on the part of the manager. The manager should have developed a good understanding of the project, given the available information. It is perfectly acceptable to be wrong in an opinion, or to say "I could not reach a conclusion with the information I had." It is not acceptable to look embarrassed when someone in the meeting holds up a purchase order (PO), when you did not even consider that POs were an issue. In other words, the manager should be in a position to propose—and admit to being totally wrong, if necessary—a complete solution or to ask questions that lead to a complete solution. Furthermore, a manager should prepare sufficient documentation of suitable quality to be able to walk the attendees through the discussion.

The final pitfall that will be discussed here is the choice of a facilitator. Not everyone can facilitate a JAD session—this requires unique skills that many managers simply do not have. Sometimes it is better to hire a contract facilitator to lead the JAD sessions. This allows an expert to handle extremely delicate discussions, and it may also allow the members in attendance to speak more freely to an outsider, who is not a direct threat or a superior.

ESTIMATING

Project plans are also used for estimating or confirming resource requirements for a project, with a focus on the following three components: time, cost, and resources. The accuracy of the estimates depends on the detail level and accuracy of a project plan.

Estimates are used for many purposes, with an emphasis on the following situations:

1. To determine fixed price bids on projects. This is especially important for consulting companies, including outsourcing firms, systems integrators, and contracting firms. These firms survive on project billings, making accuracy a paramount concern. The risk associated with an estimate is offset by a buffer amount to protect

the company. Manager compensation is often tied to how closely the estimates and actuals comply.

2. To request budget and staffing support. Estimates are used to forecast a future internal budget for a company. This can cause management to make decisions on which projects are supported and which are cancelled.

THE EFFECTIVE PROJECT PLAN

When can a project plan be described as being poorly put together? This is determined by how well the project manager completes his or her homework. There are some clearly objective conditions to identify. For example, the activities in the following project plan are not well thought out. In fact, the project manager who designed this plan has not really built a plan at all, but rather a list of "to do" items that is trying to be passed off as a plan.

The key weakness in this plan is that it is too generic. The project manager has clearly not understood the scope of the project. In fact, how would one estimate the scope, cost, or timeline of this project based on this ambiguous information? Each activity is left wide open. To improve the plan and add value to it, the following questions need to be answered:

□ What are the main functions?
□ What are the input screens?

TABLE 4.2 Project Plan: Invoicing Application

Activity	Description
1 Kickoff meeting	
2 Determine main functions for the invoicing system	
3 Design input screens	
4 Meet with users to confirm screens and functions	
5 Develop programs	
6 Test	
7 Implement	

☐ Which users will be involved in meetings? What will be done with each of them?

☐ What programs need to be written?

☐ What is the approach for testing? Who is involved in the testing?

☐ Determine dependencies between tasks.

Someone needs to investigate these activities at a more detailed level.

SUMMARY

This chapter introduced the reader to the project planning process, which involves a series of key stages leading to the development of a project plan. A key component of the project plan is the ability to describe a project in terms of building blocks—namely, phases, activities, and tasks. This allows a manageable view of a project to occur. Each task can be described in terms of a start and end date, deliverables, and resources. Deliverables are important because they provide a measurable method of evaluating a task. A project was also described in terms of milestones (major events).

Pitfalls in planning were described. The common pitfalls include lack of a project plan, requirements not understood by the project team, and insufficient funding. The use of JAD techniques for developing and communicating project plans was also described. JAD techniques can be applied to the team, as well as to seek consensus with client management.

Three graphical representations of a project plan were introduced, Gantt charts, PERT, and CPM. Gantt charts are the most common graphical representation that show task description, resources, task and overall project duration, and important dates on a project plan. The CPM method identifies the critical project tasks and shows the minimum amount of time required to deliver the project. PERT is a graphical tool to identify dependencies between tasks. The use of project plans for estimating and confirming resource requirements was described. The key components of estimating are time, cost, and resources.

Why Projects Fail

OVERVIEW

In this chapter the reader will learn about:

- Negative project events and outcomes
- Categories of project failure
- The human element of project failure
- Technological limitations
- The impact of political games on a project
- Funding limitations
- Methodology limitations
- Case studies of unsuccessful projects

DEFINING PROJECT FAILURE

Project failure can rarely be described in absolute terms. Some projects fail so badly that companies go out of business. Other projects fail, but their impact is hardly felt by the organization or the people affected. In many cases, projects are successful in some areas, while failing in others.

Table 5.1 identifies a set of events that are generally indicative of project failure. The second column in the table identifies the severity of

TABLE 5.1 Events indicative of project failure

Project Event	Severity
Cancellation	High
Late delivery	Medium to High
Over budget	Medium to High
Low quality	Medium to High
High employee turnover	Low to Medium

the project event. Table 5.2 and the legend explain the impact of the event on the careers of the manager and members of the project team. The legend also identifies impacts on the organization.

The events in Tables 5.1 and 5.2 can also be described in terms of degree. For example, a project can be a few dollars or a few billion dollars over budget. Projects can also suffer more than one event, such as late delivery and being over budget. Depending on the circumstances, some events may be more acceptable than others. For example, some projects are so important that a manager is free to go over budget, and still be congratulated for running a successful project.

TABLE 5.2 Impacts associated with project failure

Severity Code	Description	Primary Impacts
High	Worst event	Organization + Manager + Team
Medium	Career damaging	Manager
Low	Embarrassing	Manager

LEGEND
The Severity Code corresponds to the Severity column in Table 5.1. The Primary Impacts column identifies the parties directly impacted by the related severity code. Events that have a high severity code impact everyone involved, including the organization, the manager, and the team members. Events that have a medium severity impact the same parties, but to a smaller extent. In this case, companies are not expected to go out of business. Team members are rarely fired or disciplined, but do receive tarnished reputations; however, they can point the blame at someone else—the project manager. Consequently, the primary impact of the medium severity code is on the project manager's career and reputation.

Other projects can be considered to be successful, even if they are delivered late.

Why do so many IS projects fail? If projects in other industries had the same failure rate as IS projects, there would be widespread public outrage. Imagine the reaction you would have if an architect's response to a public inquiry into why a newly constructed building toppled over was "The municipal building codes kept changing." In defense of the information systems industry, municipal building codes do not change nearly as frequently as IS specifications do; furthermore, people have been constructing buildings much longer than they have been programming applications.

There is also the additional issue of magnitude and exposure to potential points of failure to consider. Many construction projects, though visually large, do not have a high degree of inherent complexity that varies dramatically from one project to another. This makes a comparison of a construction project to a typical corporate IS project unfair. However, when comparing mega-construction projects to large IS projects, more overlap becomes visible, and many of the same problems emerge.

IS projects have the additional distinction of being unlike projects in other industries in key areas. For example, the IS industry is faced with a chronic shortage of staff, an ever-evolving and changing set of development tools, a relatively high rate of employee turnover, and a very large number of working components. In fact, every line in a program, every data element in a database, every development product, and every network link is a potential point of failure.

Some standard problems result from the high complexity on most IS projects. The first problem occurs because of a general inability to recognize that a solution is correct (e.g., defining metrics). Because of the large number of components and combinations in any application, it is a real challenge to define what a successful solution should look like. For example, consider a software package like Microsoft Project. Defining metrics for all possible test conditions would be a colossal task.

A second problem occurs because phases in a project receive products from other phases, and then create ones of their own. As the number of phase levels increase, so too does the complexity. This is shown in Figure 5.1. Increasing complexity increases the potential points of

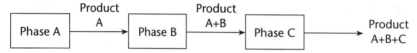

FIGURE 5.1 Phases and their projects.

failure dramatically. This creates an added challenge in maintaining the integrity of an IS project.

A final consideration is the feedback loop. This occurs when phase A builds a product that is fed into phase B. If something new is learned in phase B, a change must be made to the product from phase A, which could result in a change in phase B, and so on. This creates a moving target that can keep both phases from completing successfully. The classic example of this is the case where requirements are produced in one phase and passed into the development phase where an enhancement or a correction is identified. The impact of this is shown in Figure 5.2.

On large projects, the complexity of the work that needs to be done to complete a project can be staggering. Typically, many individuals share discrete pools of knowledge that must be combined for the project to succeed. Several factors thus come into play: As project size increases (in terms of functionality, technology, and difficulty), there is

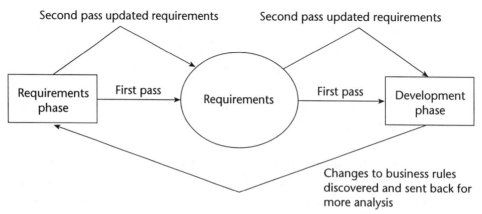

FIGURE 5.2 The feedback loop.

pressure to increase the size of the project team and the stakeholders. As these increase, so too does interpersonal complexity.

Complexity leads to chaos. Someone is needed to tie all this together. That honor falls on the project manager, who must somehow manage the project and navigate it toward success. One place to start is to understand common reasons for project failure.

This chapter identifies five broad categories, as shown in Figure 5.3, that commonly contribute to project failure. At times, a particular issue may fall into more than one category. For example, insufficient funding to hire testing resources can be viewed as a human issue as well as a funding issue. This does not affect the discussion, as the issue itself is a contributor toward project failure and its precise categorization is unimportant. This chapter also provides ways to avoid the factors that lead to project failure.

Categories of project failure are introduced in this section, with detailed explanations provided later in this chapter.

Human Issues

This broad category includes factors such as employee turnover, soundness of the business requirements, understanding of the business requirements, and technical skills. Each of these factors can destroy a project, so a project manager must become intimately aware of what they are, what the exposures are, and how to avoid them.

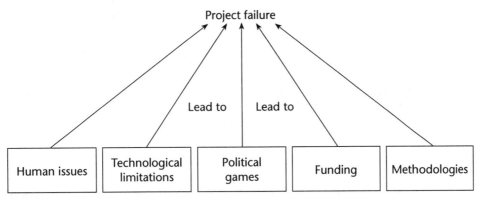

FIGURE 5.3 Categories of project failure.

Technological Limitations

Technical limitations can also cause a project to fail. This includes things like inadequate response time, not enough bandwidth for data transfer, or an inability to run certain types of software on a hardware platform. The authors' experience has been that good project management can often find a way around a technical limitation. Technological limitations will always exist, as there are some things that simply cannot be done with available technology. In such instances, manual processes are used to integrate with an automated solution until appropriate technology becomes available. This is illustrated in the following example.

> *PhysCorp International provides medical services to patients in a metropolitan vicinity. Company drivers receive a clipboard in the morning containing paper copies of service orders identifying the patients requiring service that day. The drivers sort the service orders to determine the best route for the day. At the end of the day, the drivers return to the head office to drop off their clipboards. The data entry organization updates the corporate database by rekeying everything (including comments and notes) that the drivers scribbled on the service order. Another set of service orders is printed for the next morning.*

There are several ways to automate PhysCorp International. An effective method would be to recognize situations where current technological limitations are expected to be resolved by leading-edge technology in the near future. The paper service orders will ultimately be phased out, as pen-based technology becomes reliable and affordable. But until that happens (in one year, ten years, or more), an optimized alternative solution can be designed. The bottom line is that the business of the corporation must be serviced, and solutions that jeopardize this should not be tolerated. This may mean the acceptance of an old-fashioned manual procedure.

A good project manager knows what is needed, what is possible, and when it is possible.

Political Games

Political games are played by individuals within an organization to gain rewards for themselves, or, at the very least, to take them away from someone else. In this context, their existence is hardly surprising, as most humans work for money, personal fulfillment, or to gain membership into a group. However, political games, as inevitable as they may be, have a tendency to become highly destructive to projects and even organizations. If left unchallenged, political games can cause irreparable damage to both.

Many years ago, one author was working on a project in a large organization. A 25-year veteran of the company, noticing that roadblocks were hampering the success of the project, offered a pearl of wisdom that is just as true on many other IS projects. He said, "Nobody wants the project to be implemented because it will highlight their weaknesses. They're also afraid to maintain the application on an ongoing basis because they don't have the skills required to do so." As it turned out, it was easier to keep the project going until the technology changed. When that happened, the project was quietly terminated.

To the question, "Why was the project started in the first place," the veteran replied: "As an insurance policy, and because there was money in the budget. Everyone has an agenda, sometimes it just isn't the same as yours."

The veteran also made another remarkable prediction. He pointed out who was going to be promoted, who was going to be transferred, and who would be tarnished as a result of the project's eventual failure. These rewards/punishments were not based on merit, but on how different individuals presented themselves to others in the organization. He turned out to be 100 percent accurate, less than a year later.

Political games are played on at least four levels in most organizations:

☐ Organizational politics
☐ Team politics
☐ Individual
☐ Business versus IS competition

These levels will be discussed later in this chapter.

Funding

A project that is not funded adequately is bound to fail. This is no secret, yet there are many projects that are started with the futile hope that somehow things will work out. This only frustrates project team members. Paradoxically, an overfunded project is also likely to fail for a different set of reasons.

Methodologies

One mistake that is common across organizations using project development methodologies is to view them as recipes (following the fancy process boxes without an understanding of the problem). It is easy to depend on a methodology for success, or perhaps more accurately, to place blame on a methodology when a project fails.

THE HUMAN ELEMENT

It can be argued that the human element, in one form or another, is a dominant contributor toward project failure. As a U.S. President once said: "The buck stops here." This is true of systems projects as well. The buck stops with the project manager.

Some typical human problems that can cause projects to fail are explained in this section.

Inability of Users to Agree on Business Requirements

This is like having General Motors paint a car red, then repaint it blue, then yellow, then back to red again. General Motors handles this problem by producing cars in different colors.

As another example, consider the situation where users agree that a merchandising system is required, but cannot agree on the functionality it should support (e.g., multiple languages, multiple currency types, multiple product types). This is primarily a problem in the early project phases and again in testing and implementation.

Suggested Solution: Recognize that indecision is a part of life and plan for it. Plan regular JAD sessions using an impartial facilitator who draws users and IS staff into constructive discussions. Document all communications and interpretations so that it is clear when decisions are being made or avoided. Public, friendly discussion gets people involved and encourages them to make decisions. The project manager should insist that experienced users, designers, and architects build an initial design that is iteratively modified until stakeholders agree on the proposals. It is important to have an escalation procedure that allows someone to ultimately make a decision if compromise is not reached within a project team. The manager can also use various techniques, such as prototyping, to allow users to see the impact of their decisions early in the process.

Inability of Users to Communicate Business Requirements

Another problem that is encountered on IS projects is a general lack of communication betweenl users, managers, and IS development teams.

Suggested Solution: A manager should insist that communication is maintained within a project team, no matter the size of the project. Effective methods of doing this include regular JAD sessions, status meetings, good documentation, and centrally located logs of issues, recommendations, and conclusions. Team members should be mandated to share information openly.

Inability of Users to Understand the Implications of Business Requirements

This is similar to the inability of users to agree on business requirements, however, this problem arises when users agree on a solution without fully understanding its ramifications. In other words, everyone may agree that a Canadian Purchase Order is required, but they may not understand that it is needed in both French and English. This is commonly a weak area on projects, for the following reasons:

☐ Failure of users to understand the implications and totality of their business requirements

☐ Failure of the IS team to internalize and fully understand the business requirements
☐ Failure of users and the IS team to understand and agree on the same business requirements
☐ Incomplete business specifications

Suggested Solution: There is no easy solution for this problem. Again, well facilitated JAD sessions that carefully take a project team (users, IS, management, architects, etc.) through various levels of the system, from strategic planning to system design, will allow understanding to be gained. Patience and a willingness to share details with all parties concerned will enhance an understanding of the requirements. The manager should insist that this JAD approach be followed.

Inability to Accommodate Changes to Business Requirements

Business requirements are subject to change for a variety of reasons, even after they have been agreed to by stakeholders and formally signed off. After all, how many people can walk into a department store and buy a suit without changing their minds at least a few times? It is not surprising that users change some of the requirements, even in the development phases or implementation.

Managing changes to business requirements is a complex part of a development project, and requires understanding, cooperation, and commitment from all stakeholders. The authors can remember a project where a consulting firm was brought onsite to complete a fixed price piece of work that involved migrating a standard A/R legacy application to an Oracle environment. Executive management agreed that because the migration was pretty standard, there was no need to have what was believed to be a costly and time-consuming formal requirements signoff process. It was agreed that the project would be finished when the migrated application had the same functionality as the original legacy system. The executives withdrew, and left the managers and team members from a variety of departments to interpret what this meant.

A lot of political pressure was exerted in many directions, from the business users, client development staff, and the consulting team. This made development especially difficult and open to interpretation because it was impossible to have the legacy application work exactly like the newly migrated application.

The user community was responsible for accepting functions of the migrated application during a series of testing phases. As they continued to test, the testers started asking for changes to the application. Initially, these requests came over the phone or passed-on short memos. The development team complied and maintained a quick turnover time for problem verification. Within a few weeks, several observations were made that could have seriously affected delivery of the product:

1. A change was requested one week, and reversed within a few weeks after the testers had a better chance to understand its implications. In some instances, other mutually exclusive changes were requested (e.g., move the date to position row 3, position 5 and row 4, position 65).
2. Some changes were clearly outside the scope of the release. They may have been important, but they were not part of the original contract, and could not be done by the consulting team without incurring financial losses.
3. All changes were being treated with equal priority. This meant that simple display changes (e.g., print commas inside large numbers) were being given the same priority as more serious errors that were show stoppers (e.g., a product code accounting for 25 percent of the business was not processed correctly).
4. The developers had misunderstood some requirements.

Suggested Solution: A simple process mechanism solved all of these problems. As the testing team discovered a bug or a change, they put the information into a central ASCII file. Each change was numbered, assigned a priority, and carefully described with examples. Members of the development team began to browse and update the file on a routine basis. Problems were selected based on the priority assigned by the testers—thus urgent problems were selected first. Enhancements to the scope of the release were identified, estimated, and saved for future releases. The central file allowed duplicate or contradictory requests to be quickly discovered and saved the project team a great deal of time and aggravation.

This simple file allowed the entire change management process to become more civilized and easier to manage. The file itself was used as one of the reports passed to the steering committee; consequently, there was a clear audit trail of what was happening and all participants became accountable, sometimes despite themselves. It is far easier to ask for a contradictory change over the phone, with no paper trail, than to record such a request in a file that will be scrutinized several weeks later.

The application was implemented successfully.

Insufficient Technical Skills

Insufficient technical skills can result from a variety of situations. For example, hiring resources with mainframe backgrounds for client/server projects, or vice versa, and hiring inexperienced people. Another cause of insufficient technical skills is high turnover. Depending on the length of a project, it is inevitable that some team members leave, get promoted, or are transferred to another area. A final cause could be for a lack of technical ability. This problem can occur in all phases of a project lifecycle.

Suggested Solution: Depending on the timeframe available for the project, technical skills can be learned through inhouse courses, self-training, university/college continuing education courses, mentoring/centers of excellence, and textbooks. Provide training for people who have demonstrated ability and commitment. Hire competent technical resources with demonstrated successful track records. Ensure that development standards are in place, so team members have something to emulate. Try to have access to technical gurus, as needed, and provide orientation for new team members.

Failure to Effectively Manage One or More Phases of the Development Effort

Failure in any of the project lifecycle phases (as defined in Appendix F) can cause the whole project effort to fail.

Suggested Solution: A project manager should develop a comprehensive plan showing clear deliverables, as well as clear criteria for measuring success at each step. The manager should track against these carefully, and take corrective action as soon as a problem is encountered. Quick fixes, such as expanding a timeline or just throwing another resource onto a project to keep per person time allocation under a threshold, should be avoided, as these approaches do not help the bottom line of a project's success. By developing an intrinsic understanding of a project's issues, a manager is able to take iterative action that reacts to problems when they are identified. This is what project management is all about.

Insufficient Testing

Applications that do not go through a cycle of thorough testing will probably fail in production or during acceptance testing. This phase requires preparation of test cases, advance notice, and adequate staffing in terms of numbers and knowledge. This should be viewed as a separate activity, and not as a subcomponent of the development activity.

Suggested Solution: Invest the time and money for iterative testing phases. Allow time for fixes and retesting. Impress the need for thorough testing on all team members and associated teams. Consider the implementation of Total Quality Management (TQM) programs.

Weak Implementation Strategy

Implementation requires careful planning, including a method to back out an application if something goes wrong. A carefully planned, phased approach is used by some organizations instead of an all-or-nothing effort with a significant downside, if something goes wrong.

Suggested Solution: Implementation involves risk management. Human plans, no matter how well thought out, cannot anticipate or handle all eventualities. Develop an implementation strategy that protects the whole organization against failure. Conversely, plan for success by a phased strategy that implements low-volume, low-risk, and low-priority components first. Consider things like response time and capacity issues with realistic data volumes and user demand during benchmarking activities and capacity planning, far in advance of the implementation phase.

Insufficient Resources

Projects require a specific amount of effort and materials—computers, telecommunications equipment, people, and others. A project plan should identify what is required, when it is required, and the quantity required. Since this number cannot, by its very nature, be 100 percent accurate, a project manager must draw on experience and consultation to budget resources throughout the project. The following events should be considered and planned for:

□ Architecture/design skills to get started
□ Normal turnover of key resources
□ Skills transfer
□ High-intensity deadlines
□ Short-term skills requirements (e.g., facilitator, auditor, GUI standards expert, technical guru)

Suggested Solution: Build a pool of resources, with members who have more than one skillset to offer. Plan for short-term and long-term needs. Do not fill positions with bodies, but rather with individuals who have attitudes, abilities, and skillsets appropriate to the project.

Inability to Deal with Contractors and Vendors

Managers must learn to deal with vendors and contractors—who have almost become a permanent fixture on projects. Contractors, or consultants, as some prefer to be called, generally augment organizational staff by providing specialized skills or, bluntly, additional bodies. Contractors can also build an entire project team through outsourcing, but they are still responsible to the client manager.

Vendors generally support a product that is required by an organization. This could be hardware, software, services (communication), or packages.

In dealing with contractors and vendors, managers are faced with two main challenges. The first is to ensure that their organization is properly dealt with by the vendor or contractor. The second challenge is to create an environment in which the vendor or contractor can succeed and will want to succeed.

Suggested Solution: Develop a cooperative effort with vendors and contractors. Make it clear that you want regular, open, honest communication. Develop a service agreement or at least an unofficial expectations agreement. Establish key contacts to maintain ongoing information flow. Understand that vendors and contractors have their own businesses to run. Give them enough notice to react to expectations, and treat them as human beings.

Bad Planning

Bad planning is caused by many factors. Projects require a certain amount of effort, measured in person-hours, and a wide variety of skillsets to succeed. These are also required on a specific schedule. Planning means to make sure that resources are available as needed, and that the project plan is feasible and well tracked. This is a good measure of a manager's effectiveness.

Suggested Solution: The manager should develop a realistic plan, not unduly pessimistic or overly optimistic. Be prepared to aggressively change the plan to meet the present situation. Additional planning issues were discussed in Chapter 4.

Unrealistic Expectations

This type of failure occurs when managers are not concerned with facts, but insist that some dream be fulfilled at some particular point in time of their choosing. This is not referring to an ambitious manager who is trying to get people to give their best. This situation refers to a blatantly impossible situation (such as working 2.5 full time jobs at the same time—this does happen in some consulting firms). Some employees attempt to fulfill this mandate, either because they have bought into what is being asked, or because they are too timid to contradict someone in authority. The result is that managers will find out at the worst possible time—when the deadline is imminent—that what they are asking for is impossible to deliver.

Suggested Solution: Do not expect someone with a COBOL background to learn C and UNIX overnight, or vice versa. This is not to say that employees cannot be taught new skills, but sometimes there is not enough time to do so within a project's timeframe. Other unrealistic expectations include having new requirements incorporated into a project at any time, no time allocation for training, building an application without support from stakeholders, and building an application without signed-off specifications.

Some managers also think of a workday as consisting of 20 hours and a workweek as having 7 days. The reality is people need a life outside the office to be complete and productive in the long term. A workday is really only about 8 hours and a workweek is 5 days. There are also various statutory holidays and celebrations during the year. Another accepted practice in many companies is to budget a two-to-four week vacation during the year.

Working with Poor Performers

Some people may have noble intentions, but sadly, lack the experience or ability to perform well on some projects. A manager may have to deal with workers who have made significant errors on previous projects or who have no relevant experience.

Suggested Solution: Look for opportunities to train and mentor such employees, either through your efforts or those of other members of the project team. Judge people on past performance, but understand that they can improve (or devolve) over time. Be prepared to give people opportunities in situations that you are able to control. In other words, if your trust is not met, this error in judgment should not derail a project.

TECHNICAL LIMITATIONS

Many years ago one author was working on a development project to build a shrink-wrapped piece of software for the greenhouse industry. The analysis and design of the application went strictly by the book. Standards were meticulously set and followed. Walk-throughs of the application revealed the presence of structured code, meaningful variable names, and easy maintainability. The application ran on top of an xbase database.

Presentation of the initial prototype to the business users was well received. This was in the early 1980s, and it was easy to impress users with a dash of color, specific message and errors lines, and an intuitive menu. The prototype was robust and had some functionality already completed. Additional funding was provided for the project and full-scale development began. The design of this application was innovative and exciting.

Several iterations of the product continued to improve its functionality. Several optimization and performance improvements were realized by building specific indexes, tokenizing the code, and using a RAM disk for faster access to data. However, no matter how many clever improvements were made by the development team, the PCs horsepower came from an Intel 8088 chip, and there were consequential performance limitations imposed by this bottleneck. Adding functionality to the package made it noticeably slower.

Hard disks were not yet readily available and disk drives were reading 5-$\frac{1}{2}$ inch floppy disks with 360 kb capacity. The application quickly exceeded this space and grew to fill several diskettes. Eventually the application had to be divided into physical partitions that required a user to swap the floppy disks while navigating through certain features.

The application was clearly limited by the available technology. Fortunately, use of hard disks became more popular, and a version of the application was built to run off a hard disk. A significant performance improvement was noticed; however, the underlying chip was still an 8088. The application was beta tested at greenhouse sites, but due to performance limitations was not actively marketed. Under 286+ technology and SCSI disk drives the same application runs with subsecond response time for the most heavily used transactions, but the marketing opportunity was missed. Technical limitations proved to be a show stopper for this application.

Technical limitations can become show stoppers under the following conditions:

☐ Overambitious development
☐ Insufficient benchmarking
☐ Lack of capacity planning
☐ Migration from a development to a production environment (sometimes requires changes to hardware/software)
☐ Inability to identify functionality that cannot be automated with current technology

Before selecting a technology architecture, careful benchmarks with a high volume of data should be conducted. It is important to avoid conducting a limited benchmark with only a few thousand records and then multiplying the results by a hundred or a thousand to calculate the application performance at a few million records. Performance degradation is rarely linear, which can cause a stranglehold on production systems. A full benchmark will also reveal other exposures such as disk capacity, throughput considerations, and backup/recovery rates.

Independent reference checks with the same type of business for a technology infrastructure are also highly recommended. Do not accept a vendor's claim without independent verification. For example, if running a financial application on a database server xxx under operating system yyy, with a network protocol zzz, take the time to visit a similar configuration, or at least send a questionnaire to the organization using the product and critically examine their responses.

POLITICAL ISSUES

Political issues, more often than many people want to admit, can cause projects to fail. Political issues fall into four categories, namely: organizational politics, team politics, individual politics, or business versus IS politics.

Organizational Politics

Project managers are sometimes frustrated to find a general lack of commitment within an organization to implement a project. Such situations are difficult to resolve completely. When confronted with this situation, a project manager should undertake the following activities, in the order shown:

1. Try to understand why there is a lack of commitment.
2. Try to get commitment for the project with sound reasoning and judgment. Demonstrate personal commitment to the project.
3. Limit the scope of the project until it receives commitment and does not offend anybody.
4. Document issues and concerns. Turn the project into a study with recommendations. If an application can be completed, table it with an implementation strategy. Allow executive management to make the decision to deploy or shelve the application.
5. Identify lessons learned and present them to other managers in the company.
6. Do not appear frustrated or difficult to work with. This only backfires.

An inability to function in such a difficult situation can stagnate a career and produce unnecessary stress for those involved. This is an example of politics at the organizational level. A project manager generally has no choice but to participate successfully in this type of politics. As a final resort, a manager can always make a career more, either internally or externally.

An example of this type of problem occurred on a project with a seven-figure budget. This project was started by an IS director to guarantee the integrity of the corporate database—just in case. Executive management funded the project, not understanding the technical consequences, but accepting that a database exposure existed and to make sure the project director had no excuses—just in case.

Development progressed along nicely; however, cooperation across departments was rare. For example, whenever a CICS region was required for testing or the database needed to be frozen, the project was given a lower priority relative to other projects within the organization, and consequently its deadlines kept getting pushed back. Meanwhile, pressure increased on the project manager to implement the application according to a schedule that assumed all resources would be available instantly. At some point, after many missed deadlines, the political will to implement the project disappeared. After all, a year had passed and the database had exhibited no integrity problems, so why implement a system that offered soft advantages, but could cause widespread disruption if it did not work? Furthermore, the daily work routine of the users would be changed after implementation of the system with additional responsibilities. The users could see no reason to buy into the system for the soft tangibles that were being offered. There was pressure on the manager to implement, but no desire within the organization to do so.

A situation such as this one is extremely frustrating for everyone concerned, and usually the project manager is left holding the bag. Incidentally, this system was not implemented, and the entire team was reassigned. The project manager ended up having a reputation as trying too hard and being a bit moody and was skipped over for a promotion.

The bottom line is that a lone project manager can rarely beat the system, and quite frankly, the value of a project must be measured in terms relative to the whole organization. Some projects are initiated as insurance policies against a potentially cataclysmic event. A project manager must have the political astuteness to recognize such a situation and take appropriate steps to satisfy the expectations of senior management while protecting his or her job.

Senior management should also recognize that some projects exist as insurance policies and may never be implemented. If this is the case, senior management should be honest and not set anyone up for blame. The project manager should be providing status reports and other documentation to promote this idea so that there are no surprises if the application is not implemented. This should be clearly communicated to the steering committee (e.g., a typical person spends $x on insurance. If the IS budget is $xxx, then $yy is not a bad insurance investment). As a final resort, the manager can always find another project or another job.

Generally, managers who are frustrated by organizational politics can follow some or all of the following steps:

☐ Document ideas, information, and observations. Keep a paper trail going with senior management, other departments, and team members.

☐ Do not become impatient or difficult to deal with.

☐ Start changing the visibility of the project from a tactical one to an investigative one.

☐ Write memos to members of the steering committee, politely detailing all issues and concerns.

☐ Publicize the purpose and nature of the project. Try to build internal momentum.

☐ Do not hide problems.

Team Politics

Politics can also be played within teams, with the objective of gaining the following rewards:

1. Tangible rewards. Just like birds chirping in a nest to draw their parents' attention in the hope of getting the worm, members of a team compete for the manager's attention to get a better position, pay raise, window office, faster computer, or some other perk. Managers who support this competition should not be surprised at the increased political games that result when team members learn that this attitude gets positive rewards.

2. Power and influence. Human beings love to tell others what to do. This is seen everywhere in society. Actors who are paid $8 million per picture will settle for a fraction of this salary in order to direct a movie. It should come as no surprise then, that team members will play the political game if it helps them get the power to tell other team members what to do. For example, some managers promote spying within a team. This is done by having frequent informal, one-on-one meetings with team members to gossip about what other people are doing. If a manager wants to know what Bruce is doing, why not ask Bruce, instead of going to Terry? Terry may relish the idea of having power over Bruce or influencing the way Bruce works (e.g., Bruce comes in late or talks on the phone a lot). If this has not come to the manager's attention, why is it important to hear it from Terry? And why is

Terry noticing what someone else is doing, and not doing his own work? Managers who participate in this sort of management style should not be surprised at the negative results and the lack of team building.

3. Protection against organizational politics. Many potentially good project teams are subverted by organizational politics. When it is known that this is happening, team members begin to protect their jobs instead of trying to deliver the product. Symptoms that show a growing level of politics are a surge in self-protecting memos, constant questions about responsibility, and a lack of quantifiable results.

At best, politics at the team level can encourage team members to attain peak performance, while competing with each other. In the worst and more common case, team politics degenerates into backbiting and infighting that severely undermine the project schedule. Projects can be undermined so as to fail, go well over budget, or be severely late.

Certain types of projects are more likely to exhibit this problem than others. Projects that do not delineate responsibility clearly, with poor project management and too many prima donnas, among other factors, are likely candidates. Other causes include failure to recognize loyalty and hard work, poor project management, and a high degree of workplace stress.

In the very worst situations, some team members will actively sabotage the project unless they get their way. Their message is simple: "We benefit, or the project does not succeed."

Individual Politics

Individuals play politics against other individuals anywhere within an organization. This was observed on one project, where a senior manager, who was waiting for early retirement, was primarily interested in risk avoidance. Anyone who was aggressive enough to want something done was removed from the project unceremoniously. This form of politics becomes a significant problem if the individual playing politics has a high rank within the organization, or is left unchallenged by higher management. Like a radioactive isotope with a fleeting half-life, this form of politics quickly degenerates into team politics (thus becoming a more complex problem), as individuals learn that a certain behavior is rewarded, another is punished, and that the reaction is not based on value to the company.

Business versus IS Politics

Business is taking a much more active interest in projects previously managed by IS. There are many reasons for this. Powerful, easy-to-use desktop technology (e.g., SQL tools, screen painters, xbase, decentralized computing, CASE) allows nontechnical users to build a lot of product without help from technical staff. Another reason for this trend is that projects run by IS suffer from the problem of differences between business priorities (e.g., month-end report consolidation) and IS's need to test a system. In such a situation, business typically wins, and IS cannot acceptance test a system until business users can devote time to this activity. By giving control of a project to business, IS, in fact, gives the responsibility of juggling deadlines to the department that can control it anyway.

This works well in some environments; however, this situation allows political games to be played very easily. In reality, both groups need each other. IS offers skills in system development, planning, and design that cannot be replaced by fancy screen painters on a PC. Similarly, business users have a day-to-day understanding of the business that IS cannot learn through a few weeks of intensive JAD sessions. Success or failure is clearly a shared responsibility between the groups.

FUNDING

Two project managers were discussing a sticky problem. They had a solid team working on one project, but they had just won another project. Each project offered a slim profit margin. They decided to improve the profit picture by using essentially the same team on both projects at the same time, with a few additional players. Furthermore, they determined that the project plan could be designed to fit the available budget (e.g., $100 is available, so the project would have to cost $100—whether it did or not). Items such as learning new products and client training were left out of the plan entirely. Also missing from the plan was the amount of time taken by vendors to deliver products and/or expertise to the project site. This meant that a product (a database server) was expected by a certain date. Late delivery would impact the rest of the schedule. Accommodating these items would have meant less profit, so they felt it was better to ignore the issues and hope they went away.

This planning scenario could have been catastrophic. In the end, the ability and dedication of the project team and the managers themselves pulled it off (perhaps that is what the managers were banking on). Both applications were implemented, but the stress level on the team members, especially the project leaders, was very high. Add to the picture 12-hour days and many summer weekends in the office, and one has to ask if the limited funding was reasonable. In the end, the actual profit margin was about what it would have been had both project teams been staffed properly. Perhaps, coincidentally, several key team players left the company after implementation.

A funding crunch is a serious concern in the 1990s. Organizations seemed to be much more liberal with their IS budgets during the heady 1980s. In the downsizing, restructuring spirit of the 1990s, IS budgets have been slashed and trimmed significantly. This has forced organizations to reevaluate their computer solutions by examining client/server technology and the like. Staff expenses have also been targeted as they are usually a significant portion of the budget. The problem with this is that projects are often dramatically underfunded. The resulting pressures and stress are put on the project manager, who often has no choice but to accept the mandate and guidelines of a project as laid out by senior management.

Some organizations exercise the option to pass the funding crunch pressures on to consulting firms (as discussed in Chapter 9, Outsourcing). This only begs the question in that managers with the consulting firm are faced with the same problems. Some would argue that consulting firms should be "experts" in the assignments they undertake, and so should be capable of completing the project within a smaller budget. While this is true, any competitive advantage derived from being an expert is soon lost when more than one consulting firm is bidding on an assignment. Since the firms are both experts, their respective bids will be cut appropriately.

FAILURE TO SUCCESSFULLY APPLY PROJECT DEVELOPMENT METHODOLOGIES

There is certainly no shortage of development methodologies available. Each of them undoubtedly offers implementation success stories. However, can anyone recall a project in which a methodology was followed, but success was not attained? The authors can.

Development methodologies are often used as cooking recipes or connect-the-dot puzzles. Without a complete picture of a project's issues, development methodologies are exposed to failure. Development methodologies are not magic and they do not operate in a vacuum. There are many activities taking place inside the boxes that require experience, analysis, and ability to complete. If a manager does not have a handle on a project at every stage of the development cycle, meticulously following a methodology only postpones the inevitable realization that a project is not on track. The sooner a manager realizes this and takes corrective action, the better it will be for the success of the project.

Chapter 7 describes a new methodology called the Iterative Project Development Methodology (IPDM), which has successfully delivered a broad range of projects. This methodology differs from many other commonly used development methodologies in terms of its flexibility and also its attention to deliverables, rather than processes. IPDM depends on four factors:

☐ Extensive utilization of JADs
☐ Reusable, functional prototype(s)
☐ Meaningful dialogue between stakeholders
☐ Professional facilitation

Some basic strengths of IPDM are that it supports communication between all players involved on a project, builds a broad base of commitment, and shortens the time for deliverables to be implemented (early payback).

PROJECT PROPERTIES

This chapter has presented a group of factors that can cause a project to fail. The existence and reference of these factors depends on the type of project being managed. Any given project can be described in terms of four properties: functionality, duration, scope, and size. Tables 5.3, 5.4, 5.5, and 5.6 identify expectations in terms of human reaction, technical impact (on the project), and the management challenge for each of these properties. These tables can be combined for a combination of properties on any given project. For example, a project that has medium functionality, a short duration, limited scope, and medium size has the possibility of failing, because a stressed-out project team builds a low-quality product to meet a schedule. A project manager can avoid this problem by recognizing that the relevant architecture must be available at the appropriate time by communicating this requirement to the vendors. The project team should also be freed from unnecessary tasks (e.g., do not waste their time by having them fill in countless timesheets or follow bureaucratic procedures that do not add value to the delivery of the product). The team should be encouraged to work without distractions, with clearly defined rewards for a successful delivery.

The medium category in each factor offers a better chance for success than the other two categories. This is consistent with the results of the management survey that suggests dividing large projects into consecutive medium-sized projects of 6-month durations each.

TEN WAYS FOR A MANAGER TO SPOT A PROJECT THAT WILL FAIL

1. Your team only gives you good news at every status meeting.
2. The implementation date is only a few weeks away but you, the manager, have never seen a hands-on demonstration of the application.
3. Most of the memos your team sends to you complain about the lack of skills in the other team members.
4. Team members continue to play the fine act of protecting themselves at every opportunity.

TABLE 5.3   Functionality

Project functionality refers to the business requirements that are incorporated into an application.

Functionality	Human Reaction	Technical Impact	Management Challenge
Simple (few screens and program logic and rules)	Overconfidence. Sloppiness with details.	Buy only the architecture that is needed (no need to overspend).	Make the team understand the importance of the project, despite its apparent simplicity. Need to hire appropriate resources.
Medium (a few dozen screens and programs and rules)	Reasonable opportunity to study the problem and develop a good solution.	Limited impact on architecture selection. Consider a scalable solution.	Ensure that good documentation and testing is developed.
Complex (no limit on screens or program number and size and rules)	Overwhelmed by information overflow. Concentration on overviews, instead of value-added details. No understanding of all that is required. Request for more staff. Concentration on the easy stuff, while avoiding the complex issues.	Performance problems may result as many rules are implemented. Potential for many program bugs.	Understand the task and ensure that the team is not always avoiding the difficult parts of the application. Keep on top of what the team really knows. Ensure good documentation is created from the beginning, and cross-reference with the team.

TABLE 5.4 Duration

Project duration refers to the length of the project. While this is often expressed in terms of months or years, any time period can be used.

Duration	Human Reaction	Technical Impact	Management Challenge
Short (less than five months)	High level of stress. Quality ignored while trying to just get the job done.	Opportunity to acquire proper architecture may not be available. No opportunity to shop for best prices. Risk that architecture cannot be established in so short a timeframe.	Ensure that all hardware, software, and other resources are exclusively available to meet the deadline. Protect team from unnecessary inevitable stress. Try to keep the whole team intact for the duration of the project. Avoid non–value-added activities.
Medium (between five months and one year)	Ability to plan. Competition for promotions.	Ability to shop for the best deal.	Ensure that staff is concentrating on deliverables. Have a short-term plan to accommodate occasional turnover.
Long (more than one year)	Procrastination. False starts. Duplication of planning efforts. No pressure to get started. Politics to avoid blame.	Architecture could become obsolete before the project is completed.	Divide the long project plan into manageable phases to deliver usable functionality every six months or so. Measure success at frequent intervals. Need to handle staff turnover.

TABLE 5.5 Scope

Project scope refers to the number of business areas touched by a project. This is one level higher than functionality.

Scope	Human Reaction	Technical Impact	Management Challenge
Limited (one department or area)	Internal competition for turf.	Ability to use architecture of choice.	(See simple functionality)
Broad (many departments or areas)	Competition for control of the project between departments or areas. Who's really in charge and responsible?	Requirement for architecture standards or open systems.	Maintain regular communication with management in the other departments.
External (broad, includes areas outside the company)	Possibility of chaos, as scope of a project may get out of control. Disturbances to a project team.	Possibility of multiple architectural standards and incompatibilities.	Understand external influences to ensure they do not hinder the project. Protect the project team from the unnecessary stress of a large scope.

5. Team members are resigning on a regular basis.
6. Team members are either frustrated and constantly on edge or, conversely, feel no pressure to get the job done.
7. The project has already missed several deadlines and is well over budget.
8. There have been no detailed walk-throughs of the application design and code by independent reviewers.
9. When you think of your project, there is no thought of team, but only separate individuals.
10. The user community is not even aware of the project.

TABLE 5.6 Size

Size refers to the physical size of the application (number of screens, programs) and data volumes.

Size	Human Reaction	Technical Impact	Management Challenge
Small (measured in megabytes)	Efficiency of design and code ignored.	Simple low-capacity architecture.	Invest in a solution that can be reused if size increases.
Medium (measured in a few gigabytes)	Focus on design and code.	Wide range of suitable products are available.	Invest in a scalable solution.
Large (measured in many gigabytes)	Too much time spent on optimizing design and code.	Low response time. Not enough capacity. Constant equipment upgrades.	Invest in a scalable solution. Insist on true benchmarks of performance and capacity early in the project.

CASE STUDIES: INGREDIENTS OF FAILED PROJECTS

Case Study A

The objective of the project was to build an application for removing certain types of data from an online relational database that contained tens of millions of records. Some of the removed records were to be archived and reinserted into the database upon request (within a 24-hour period). Other types of records were to be purged from the system forever.

This project was initiated as a response to the rapid growth of data in the database, whose volume was projected to exceed the upper bound recommended by the software vendor. No clients of the database had ever exceeded this limit; consequently, the software vendor could not guarantee that the application would continue to run successfully, in terms of response time, utility support, data access, and overall integrity of the data after this limit was reached. Because the application was highly visible and mission-critical, supporting millions of users, this uncertainty was unacceptable to the organization's executive management. They determined to offset the growth in data volume by removing data that was no longer needed by systems or users within the organization.

The project mandate had several intrinsic factors that led to the failure of this project. These were the following:

1. Aligning IS and business concerns. Business units were happy with the current application and were slow to buy into the project. These business units were not offered immediate benefits for their participation in the project—except to be told that the application would continue to run in the future. Since it was currently running successfully, the risk of inaction could not be adequately conveyed to them. In the meantime, they had other priorities, such as statutory requirements.

    Business units were forced to support the project, but they consistently focused most of their resources on other projects. Projects that were deemed to be more important (e.g., those that satisfied the public or statutory requirements) had a higher priority in getting resources. This was important because the project was impacted several times from a lack of getting testers, business analysts, and physical space in the computer system. On one occasion, business analysts were removed from the project and reassigned to a more visible one with higher priority. The project was clearly seen as an IS project.

2. Inherent project complexity. This was a challenging project that required an understanding of a multitude of factors to design an effective solution. Business rules that needed to be incorporated in the system represented the most complex part of the product. This part required full input and support from the business community, which was never forthcoming. Since they were happy with the current system, they were reluctant to consider changing it in any way.

3. Risk aversion. Finding end users to define data that was no longer needed by applications proved to be an impossible task. Furthermore, they had to determine if such data would ever be required in the future. If this was so, the data could be archived on tape (meaning it could be brought back into the database within a day), otherwise it would be purged forever. The complexity of the business rules also frightened the business community from participating fully. No one wanted to take responsibility for removing data that could be needed by someone, at some time in the future. This potential risk destroyed whatever interest there was in the business community to actively support a project that could protect their investment in an application by removing the risk of physical database problems.

An examination of this project in hindsight also shows many other problems that foreshadowed its eventual failure. The project started with an artificially tight schedule in the hopes of saving money. This forced the application architects to propose a solution that was not investigated fully, because there was no time to do so. The business requirements were also loosely defined. Although the executive sponsor was identified, key users were not. This forced the business analysts to build requirements and conditions that were not confirmed with authorized users. The first release of the application was developed in two months. Unfortunately, with no key users, it was not clear whether the application satisfied business requirements. Furthermore, without key users, it was not clear that the defined business requirements were valid. Consequently, most of the organization had not bought into the application. There was some ensuing discussion to determine how to proceed. The executive sponsor made the strategic decision to allocate physical and user resources to the project. Before this happened, another project with a more defined mandate took the users away, with the result that the project stayed in limbo for three months. While development continued during this time, other key groups (e.g., database services) became uncomfortable with the idea of taking responsibility for the project's implementation. Quite simply, they were happy with the status quo, and they did not want to assume responsibility for new risks.

During the three-month delay, the project team had time to review the basic architecture of the system and several weaknesses were discovered as a result. The original concept of saving money by rushing the application through the design process had two weaknesses: The rest of the company was not ready for the project, and the design was substandard. A redesign was initiated with good results, requiring a rewrite process that lasted six weeks.

Organizational politics led to team politics. Several key members of the team adopted a siege mentality, as did members from other departments of the organization who were loaned to the project. This made every major decision slow, as everyone covered himself or herself and refused to make decisions.

The project dragged on for an additional six months. During this time, user teams were brought into the project, and yanked, without warning, to other projects. The application was developed according to the specifications that were drawn up and signed off by the business community, and it passed unit testing. Executive and senior management reluctantly agreed to consider implementation. Unfortunately, they could find no users who were willing to validate the written business requirements, nor supply any of their own. After several weeks of posturing, management decided to make a decision. In a single day, they determined that since the database had not failed during the year of development, perhaps the answer was simply to purchase additional disk drives. This allowed everyone to avoid assuming responsibility for implementation. The project was basically shelved until a future date.

The major errors made in this project are summarized in the following list.

□ Key users were not mandated to describe requirements and conditions for the project on a full-time basis. IS was responsible for the project and so the user community never bought into it. Perhaps it would have been better to have given responsibility to the user community.

□ Users who were assigned to the project were moved to tactical projects without warning. Other users were allowed to procrastinate until they too were transferred to other projects.

□ Two business analysts were alienated during the requirement definition phase by management, so they both quit at the end of the first phase. Their business requirements were left without any takers or defenders.

□ All possibilities, such as true database limitations, benchmarking with high data volume, and additional hardware, were not exhaustively considered before a design and approach were finalized.

□ Benefits of the application were not clearly investigated and defined for subsequent measurement.

□ Constantly changing business users resulted in changing business requirements (e.g., conditions under which records were archived).

□ The pilot project duration was too long. It should have been shorter, with less detailed functionality.

□ A pilot should have been used to excite the user community. This offered the best opportunity to make this project a success, as users would have been able to see what the application would look like, with a minimum of effort. This would have given them more time to buy into the process.

□ The project team consisted of contractors and in-house resources. Some confrontation existed between the groups, as in-house resources were concerned that they would be held responsible if the project did not succeed. The loose mandate made this a likely event.

□ Some of the team members were ineffective (but not disruptive).

□ The project plan left out key steps.

□ Milestones could not be met due to lack of support within the organization.

This project failed due to the following factors: organizational politics, project team politics, lack of communication, requirements not clearly understood, and insufficient commitment to project.

The project manager could have taken the following initiatives to save the project:

1. Build a downsized version of the system that only removed terminated records that would never be required again. This would have allowed the business community to accept the application because of reduced risk. More management support would have resulted for implementation. After a period of time, management may have approved an expanded version of the application and staffed it appropriately.

2. Sponsor additional feasibility studies.

3. Benchmark high data volumes.

Case Study B

The objective of this project was to build a client/server-based sales analysis system for a software house that was building a retail package. The overall project was managed by a marketing director who had contracted a beta site to partially pay for the development effort. The sales analysis project was managed by a partner in a consulting firm. The project team consisted of a project leader and four programmers, all alumni from other highly successful client/server implementations. Due to budget restrictions, the project plan was compressed to make a profit. The first phase was defined, while the second phase would remain ambiguous until beta implementation of the first phase.

Phase 1: Sales Analysis System

Activity 1: Build specifications (1 week)

Activity 2: Get specification approval from clients (1 week)

Activity 3: Build client/server infrastructure (1 week)

Activity 4: Develop code (5 weeks)

Activity 5: Unit test (1 week)

Activity 6: System test (1 week)

Activity 7: Acceptance test (1 week)

Phase 2: Integration with Retail Package

no details

The schedule was clearly ambitious. The sales analysis system consisted of four major processes with about a dozen screens developed under C and SQL Server. Program specifications were written and quickly approved on schedule. The first problem occurred when the client/server infrastructure deployment was delayed because the hardware and software was not available when promised by the vendors. This delayed Activity 4, Develop code, by a week or so. The project team developed a prototype that was demonstrated to the clients. It became clear that the approved specifications did not fully represent expectations. In particular, there seemed to be shifting requirements, in that the client wanted a generic user interface such as that supported by Excel, Lotus 1-2-3, and dBase4, with the flexibility to adapt to specific requirements. Furthermore, they wanted an application for resale. This was a new requirement. The trouble was that such an interface would take far longer than two months to build, and a team that was considerably larger than five.

The program specifications were revised to satisfy the new requirements and the project team iteratively developed the application. It should be mentioned that the development team worked with great dedication, through head colds and fevers, and with 60- to 70-hour weeks. Unit testing was completed on schedule. As system testing started, it became clear that a retail package was not going to be developed. With no retail package, there was no need for a sales analysis system. The project was quietly canceled, resources were reassigned, and only part of the bill was paid.

This project failed due to a number of factors that were mentioned earlier in this chapter: insufficient funding, insufficient time to complete the project, lack of a project plan, requirements not clearly understood, unrealistic expectations from stakeholders, and not learning from past experience.

Case Study C

The objective of this project was to manage the IS facilities of a client in the insurance industry. The client expected the service bureau to handle all day-to-day operations, including support of the online report generation, backup/recovery, and other facility management concerns. The client also maintained a project portfolio that contained enhancements, modifications, and fixes to the mainframe application software.

The service bureau allocated one project manager, a project leader, and seven developers to satisfy the client. The service bureau staff selected projects from the project portfolio, and implemented them on a schedule that was agreed upon by the two companies. This is a typical service bureau/client relationship.

The client continually complained about the lack of employees in the service bureau who fully understood the client's systems. This issue threatened their continued relationship. The cause of this problem was straightforward. The service bureau, as a whole, had a very high turnover (50 percent within six months). The project team had a rate worse than this. This meant that no one stayed on the project team long enough to become an expert on the client's systems.

The service bureau management was directly responsible for the high turnover rate for the following reasons:

☐ Employees were not treated as professionals (e.g., no flexibility in working hours, dress code)
☐ No employee training
☐ Ineffective management techniques (e.g., management could not be reached for help, even in a crisis)
☐ Low pay

The sum of these factors discouraged many employees from working with the service bureau for an extended period of time. Once staff started to leave, a bandwagon effect started that was difficult to curtail.

The project manager was an active contributor to the high employee turnover. The manager's style alienated many employees. He was authoritative to the point where staff members resented being watched so closely in terms of when they arrived for work, what they talked about, and when they left. The project manager was not a problem solver, either. He did not encourage the project team to approach him with problems.

This project manager could have prevented the high turnover quite easily. A good place to start would have been by developing his own management skills through courses and/or seminars. He should have also concentrated on developing his staff, finding out their concerns, adding value when they approached him with problems, delegating more responsibility to those who were capable of shouldering it (some definitely were), and encouraging team building. A clear career path for his team would also have encouraged many to stay.

Case Study D

The objective of this project was to reengineer financial services in a large company. The project team consisted of a project manager, six business analysts, and some administrative staff.

The following project plan was identified, with a duration of six months for the first phase.

Phase 1: Business Analysis

Activity 1: Select key users

Activity 2: Interview key users

Activity 3: Design new processes

Activity 4: Identify IS projects

Activity 5: Publish recommendations

Activity 6: Present recommendations to steering committee

Phase 2: IS Projects

Activity 1: Identify projects to initiate

Activity 2: Select project managers

Activity 3: Scope projects

Activity 4: Present design documentation to steering committee

The project was successful in producing recommendations, however, it was unsuccessful in gaining steering committee approval to initiate them. The project was initially started to address a tactical problem. Within the space of a few months, responsibility to resolve the tactical problem was given to another department. This happened through no fault of the project team, which was suddenly left with only a vague mandate.

There is almost nothing the project manager could have done differently to make this project successful in its original mandate. The project manager instead focused on changing and reducing the project scope. The project team was diverted into another useful activity that would provide value to the organization—to study architectural alternatives. The manager lobbied the steering committee to accept the change in scope, which they did. Future problems were avoided by keeping them informed about the project on a weekly basis.

The project team took the initiative and actively interviewed key individuals within the organization and managed to build a strong set of recommendations that were presented to the steering committee on the original schedule. Unfortunately, none of the recommendations were accepted, so the project team was disbanded and moved to other projects.

This project provides an example of a project manager salvaging the careers of a project team by making the best of a bad situation. By most project criteria, this project did not succeed, as none of the recommendations were accepted. However, the result could have been far worse, had the project manager not taken the correct steps.

SUMMARY

Five categories of project failure were defined in this chapter, namely: human issues, technological limitations, political games, funding, and methodologies. Factors that can cause project failure were discussed in terms of these categories. Suggestions to avoid these problems were also provided. Empirical evidence for the arguments provided in this chapter was drawn from a comprehensive survey that was completed by managers and executives in the IS industry, and is included in Appendix C, Management Survey Results—Why Projects Fail.

Several case studies of failed projects were provided in this chapter. The first case study was described in terms of a business scope and involved mainframe architecture. General errors which were made in managing this project were described. Errors in each of the basic project phases were also described to allow the reader to gain a broader perspective into why this project, representative of many others, was not successful. Most of these errors involved factors that could have been avoided given the appropriate foresight.

This project involved client/server technology and a very short duration. Although the project began with several advantages, such as a winning project team that had worked on previous successful assignments, these were not enough to make the partner software house fulfill its mandate. Quite simply, the project was unsuccessful because the project manager could not affect the larger software house and its ability to deliver the parent retail system. In such an instance, a project manager must take appropriate steps to respond to an anticipated failure to avoid personal career shock, and also protect the careers of the project team. This is, in fact, what the project manager was able to do by following steps that were discussed in this chapter.

The second case study clearly shows that some projects cannot succeed no matter what a manager does to make it so. In such instances, the project manager is faced with many choices, not the least of which is to protect his or her own career.

This chapter also provided a list of ten ways for a manager to know that a project is going to fail. The chapter concluded by describing projects in terms of four properties: functionality, duration, scope, and size. Management responses to these properties were also provided for a variety of attributes.

Why Projects Succeed—Case Studies

In this chapter the reader will learn why projects succeed. The chapter also presents case studies of successful projects, including mainframe development projects, client/server projects, and open systems projects.

WHY PROJECTS SUCCEED

Projects succeed when enough factors go well to allow a project's objectives to be satisfied. This is not the same as doing the opposite of the information contained in Chapter 5, Why Projects Fail. The following steps define a practical approach for understanding why some projects succeed:

1. Understand and avoid the reasons for project failure
2. Understand and implement project success factors
3. Learn from other people's experience
4. Learn from personal experience

Project success can be measured directly in terms of budget, requirements, timeliness, quality, and customer satisfaction. A project is deemed 100 percent successful when these fit within budget and specifications. Although 100 percent represents the whole pie, projects can also come in significantly under budget, or before the dead-line. These terms are described in the following list, then shown in Figure 6.1.

1. Budget. Measured in terms of dollars (or some other currency of the land), budget is generally allocated as a fixed quantity for a project or its components.
2. Requirements. Project requirements are identified and captured in some medium. Historically this has been done in a series of paper documents from data models, ER diagrams, flowcharts, dataflow diagrams, pseudo code, decision tables, and significant wordage. A trend in the 1990s is to use a working prototype to capture the look and feel of the functionality a project is expected to support. The breadth of this factor is large and can include such considera-tions as longterm infrastructure.
3. Timeliness. This refers to the deadlines for the project, milestones, and phases. Deadlines are expressed in terms of a fixed day of the calendar, and can also refer to duration and total hours of effort.

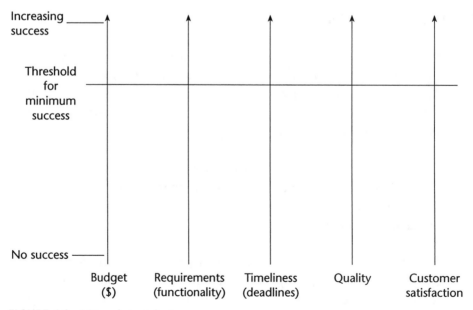

FIGURE 6.1 Measuring project success.

4. Quality. This measures the reliability of the finished product. Reliability in turn is measured in terms of a minimum bug or problem count and the frequency of product failure.

5. Customer Satisfaction. The customer satisfaction factor is simple: "Is the customer happy with the delivered product?" This is arguably the most important consideration and can be ascertained with two simple questions: "Would you recommend the project team unconditionally?" and "Can we do more work for you?"

The effectiveness of a manager can be measured against the attainment of these factors.

Soft success factors include such items as a happy staff, low staff turnover, and responsible training programs. Although it may not be obvious, these factors can lead directly to failure conditions, so they too should be optimized for success.

Projects do not require absolute perfection in order to be successful. It is up to the management team and the customer to determine which factors must be 100 percent met and what value the others must attain in order to deem a project a success.

This chapter provides case studies of successful projects and attempts to identify specific factors that were responsible for their success.

CASE STUDIES: SUCCESSFUL IS PROJECTS

The case studies included in this chapter have been generalized to protect the privacy of organizations. Individual names, where provided, identify real people who have agreed to have their names included in this book.

These case studies were selected based on technology, budget, project length, complexity, and team size. Both mainframe and client/server technology are represented. Three of the projects have multiple phases totaling several years of effort with multimillion dollar budgets and teams with several dozen staff members. The remaining projects have durations of less than six months from initiation to implementation, with project teams of less than a dozen people.

Case Study E

One project with a multimillion dollar budget was the epitome of how a successful project should be run. The client, the consulting company, and the individuals on the development team found the experience to be profitable and fulfilling. The application is currently serving tens of millions of customers each year. Customers of the client who have seen the system serving the public have commented on the high satisfaction level it has achieved.

The project's mandate was to develop a mission-critical, online ticketing application for an overseas client. This was a pioneer client/server project that had Sybase SQL Server supporting 100 PC client machines running an application developed using JAM from JYACC and functions coded in C language. The clients were connected in a LAN/WAN environment through Ethernet boards, and a TCP/IP interface. Each PC was connected to a thermal ticket printer and an optional ticket scanner.

An experienced two-person management team led the project from the start. The project director had the ability to understand the business requirements and the foresight to hire an effective technical architect to pull the pieces together. Using a rapid development tool to quickly build a usable prototype of the application, the architect quickly gained the confidence of the client. The hardware/software products were selected by the client and the consulting group based on established criteria (e.g., vendor support capability, price of the products, functionality of the products, reliability, and fault tolerance, among others). After gaining the client's approval to proceed, a project team was quickly assembled. An organization chart for this project is shown in Figure 6.2.

A project plan was developed based on the prototype and parameters received from the client. Implementation of the product was separated into three phases or releases. The first release was mandated to implement a small portion of the client's business portfolio. A mistake at this level would not be devastating (but would be extremely embarrassing and inconvenient). Specific screens were selected for full functionality development.

A development platform was leased and placed at the consulting site. The client also set up a testing environment for its staff. At the start

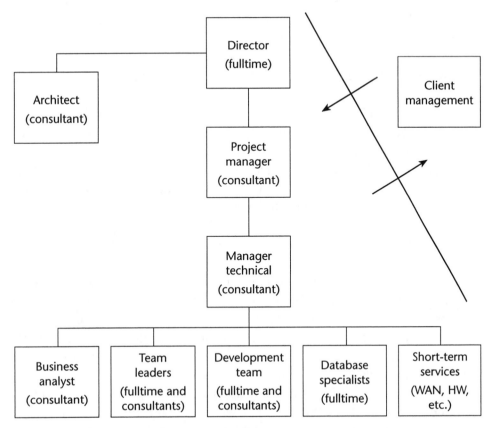

FIGURE 6.2 Organization chart—Case Study E.

of the project, the team consisted of generalists. Original team members were sent on Sybase SQL Server training courses. Developers focused on selected areas and within a short period of time built up a substantial level of expertise. There was a Sybase specialist, a C specialist, a DBA, a hardware specialist, and so on. Cross training was encouraged among the team.

The ability of the team to work together was perhaps the strongest component of this project. There were no visible destructive politics being played, yet many members were highly interested in attaining personal success. Management was results oriented, and there was no time for delay in the project deadlines. Information was actively shared and turf-protecting was not visible.

The project was adequately funded. The budget was analyzed on a weekly basis for time and materials and explained to a client that had been disappointed by another consulting company. Team members were paid for all hours worked, or given time off (at some distant point in time).

Team building was also encouraged on this project. Team members regularly went to lunch together. (Having lunch does not automatically make a project successful. In fact, teams that socialize too much can be harmful to project success. However, lunches and other social activities that are used in the context of team building and opportunities for reflection have been shown to be beneficial.) One of the senior members of the team would frequently take the whole team to lunch. This provided several benefits to the project that easily outweighed the $300 to $500 lunch tab. First, team members became closer and friendlier. Lunches became an opportunity to discuss world topics and issues, and also to look at another perspective of the project on a regular basis. These lunches were also an opportunity to treat team members as professionals and thus all started acting as professionals. Lunches appear to be a better team-building method than weekend ballgames or dinners.

An important factor in the success of this project was the development of a solid relationship that was built with the client's management. This was done by building trust, delivering products and containing functionality as promised. Weaknesses in the functionality were clearly described in the release notes. Functions within each release were delivered to the client on a regular basis to allow management to see what they were getting, to become comfortable with the product, and to begin testing. The project team also respected the feedback provided by the users, prioritized requests, and made relevant modifications to the product.

The project architect focused the team on building the significant functionality first, and left routine functions (such as table updates and maintenance screens) for later releases. This allowed the client to build confidence at the outset of the project. After all, if the difficult functions are basically working in the first three months of a project, the client can lay the infrastructure, train the staff, and make the other investments necessary for a future implementation date. Without this confidence, a client may not make the commitment necessary for a successful implementation.

The project team also tended to be proactive rather than reactive. This was seen in many instances. A user guide was started at the outset to force good documentation and to give the client something to evaluate. Problems were anticipated as far in advance as possible. Benchmarking was done early because it was known that response time would be a critical issue. This process taught the team several techniques that reduced online transaction response time for frequently used functions from ten seconds to two seconds.

The management team was experienced and willing to play many roles. The technical manager routinely walked around and spoke to each team member. This allowed him to offer advice, while also knowing firsthand what was being done and the actual capabilities of each team member.

The team also established standards early during development. This involved screen layout, navigation, change control, code style, messages, report layouts, and other areas.

For personal or other reasons, several key members left the project. This did not cause a major disruption because other team members rose to the challenge of replacing the skills that were lost, and management had the foresight to cross train from the beginning.

Release 1 was implemented successfully. Release 2 was implemented and required optimization and finetuning. Release 3 was implemented successfully.

Interestingly, this project also demonstrated the use of several philosophies that are popular at the time of writing, namely, re-engineering, team empowerment, and rapid prototyping.

Re-engineering The original system had dozens of core screens to support the human process of selling tickets to the public. The new application was built around improved processes, and consisted of about six core user screens with enhanced functionality.

Team Empowerment The members of the team were empowered on many levels. Most team members were process owners. They completed the analysis and specifications, sought approval, coded, and tested their process. Development was done in parallel.

Rapid Prototyping This played a big part in the project. To allow the client to touch and feel the completed application before developing anything, the project architect initially completed a data model and prototyped all the screens in the application. These were presented to the client, who made useful suggestions that were incorporated into the prototype. This process was iterative, until consensus was reached with the users. The client found this exercise reassuring, especially since a previous consulting company had attempted the project without using this technique and achieved no measurable success.

Rapid prototyping was used throughout the remainder of the project. All screens and reports were prototyped and demonstrated to the client, iteratively enhanced, then developed. This allowed several benefits, as discussed in Chapter 7, Iterative Project Development Methodology.

Summary of the Reasons for the Project's Success This project was successful for the following reasons:

☐ A clear mandate was articulated
☐ There were talented resources on all levels—client, development, and management
☐ Appropriate funding was provided
☐ Requirements were understood clearly, and were flexible enough to accommodate modifications
☐ A minimum amount of politics existed
☐ The project plan was effective
☐ Project management was excellent

Case Study F

The project involved an outsourcing company (the "vendor") that was serving a property and auto insurance company (the "client"). The relationship had become progressively strained for several reasons, most of which started innocently enough. The outsourcing contract specified that the vendor was responsible for running the client's mission-critical applications on the vendor's IBM mainframe. The vendor was responsible for all operations, including backups and the generation of daily reports. Frequent enhancements to the application were required and completed by the vendor on a contractual basis. The client was responsible for acceptance testing. The vendor was paid for computer time, overhead costs, and hourly rates for all vendor employees on the project.

The client asked for some major enhancements to the insurance rating system with a three-month deadline. This date was publicly announced, so it could not be readily shifted because other departments made their plans according to this date. The technology was an IBM 3091 running JCL XA, Cobol, CICS, and VSAM.

The project team consisted of three business analysts from the client side. The vendor provided a senior consultant and three developers. These were responsible to an account manager who hired the contract senior consultant to build a good relationship with the client. The project plan was built to satisfy a three-month schedule, with a comfortable margin for unforeseen circumstances.

The senior consultant became the project champion and the acting project leader. Initially, the client mandated an approach they felt should be followed. The senior consultant evaluated the approach, and at once felt uncomfortable with it because it involved populating rate tables without going through the standard edits in the front-end CICS screens. After some investigation, with the tight timeframe in mind, the consultant raised this issue with the account manager, citing the danger of trying to change procedures that had taken a decade to develop within a three-month timeframe. The account manager sided with the client's approach simply because they were the client. At this point the senior consultant had a crucial decision to make. Feeling that the suggested approach was not viable and realizing that the client, in the final analysis, was interested in a successful implementation, the senior consultant decided to defend his position. Again the account manager acquiesced to the client, basically brushing the consultant aside with some veiled mention about exceeding his authority.

The consultant, analyzing his career, and realizing that the marketplace offered other opportunities, took a risk and continued defending his position because the alternative would have resulted in a failed project. Approaching the account manager, the consultant essentially said: "If you are ordering me to follow the suggested approach, I will. But first, I will document my misgivings and copy them to your boss, the director, the client director, and the president of this company. Then in three months, when the system is implemented and the online crashes, I can point to my memo when people point at me. The memo will point them to you." The account manager agreed to a feasibility study of the two approaches.

The consultant spent two days completing the feasibility studies and e-mailed them to the client director, who approved the new suggested approach within a day. It seems that the client was, in fact, more interested in a successful implementation than an approach.

The consultant then led the team through standard development phases, namely analysis, specifications, approval, coding, and testing. These were completed, after consistent hard work, one week shy of the deadline. Although 60-to-70-hour weeks were standard during this project, overtime was not requested because of the existing strained relationship between the client and the vendor. Implementation of the application proceeded smoothly—with the exception of one disk file overflowing because more than double the data volume identified for conversion was placed into the file—without communication to the development team. This was a harmless problem and fixed painlessly. The enhancements went live with no further problems on the designated implementation date.

The client was very pleased with the results of the project. A reference letter was e-mailed to the consultant, the account manager, the director, and various other senior members of management in both companies. The account manager's reaction? After taking a holiday during the week of implementation, the account manager only commented on the disk file overflowing.

Summary of the Reasons for the Project's Success This project was successful for the following reasons:

☐ Commitment of the development team
☐ A good project plan
☐ A talented project champion

Case Study G

This project involved a consulting company (the "vendor") that was contracted to build a property and automobile insurance application from the ground up, using new hardware and software technology, for the "client." This was a large multimillion dollar venture with some unique challenges.

The vendor management team consisted of a senior manager and two technical managers. The rest of the team consisted of a few dozen business and technical people at various levels, from entry to project leader. The client also provided about eighteen staff who were divided into several key areas. The first area consisted of overall project management, where one client manager was in charge of technical management and another was in charge of business management. Several junior client managers reported to these two. The second area consisted of an extensive client testing organization that reported to the business manager. This group was responsible for ongoing testing of the application, acceptance of new modules, tracking of bugs/problems, and enhancements to the application. Client technical staff were included on the development team to facilitate skills transfer from the vendor to the clients.

This technical and human organization posed two challenges. First, the vendor staff had to reside onsite at the client building. The vendor staff had built a lifestyle around flexible hours, relaxed clothing, eating at their computer terminals, and reading hex dumps for fun (no kidding). The client staff started work every day at 8:30 AM, took a ten-minute coffee break at 10:00, lunch at 12:00, and another coffee break at 2:30 PM. The workday ended at 5:00. There was an immediate culture clash between the two groups. The client insisted that the vendor adopt its work ethic. The vendor management, looking at the importance of the client, reluctantly agreed to the terms. Key players of the vendor development staff immediately threatened to resign. The trouble was that some of these folks were brilliant and incredibly dedicated workers. They were also serious about quitting. The vendor went back to the client and explained the situation. The client acquiesced.

The second challenge faced by the project team consisted of deploying a fairly sophisticated application on new technology under a tight development schedule. Several client references existed with the same technology, but these were much smaller versions of the system. This challenge was handled by studious prototyping and extensive benchmarking. Consultants with excellent track records were involved in determining the feasibility of the solution. With their determination that the system was possible, the project proceeded.

Development was achieved in two phases. Phase 1 implemented the automobile insurance component of the application; phase 2 implemented the property insurance component of the application.

Summary of the Reasons for the Project's Success This project was successful for the following reasons:

☐ Commitment of the development team
☐ Good project plan
☐ Excellent project management
☐ Effective understanding of the business requirements
☐ Thorough testing

Case Study H

This project was intended to accommodate several hundred store locations nationwide for a large retail store. The business requirement was to support price changes to products carried by the retail chain on a weekly basis. Pricing had to be approved by several departments in the organization.

The technical architecture consisted of an IBM 3090 running MVS XA, Cobol, CICS, IMS, VSAM, and a 4GL. The 4GL was new to the organization, and had no internal experts to support it. The new application was intended to accept input from a nightly batch job, produce various results, and then feed other systems in the company.

The project team consisted of a project director, a project leader, a business analyst, a systems analyst, a user director, and several users and developers. The team was small, but the mandate was highly visible within the organization and just as important.

The project length was a comfortable six months. The systems analyst effectively led the development and built the project plan to have a duration of four months, leaving a margin of two months to handle unexpected circumstances.

The business analyst completed some paper specifications and left the company. The systems analyst set up a series of JAD sessions with the user director to discuss the project requirements. Other technical staff and users were also invited to participate in these sessions. The result was a set of paper specifications and a prototype using the 4GL product. These were approved by the user director.

Development proceeded smoothly. The user director was regularly informed of progress. Hands-on demonstration of the application was also provided to the users. New requirements were incorporated where possible, without impact on the project plan. During system testing, the user director requested that the project be implemented six weeks early, asking if this would be a problem. As the project was proceeding on schedule, it would be ready at least a few weeks prior to this. The request was easily accommodated.

The application was implemented with a plan to back it out if problems were encountered. The development team was onsite to address any difficulties. Not a single problem or bug was detected when the application went live.

Summary of the Reasons for the Project's Success This project was successful for the following reasons:

☐ Commitment of the development team
☐ Good project plan
☐ A talented project champion

Case Study I

This project was intended to satisfy legislative requirements for a large government department. Geographically separated offices required a common application processing system for the health industry. There were literally hundreds of online users with extensive batch reporting requirements.

The technical architecture of the system consisted of a DEC VAX running Ingres and a 4GL forms tool in each of the dozens of offices.

Faxing requirements were handled through Intel-based processors running Windows, Winfax, and Microsoft Access.

The project team consisted of a project director, several managers, several DBAs, a pool of developers, and occasional contract staff. The overall team size would have to be classified as large.

The project duration spanned several years. Because of this long length, an iterative approach was used to deliver functionality in phases. Rollout was initially limited to a few pilot sites that were able to test the full application under real business conditions.

The application was developed using an iterative approach. The 4GL tool was used to prototype the basic screens after a data and process model were developed. Regular JAD sessions were scheduled to iteratively develop the prototype into a working application, complete with reports and interfaces to other applications.

Summary of the Reasons for the Project's Success This project was successful for the following reasons:

☐ Commitment of the development team
☐ A talented project champion

Case Study J

This limited project was intended to do a massive conversion of claims and policy data from an IBM mainframe to a GEAC mainframe at a medium-sized property and casualty insurance company.

The project team consisted of a project manager, a project leader, several users, and junior developers. The project leader was responsible for the planning and execution of the conversions.

The project duration was a comfortable six months. Two basic deliverables were defined: policy conversion and claims conversion. Due to the heavy volume of data and the consequential impact on the online application, the actual conversions were done on the weekends when the online was not active.

The basic operation of this application was to accept an input tape in IBM EPCDIC format with a tape header and tens of thousands of corresponding records. A relatively small number of policies, about sixty thousand, were available for conversion. In addition to this, several hundred thousand claims were available for conversion. The header record indicated whether the subsequent records were to be policies or claims. This value selected a C-like program that mapped each record into a new format for a relational database. Control reports were produced for the audit department.

After the programs and batch procedures were developed, a substantial testing procedure was completed to ensure that each mapping step was correct. The conversions were planned over a period of successive weekends, beginning with the policies. The actual process ran smoothly and the control reports proved that what went in came out. The following weekend, about twenty thousand policies were copied to tape for the conversion. Unfortunately, the actual conversion crashed. The project leader was called at home, and trying to be helpful, suggested a solution without properly thinking things through. On Monday morning, it was discovered that the entire weekend conversion was botched. In fact, the advice offered over the phone by the project leader had made things far worse than they were because of the first crash. At this time, everyone in the user and IS community became involved looking at the control reports. Executives and auditors who had never been seen before entered the picture. This was an online disaster and everyone wanted to know what went wrong. Duplicate copies of several claims were created. One claim was copied 57 times in the production database!

The problem was quickly traced to bad sectors on a defective input tape. This was a physical problem that had never been tested. The testing process used two tapes, one for policies, the other for claims. In both cases, the actual tape medium was not defective, and so logic was never considered to handle this possibility. Having discovered this, the problems caused by the weekend conversion were reversed within two days. Although it was a remote possibility that another defective tape would turn up, the conversion programs were changed to protect against this. Conversion of the claims on the next weekend went smoothly, much to everyone's relief. The remaining claims were successfully converted over the next month without incident.

The project became a success and several people learned valuable lessons. The first of these was to test for even remote, ridiculous conditions. The second lesson was to refrain from offering quick, off-the-cuff advice over the telephone. The final lesson was not to underestimate the risks in any production level implementation.

Summary of the Reasons for the Project's Success This project was successful for the following reasons:

- ☐ Commitment of the development team
- ☐ Ability to react to unexpected problems
- ☐ A talented project champion

SUMMARY

This chapter analyzed reasons for the success of some IS projects. Clearly, successful projects involve avoiding factors that can cause project failure, but the chapter also demonstrated that project success involved additional factors. Six case studies of successful projects were examined in an attempt to gain a more thorough understanding of project successes, and to provide a broader perspective for the reader. Three of the case studies involved multimillion dollar budgets with multiyear project plans, divided into consecutive six-month phases. The project teams were large. In contrast, the remaining projects had less than six-month durations with small, fully empowered teams.

It appears that the presence of a project champion with suitable authority is significant for a project's success. Project leaders, architects, or managers are appropriate choices for this role.

Many of these projects followed one project methodology or another. Chapter 7 describes a methodology called Iterative Project Development Methodology (IPDM) which has been used on many successful IS projects.

Iterative Project Development Methodology (IPDM)

OVERVIEW

In this chapter the reader will learn about:

- A results-oriented view of project management
- Iterative project development methodology (IPDM)
- Detailed processes of IPDM exploded to two levels
- Ten steps for getting started
- History of development methodologies
- Strengths and weaknesses of general methodologies

BEYOND A PROCESS-ORIENTED VIEW OF PROJECT MANAGEMENT

Project management involves the difficult task of balancing multiple factors in order to produce project deliverables. Many managers have historically met this challenge by adopting a process oriented approach to their jobs. The process-oriented approach follows some particular development methodology in a precise way and requires regular status meetings (most of which report that work is progressing well) to track the project. A substantial number of projects still do not get delivered on time and within budget. A majority of those that seem to be on track often only satisfy a subset of the original business requirements. The authors are aware of one multimillion dollar project that implemented a large application that produced no reports, even to satisfy auditing requirements. The opportunity for human error and fraud in this situation was significant.

Many organizations define rigorous detailed internal management principles for their managers. Much of the energy spent on these activities adds no value to the project deliverables, even though the activities may satisfy the needs of someone else in the organization. The end result is that a substantial amount of time is spent judiciously following the processes of project management, yet in the end, organizations are still plagued with chronic overruns and a general lack of project completion. In fact, many projects become revolving doors for managers, who take charge of a project, do all the right things according to generally accepted principles of project management and development methodologies, but end up achieving no tangible results even after many months or years into a project. Eventually the managers move on to other things hoping to avoid damaging their careers, or they continue making the same mistakes and spend many years on the same project.

The authors have personally seen many examples where generally accepted project management principles were applied to information systems projects, yet after several years of effort nothing but reams of paper specifications, minutes of meetings, and isolated fragments of code were produced after millions of dollars were spent. A close look at the participants generally shows hard-working, intelligent, dedicated professionals. Yet there are countless examples of problems in organizations all over the world.

But the situation is far from hopeless. Many examples of successful IS projects are also found around the world. Some of these were discussed in Chapter 6, Why Projects Succeed—Case Studies. The purpose of this chapter is to describe a powerful development methodology that has evolved over a variety of projects undertaken by the authors. The iterative project development methodology (IPDM) has been successfully used on both small and large development projects, including a variety of architectures such as mainframe, midrange, client/server, open systems, and others. IPDM also supports custom development, outsourcing, package search, and other IS development projects. One of its principal attributes is to change the traditional process-oriented view of project management to a results-oriented view. This requires a fundamental change in the current method in which projects are planned, as described in IPDM.

PROJECT DEVELOPMENT METHODOLOGIES

Project development methodologies have been around for centuries, and were used to construct such objects as ships, houses, dams, and factories. In the last few decades, these methodologies were refined specifically to guide information systems projects. A project development methodology is like a recipe in a cookbook intended to allow the cooks to whip up a successful project. Many of these recipe-like methodologies read like "spend one week reviewing the code, mix with an auditor, shake with an implementation schedule . . . ." Inevitably, some recipes are better than others, and sometimes successful projects are implemented by strict adherence to a development methodology.

Strengths of More Popular Methodologies

1. A clear step-by-step roadmap from point A to point Z: Methodologies provide an ordered list of all the activities that should be followed to complete a project. The difficulty with this is that a list of generic activities cannot be comprehensive enough to satisfy all possible types of projects.
2. A tried and proven path to project implementation: Methodologies generally have proven track records. That is the reason they are packaged and distributed in the first place.
3. Important project deliverables are anticipated far in advance: Projects that are conducted according to a methodology provide a manager with a list of expected deliverables at the start of the project, thus giving the manager something to work toward (e.g., data model, ER diagram) on a project plan.
4. A checklist for project managers to follow: A methodology allows project managers to build an inventory of the activities that lead up to the deliverables, and subsequently check off completed items.

5. A starting point: Methodologies allow managers to start their projects without having a complete understanding of relevant issues.

Weaknesses of More Popular Methodologies

1. Lack of flexibility in dealing with unexpected problems: Managers who are following a methodology from A to Z may be incapable of handling an unexpected occurrence. For example, during acceptance testing, what happens if an operating system has a bug that disrupts communication to some PC clients? Similarly, other unexpected and complicated issues arise that cannot be resolved by looking for advice in a process box on a methodology document. The only answer is to have a hardworking, experienced project team tap into creative thinking.
2. Focus on procedures, sometimes at the expense of results: Procedures are intended to offer an effective approach for solving complex problems. This may be true; however, sometimes procedures can become a crutch for people trying to avoid making difficult decisions. Over a period of time, procedures can also become inefficient. Consequently, staff who follow procedures without questioning their applicability may be sacrificing results in their pursuit of dotting every "i" and crossing every "t."
3. Unnecessary steps that are often ignored by project teams: Methodologies are intended to be all-inclusive and universal. Such methodologies, by definition, will contain a comprehensive set of processes to support this. This is in direct conflict with being streamlined.
4. Long durations for deliverables: Deliverables in most methodologies are the end product of a sequential, nonoptimized series of steps.

Things That Project Methodologies Will Not Do

Project methodologies are not a magic wand for project development. They are simply roadmaps that could lead to successful projects. Some managers expect far more from them. In fact, some feel that the use of a methodology will pretty much guarantee the success of a project, with minimal effort from them. This would be similar to interviewing a few very successful people like Bill Gates to find out how they made their fortune and then expecting to repeat the process and achieve the same results. Of course, there is no guarantee that this would happen. The results will depend on many factors, such as opportunity, the state of the economy, personal contacts, starting capital, the product being sold, and of course, the abilities of the people involved. It is the same with project development methodologies. They will not do the following things:

1. Instill a manager with vision. A methodology may identify the need to do this, but it will only happen if the manager strives to make it so.
2. Turn someone into a good manager. A manager must develop multiple skills and experiences to make this happen.
3. Build an actual deliverable. Deliverables require effort from the project team to develop. Teams must be motivated and be able to produce deliverables. A manager must take responsibility for making this happen.
4. Implement the project by automatically making things happen. A methodology is not an animate entity that makes things happen by itself. Without input, a methodology produces nothing.
5. Replace a talented project team. The project team will make a project successful. A good project team will often develop or refine a methodology as needed. A weak project team will not gain much value from any methodology, no matter its strength. Instead, it will serve as a crutch to the team, who will come to work every day and have something to work on until it becomes clear that the project is not on track. Some methodologies delay this for quite some time.

One final example that disproves the notion that a methodology replaces the need for a good project team is to consider a canvas, paintbrush, and a how-to-paint book. Two artists using the "artistic methodology" in the book will probably produce two very different paintings. Ultimately, their talent will determine the quality of the final painting, even though they are using the same methodology. In fact, if they are not artists, they may end up producing garbage.

IPDM: A NEW PROJECT DEVELOPMENT METHODOLOGY

The iterative project development methodology is a derivation of the rapid application development (RAD) methodology that gained widespread popularity in the 1980s and 1990s. IPDM has the following main characteristics.

Look and Feel Prototypes of Applications and Processes

This is a key component of this methodology. Prototypes allow clients to have a view of the final solution with minimal investment. In most non–IS projects, detailed models or prototypes are developed before full-scale construction is authorized to start. This is true of buildings, bridges, rockets, and even movies (e.g., demo tapes). None of these objects is generally purchased directly from drawings or scripts. Yet historically, many IS applications are built from nothing more than paper specifications. Users are expected to visualize a solution based on flowcharts, decision tables, and words. Strangely enough there is surprise and disappointment when users look at the solution, which is sometimes delivered years later, and want something different.

There is also a widespread misconception that prototypes are an open invitation to users and project teams to design on the fly. In such cases, a prototype is built and demonstrated to users. The users accept the prototype and development begins. When users want to modify or add requirements, these are simply prototyped and incorporated into the development process. As this process repeats itself, the project team suddenly finds itself trying to hit a moving target. Requirements are coming in from all over the place and there simply is not enough time to finish development. This results in a bug-infested application, bruised egos and missing requirements. Prototyping gets a bad reputation, when in fact, its purpose was misunderstood from the start.

Prototypes should be used as another tool to capture business requirements. IS prototypes should be used in the same way as models and prototypes are in non–IS industries. The prototype serves as a working model of the final application that the users can touch, feel, and understand. When they agree that the prototype is an accurate solution to the problem being addressed by a project, the prototype becomes the fixed requirements definition. Any changes to the prototype must be assessed to determine their impact, just as changes to requirements were historically handled in development projects that did not rely on prototypes.

Iterative Approach to Product Development

This is another important part of this methodology. Iteration is used to select a starting point, then repeatedly build on a solution until it is satisfactory. This is like going to a really dirty pane of glass, wiping it with a cloth, and noticing that it looks cleaner. Stopping this process will still result in the glass being cleaner than it was before the first swipe of the cloth. The glass can be shown to a client, and approval can be sought to continue. Additional swipes of the cloth across the pane of glass will continue to make it cleaner. Stopping at any time will result in a cleaner pane than it was at the beginning. Effort can be expended in this way until the client is satisfied with the cleanliness of the glass. Iteration on IS projects works the same way.

Flexibility in Dealing with Requirements

The objective of a project is to build the best and most useful product possible. Users will always remember additional requirements, even after signoff of the business requirements. The iterative nature of this methodology allows some flexibility in accommodating additional requirements within the project schedule. Requirements that cannot be incorporated without affecting the project plan can be rolled into a subsequent phase.

Direct Involvement of Users

Users have always been involved within the development cycle. But historically this has been limited to activities like answering interview questions and reviewing paper specifications. Users have not typically been sitting in a JAD session or at a PC actively painting GUI screens. By involving them in the design of the prototype, they are brought into the development process. This offers several benefits. First, they are able to actively lend their expertise to the process. Second, they become involved and thus become closer to the project and fight for its success. They gain a sense of ownership and familiarity. Lastly, the users are able to test drive the application from the beginning, eliminating or dramatically minimizing surprises at the time of delivery.

Other Goals

IPDM has been shown to achieve the following additional significant goals: (1) deliver a completed application in a shorter period than was previously possible; (2) increase user acceptance of the final product; (3) support a phased approach to implementation, where selected components of an application are delivered to users at regular time intervals instead of at the end of a long development process; (4) achieve unconditional client satisfaction with the final product. In addition to meeting these goals, projects can be delivered with reduced costs and development time.

Despite these benefits, IPDM should not be viewed as a magic wand, but rather it should be given careful consideration as a development methodology.

A DESCRIPTION OF IPDM

The IPDM has evolved over a span of many successful projects encompassing a broad range of business and technical environments. This methodology has successfully salvaged numerous projects that have gone grossly over budget and missed deadlines. It was successful in winning over badly scathed users and clients who had spent millions of dollars and many years without getting anything of value in return for their investment or patience.

The methodology contains fifteen high-level processes that are manipulated in an iterative fashion. Some of these processes can be conducted in parallel, but this largely depends on the project specifics.

Level 1 (Highest Level)

Figure 7.1 provides a high-level view of the iterative project development methodology. Input/output files are not shown on this level, but they are included in the figures containing lower-level views of these processes later in this section.

An overview of the fifteen processes in Figure 7.1 is provided here.

Confirm Project Orientation Process This orientation opportunity should be used by a project manager to become familiar with a project. Specifically, a manager should determine the importance of a project to the organization, identify the project sponsor, and ensure that an active

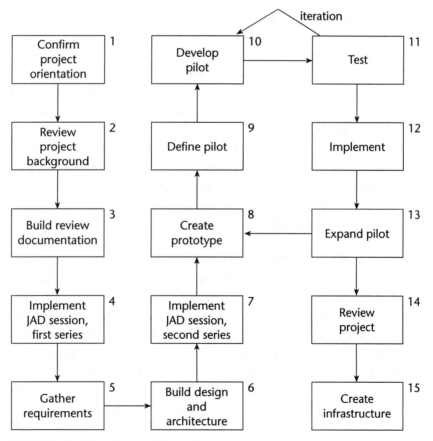

FIGURE 7.1 IPDM: level 1 (highest).

steering committee exists. The manager should also get to know the people who will play key roles in the life of the project.

Review Project Background Process All relevant background information concerning the project should be reviewed by the project manager. This includes the project mandate statement, written documentation, business documents, and the results of previous attempts at the project.

Build Review Documentation Process The project manager should digest all the available project information and reformat it for discussion and JAD sessions. This allows the manager to begin sharing information with key players in the company and begin to build a consensus. The manager should not hesitate to involve other staff in this task if it is too large.

Another point to remember is that most people do not like to write documentation, which tends to be a time-consuming and arduous task. This step gives anyone an opportunity to begin this process and immediately make a positive impact that tends to mobilize others. An example of this was seen on a project that had been active for years, but with few written requirements being developed during that time. This was a point of great consternation for some members of the project team, who needed a definitive statement of business requirements to begin to satisfy their responsibilities. A new consultant on the project simply acted as facilitator and started recording requirements based on what was said by the players during JAD sessions. This act proved to be a great catalyst in moving the project forward.

Implement JAD Session, First Series Process This is an iterative process that begins with the manager approaching key players (e.g., directors and managers of relevant business areas or departments) in one-on-one meetings to verify the documentation that was produced. The manager should assume that this documentation is incomplete or wrong, and should use these meetings to get a better understanding of the requirements or direction that the project is expected to take.

When the manager is comfortable with the documentation and information resulting from the small meetings, JAD sessions should be used to bring key users and IS staff together to revise and confirm what is known about the project.

This is an important planning process that will allow a project manager to build a reasonable project plan, ascertain resource requirements, determine infrastructure requirements, and have a first approximation of estimates.

Gather Requirements Process This is a traditional process that builds business requirements and sometimes technical requirements. A project manager can appoint business analysts, consultants, or other staff to assume responsibility of gathering and documenting this information.

Build Design and Architecture Process This process involves technical staff, designers, and architects to build a solution to the project within the constraints of the organization. This will lead to a list of hardware and software tools for the project. The team may rely on feasibility studies and benchmarks that have already been done, or commission new ones to support the design and architecture process.

Some portions of the infrastructure solution will be implemented immediately (e.g., database creation scripts) to support development.

Implement JAD Session, Second Series Process The solution being proposed for the project is shared with key individuals in the company to obtain the following benefits:

- ☐ Get their input and benefit from their expertise
- ☐ Gain their support
- ☐ Share information with them
- ☐ Get confirmation for the decisions already made on the project
- ☐ Confirm detail design

Create Prototype Process A functional, reusable prototype is developed to support the requirements documentation produced in the previous processes.

Define Pilot Process The business requirements are divided into phases. Each phase is allocated a milestone called a pilot. This is an implementation of the core functionality within a phase without the bells and whistles. The pilot deliverable should be used as a proof of concept that runs a subset of the total data required for a phase. The completed pilot should be demonstrated to decision makers. Changes to the requirements should be anticipated, but they should be evaluated in terms of cost and impact on the schedule before being accepted into the current phase. If they cannot be handled, they should be incorporated into a future phase.

Develop Pilot Process This traditional process requires analysis, design, specifications, coding, and unit testing for deliverables in the phase. This is an iterative process that involves building the pilot, going to the testing process, getting approval for the pilot from executive management, then completing development for the remaining functions in the phase.

Test Process This is a rigorous testing process that includes system testing, regression testing, and acceptance testing.

Implement Process A plan is developed and followed to implement the application. A backout plan is also developed in the event that the implementation is unsuccessful.

Expand Pilot Process Following a successful implementation, the functionality in the remaining phases is split off into additional pilots. This is an iterative approach that branches back to the prototyping stage.

Review Project Process Following any implementation, a formal evaluation should be conducted to learn from the experience.

Create Infrastructure Process After a successful implementation, project staff is generally moved off the project. A manager should ensure that there has been appropriate skills transfer to allow this to happen smoothly.

Level 2

Confirm Project Orientation Figure 7.2 shows a level 2 view of confirm project orientation process, which should be used to confirm the project mandate and the project sponsor.

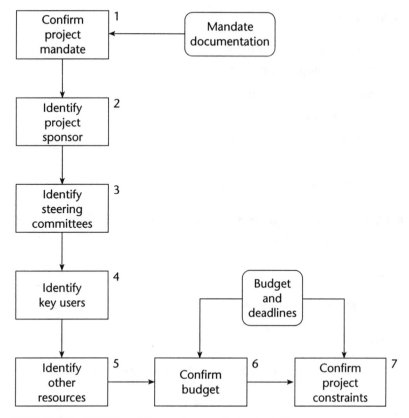

FIGURE 7.2   IPDM level 2—confirm project orientation.

Input

    Documentation mandate

    Budget and deadlines

    Project vision

Output

    Project confirmation

    Steering committee(s)

    Identification of key users

Subprocesses

Confirm project mandate

Identify project sponsor

Identify steering committees

Identify key users

Identify other resources

Confirm budget

Confirm project constraints

Review Project Background Figure 7.3 shows a level 2 view of review project background process.

Input

Project documentation

Output

Understanding and confirmation of the project

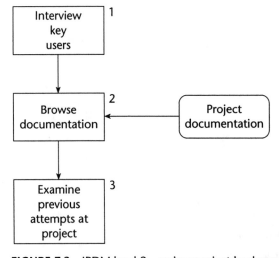

FIGURE 7.3 IPDM level 2—review project background.

Subprocesses

Interview key users

Browse documentation

Examine previous attempts at project

Build Review Documentation Figure 7.4 shows a level 2 view of build review documentation.

Input

Project documentation

Output

Data models

Requirements

Process models

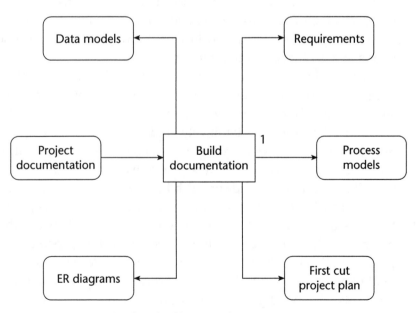

FIGURE 7.4 IPDM level 2—build review documentation.

ER diagrams

First cut project plan

Subprocess

Build documentation

Additional Information There is no secret to doing this properly. It takes hard work and talent. This is the hardest thing to do and often the weakest link in a project. Business requirements are rarely straightforward, and users often need assistance in establishing them. To understand this, imagine a person buying a car. The person may have decided to buy a sports car, but needs assistance in choosing one model over the others. Even then, the buyer also needs assistance in understanding the implications of getting a lease or a loan, insurance options, mileage considerations, and warranty possibilities.

An ineffective method of capturing business requirements is for an analyst to ask a user a set of questions and to meticulously write down what was said exactly and go away believing that a good job was done. Instead, an analyst should show initiative, internalize the requirements to determine consistency, and offer suggestions to the business users. This process is iterative in that the requirements are finetuned over a series of passes, improving each time.

The business analyst (BA) must be careful to avoid confrontation during the process of defining business requirements. After a few projects, effective business analysts learn enough about a set of business cases to allow them to intuitively understand and develop business requirements for a wide variety of business cases. The analyst, who often acts as a consultant in this phase, has a backlog of knowledge that allows him or her to distinguish between what has been known to work, and what has not been known to work. During this process, the business analyst should also endeavor to be consultative rather than combative. A BA/consultant should also avoid being perceived as too passive or having little to offer in this phase. A BA/consultant must lend experience and wisdom to a project without becoming overbearing. This can be done by organizing a series of Joint Application Design (JAD) sessions with the users.

A manager should be careful to ensure that a business analyst is performing this job function correctly. Managers that do not have the technical or business skills to ensure this is happening should seek out a suitable project leader or architect for assistance.

The common method of conducting this phase consists of empowering a one- to three-person project team. Outside expertise is sought as required.

Skills Required: Architects, business analysts, systems analysts, data modellers.

Implement JAD Session, First Series Figure 7.5 shows a level 2 view of implement JAD session, first series.

Input

ER diagrams

Data models

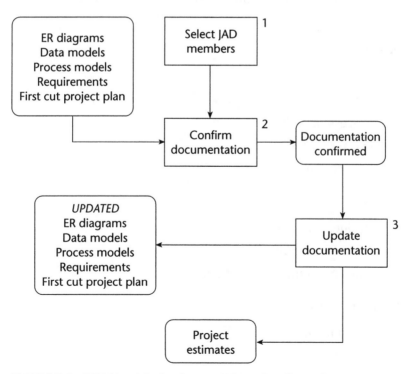

FIGURE 7.5 IPDM level 2—implement JAD session, first series.

Process models

Requirements

First cut project plan

JAD members

Output

Confirmation of documentation

Updated versions of input

Project estimates

Subprocesses

Select JAD members

Confirm documentation

Update documentation

Gather Requirements Figure 7.6 shows a level 2 view of gather requirements.

Input

ER diagrams

Data models

Process models

Requirements

Project plan

Output

Business requirements

Technical requirements

Draft program specifications

Subprocesses

Select team

Identify key users

Build interview strategy

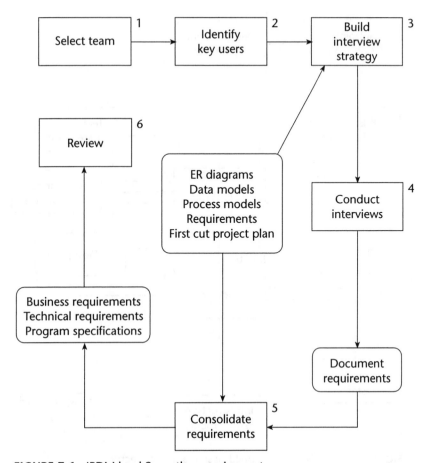

FIGURE 7.6 IPDM level 2—gather requirements.

    Conduct interviews

    Consolidate requirements

    Review

Build Design and Architecture Figure 7.7 shows a level 2 view of build design and architecture.

Input

    Business requirements

    Technical requirements

    Corporate infrastructure

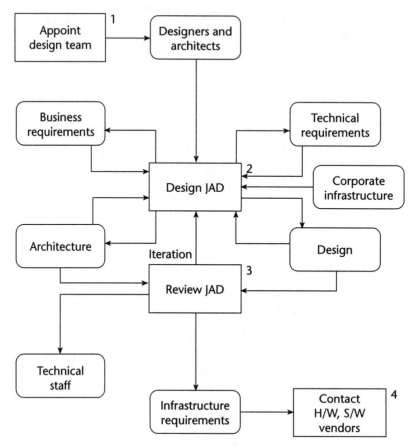

FIGURE 7.7 IPDM level 2—build design and architecture.

Output

Updated business requirements

Updated technical requirements

Architecture

Design

Infrastructure requirements

Subprocesses

Appoint design team

Design JAD

Review JAD

Contact H/W, S/W vendors

Additional Information Conduct careful reference checks and analyze benchmarking results in selecting the technology. Establish performance criteria and system availability requirements (e.g., Is a fault tolerant system required? What is online response time? Throughput requirements?).

Just as the act of gathering business requirements is not a "by-the-recipe" process, this step also involves hard, but properly focused, work that cannot be done by following a recipe. If the knowledge and experience to do this effectively is not available in house, it is wise to hire consultants to bring it in. In the 1990s, there are many technology options available, such as client/server, legacy systems, pen-based systems, voice systems, and distributed systems, to name a few. Each of these can be the subject of at least one textbook. An error in judgment in this stage can have costly repercussions in the other phases.

Skills Required: Architect, systems analyst.

Implement JAD Session, Second Series Figure 7.8 shows a level 2 view of implement JAD session second series.

Input

Project plan

Design documentation

Architecture documentation

Output

Approved documentation

Subprocesses

Select review team

Implement JAD sessions

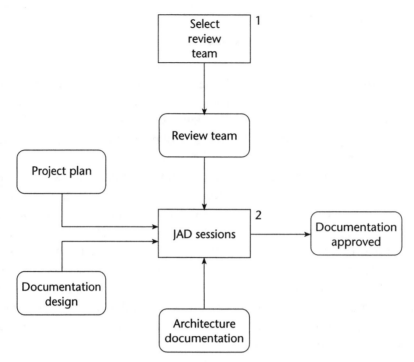

FIGURE 7.8 IPDM level 2—implement JAD session, second series.

Additional Information Confirm that the business users understand the business requirements and their impact (through JADs, functional prototypes, ER diagrams, dataflow diagrams, process charts).

Remember that change appears to be a big and unavoidable part of life. Changes to business requirements should then come as no surprise, and a mutually agreed method between users/clients and the development team should be established at the onset of the project. Perhaps the project team can accept changes, but only apply them in a subsequent release. Implementation can be done in phases of six- to eight-month durations.

Skills Required: Architects, systems analysts, business users.

Create Prototype Figure 7.9 shows a level 2 view of create prototype.

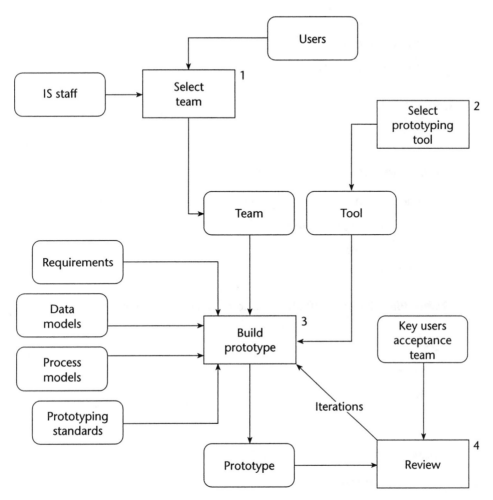

FIGURE 7.9 IPDM level 2—create prototype.

Input

IS staff

Users

Prototyping tool

Key acceptance team

Requirements

Data models

Process models

Prototyping standards

Output

Prototype

Subprocesses

Select team

Select prototyping tool

Build prototype

Review

Define Pilot Figure 7.10 shows a level 2 view of define pilot.

Input

IS staff

Key users

Project plan

Output

Pilot requirements

Revised project plan for pilot

Multiphase plan

Subprocesses

JAD

Revise pilot project plan

Revise project plan

Additional Information Every project can be divided into several subreleases. The nature of application development in the 1990s has evolved from earlier decades. Traditionally, projects tended to be an

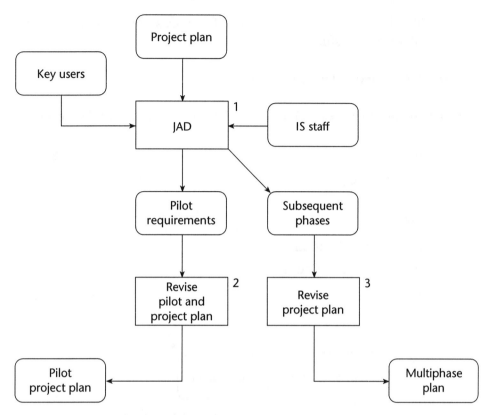

FIGURE 7.10 IPDM level 2—define pilot.

all-or-nothing proposition. Large projects required large budgets, lots of staff, and long development cycles. The current approach is to support full development through a series of phases in order to provide value to the customers, as soon as possible. Each phase has deliverables that can be implemented so that users can start testing, parallel running, and using them. The first phase could be designed to serve as a pilot.

A pilot should include the critical functionality of the whole project, but limit the number of test cases and noncritical features. A pilot project does not need to be implemented, but should be presented and confirmed with key users. Changes should be encouraged and incorporated into the application through normal channels at this time, in order to build a superior product.

The project plan should lead to full release implementation after the pilot is successful.

Skills Required: Full project team.

Development Figures 7.11 and 7.12 show a level 2 view of development.

Input

Specifications

Output

Revised specifications
Physical program design
Unit test plans

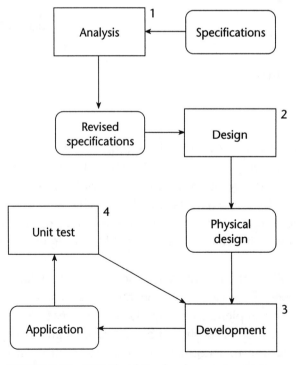

FIGURE 7.11 IPDM level 2—development, part A.

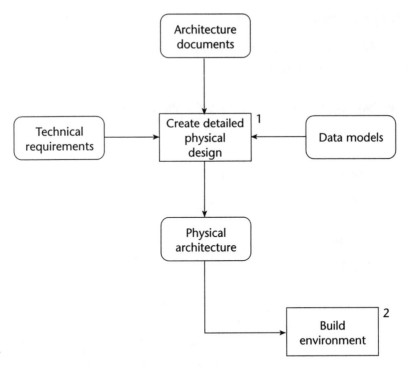

FIGURE 7.12 IPDM level 2—development, part B.

Subprocesses

Analysis

Design

Development

Unit test

Input

Architecture documents

Technical requirements

Data models

Output

Physical architecture

Subprocesses

Create detailed physical design

Build environment

Testing Figure 7.13 shows a level 2 view of testing.

Input

Test plans

Key users

Test team

Volume data

Application

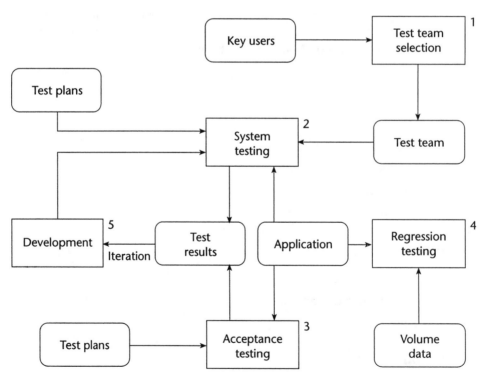

FIGURE 7.13 IPDM level 2—testing.

Output

Test results

Updated application

Subprocesses

Test team selection

System testing

Acceptance testing

Regression testing

Development

Additional Information Never accept a piece of code from a developer if it is not unit tested. In fact, it seems silly at team meetings to hear someone say that they are 75 percent finished, all programs are compiled, and unit testing will be starting soon. In fact, such members are 0 percent finished, but have just keyed everything into a file. Managers must be careful to resist accepting these statements at face value. Insist that all programs be unit tested as they are written, and not at some point in the future.

The testing process should be divided into phases. The generally accepted breakdown consists of the following items:

☐ Unit Testing. This form of testing is conducted by developers on their pieces before they can be deemed complete.
☐ System Testing. This is a formal testing phase that involves users and developers to test the entire application in a managed format.
☐ Acceptance Testing. Acceptance testing is managed by users to formally determine whether a system satisfies the formal requirements agreed to by management.
☐ Regression Testing. This involves running test cases through an application to ensure that changes do not disrupt other functionality. For this reason it can also be used to test high data volumes.
☐ Parallel Testing. If there is a legacy system that is being replaced by the application being developed, parallel testing involves comparing the results from both systems to determine the validity of the new system.

Testing is often done in teams led by a resource external to the project team to get objective results.

Skills Required: Testers, business users, technical backup.

Implementation Figure 7.14 shows a level 2 view of implementation.

Input

Implementation plan
Backout plan

Output

Implemented application

Subprocess

Implement application

Additional Information An implementation plan should gradually bring an application online while ensuring that an organization is protected against any type of system crash. This is often done by running a previous system (if there is one) or a manual process in parallel with a new system until it is deemed acceptable.

Implementation is also frequently done on different hardware than development, especially in client/server projects. This means that all operating software and connections must be reestablished on

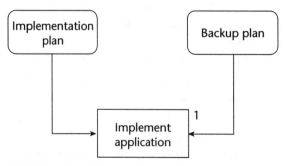

FIGURE 7.14 IPDM level 2—implementation.

the new hardware. Other issues, such as licensing agreements and vendor support, must also be considered. The development environment may still be required, so it must be kept intact and in sync with the production environment. The project manager must also determine which team members are required to stay on the project, which are required part time, and which not at all.

Skills Required: Development team + implementers.

Expand Pilot Figure 7.15 shows a level 2 view of expand pilot.

Input

    Application
    Key users
    IS staff

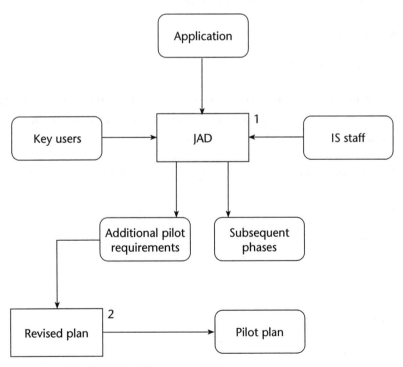

FIGURE 7.15 IPDM level 2—expand pilot.

Output

New pilot plan

Updated project plan

Subprocesses

JAD

Revised plan

Project Review

Input

Test plans

Error list

Output

Lessons and recommendations

Subprocess

Project review

Additional Information This is a review of the project, perhaps in the form of JAD sessions, with a view to improve future projects. This should be passed to the next release.

Skills Required: Project manager, business analysts, system analysts.

Infrastructure

Input

Trainers

Team

Output

Standards

Operational plans

Subprocess

Infrastructure

15 STEPS FOR GETTING STARTED

Using this methodology, the following steps were used for a one-year project. A six-month pilot was successfully developed and implemented, followed by the other phases of the project.

1. A project sponsor was selected. The sponsor selected a project manager and a steering committee.
2. The project manager selected a lead architect to oversee the design aspects of the application.
3. Prototyping tools were selected. The following tools were evaluated: JAM from Jyacc, Powerbuilder from Powersoft/Sybase, Vision from Unify, SQLWindows from Gupta, and Microsoft Access.
4. The architect worked with the users to build and confirm business requirements.
5. The project manager worked with a technical team to select technical architecture that was consistent with the organization standards.
6. The principal users of the project were identified.
7. The architect facilitated JAD sessions to confirm the business requirements. The architect ensured that the users understood the business requirements. The users ensured that the architect understood the business requirements, as well. This enabled both groups to have a common understanding of the project.

   The architect worked with the project team to accomplish the following:

   a. Talked with the users, read background documentation about the project
   b. Developed dataflow diagrams, ER diagrams, flowcharts, and a project plan to describe the project's business requirements
   c. Modified documents to reflect changes identified during the JAD sessions
   d. Built a project plan

e. Identified a six-month pilot

f. Built a multiphase project plan

8. The architect worked with a team to build a reusable prototype that reflected the business requirements

9. The prototype was confirmed with the users

10. The prototype was enhanced and reconfirmed with the users on an iterative basis

11. Program specifications were written to accompany the prototype

12. The project manager selected a project team

13. Training and support was provided for the project team

14. The project plan was divided into milestones that delivered the application in short phases of a few months or less

15. The deliverable from each phase was given to the users so that acceptable testing could begin

Regular status meetings and memos were used to inform the project manager and the project team about issues and status.

POTENTIAL PITFALLS

IPDM is unlike many other development methodologies in that it focuses on deliverables instead of processes. This could leave an exposure for managers who are dependent on following a recipe-like approach. IPDM is unsuccessful when used incorrectly, as shown in the following cases:

1. Prototyping should not be equated with having no defined requirements. A prototype in the computer industry is similar to what is created in other industries. An architect builds a scale model of a building to show clients what the product will look like, without incurring the total costs of actually constructing the building, only to discover that rooms or hallways are too small. Similarly, engineers build various specifications on paper, on CAD, and scale models to show what a car will look like before actually starting up the assembly lines.

In the IS industry, prototypes are often not used in the same manner. They sometimes become a license to be lax with business requirements. A prototype should be built iteratively until it is signed off. From that point on, the prototype becomes the functional specification for the project, and any other changes to it should be carefully assessed for impact on the project plan.

2. Choosing the wrong development tool for building the prototype. A prototype should be developed using the same development tool as the rest of the system. This will make it reusable. The development tool should have the following features:

☐ Easy-to-use painting tool supporting GUI or character-based screens. The character-based screen methodology is useful in applications that must be ported across platforms for a variety of clients (some of whom do not have architectures capable of supporting GUIs) and also in applications that require quick response time.
☐ Broad database support (e.g., Informix, Oracle, Sybase, Ingres)
☐ Event-driven functionality
☐ 4GL support

OTHER CONSIDERATIONS

Select Project Team

This requires a careful mixing of skills and attitudes, based on the business requirements and the technology. A project manager must be careful to hire a mix of full-time staff and consultants that work well together, and offer the technical skills that are necessary to implement a project. Project managers should not be bashful at this point. Prepare a detailed questionnaire or quiz to gauge a candidate's set of skills. Also keep in mind that bright professionals with good attitudes are capable of learning new skills relatively quickly. For example, a consultant who had one year of C experience was hired as a senior developer on a client/server project. Within three weeks, the developer was able to learn entirely new skills, without specific training, in areas such as Sybase SQL Server, TCP/IP, JAM (a screen management product), and a new operating system, sufficiently to fulfill the requirements of the assignment. The attitude and the aptitude were the important characteristics this developer offered, and hiring someone with more specific experience may not have saved time and money. Many such examples justify the position that soft skills are sometimes more important than specific skills. The best fit may be a candidate who can offer both soft and specific skills to a project.

Skills development should be an ongoing process during the development cycle. This can be done through a variety of means, such as magazines, text books, and inhouse training courses.

Skills Required: Project manager.

Regularly and Critically Monitor Progress

In a meeting, a project manager inviting disaster goes around the table and asks everyone to give his or her status as a way to measure the overall status of the project. In many environments, the most wonderful things are said, such as: "There is no inflation," "World peace is around the corner," "Only ethical politicians are elected," and "Everyone is competent in his or her job." Yet, at implementation time, every conceivable problem confronts the project team.

The reality is that human beings have an affinity for wanting to do the easy things first and ignoring the difficult ones for as long as possible. The weekly status meetings that report continued progress often cite only these successes, and the classic "almost-done" syndrome easily applies. The manager should not be surprised to find that the project will always remain 80 percent complete and 20 percent incomplete.

A manager can solve this dilemma by complementing weekly status meetings with regular walkabouts and demonstrations of work in progress. Managers that are too senior or uncomfortable to do this can have a team leader or other team member do it instead. One effective manager the author worked with used to walk around every several days, look at what was being done, and talk to all the team members on a one-on-one basis. This allowed him to see the current state of the application, the ongoing ability of the developers, and also allowed the developers to gain from his experience. In one instance, a developer was working on a user interface screen using JAM from Jyacc. Functions coded in C language were connected to events on the screen. The application was connected to Sybase SQL Server. The developer unit tested the application and declared that he was finished. The manager walked to the screen and performed what all the team members affectionately began to call the "Mitch test." This involved holding down a key at random and filling all the fields on a screen completely. Without exception, this test has always uncovered a problem somewhere in an application.

Managers who adopt this walk about strategy should be careful to be noncritical. If done incorrectly or harshly, your team will spend more time dreading your presence and less time actually getting work done.

Skills Required: Project manager, architect, project leader.

Build Team Synergy and Loyalty

A group of individuals working together as a team will produce a better product than individuals looking after their own interests. A manager should consider different forms of team building, perhaps bringing in a facilitator to promote this. It is important for the members of your team to respect each other's abilities.

In the computer industry it is possible to build loyalty, but do not expect to keep all your key players on the team for the length of a project. Ensure that at least two team members (who are not buddies, as they often leave during the same time period) share the same knowledge. Also insist on good ongoing documentation that must be shared with all the members of the team. Implement a regular review of the documentation so that team members have an incentive to keep it current.

Skills Required: Development team.

SUMMARY

This chapter introduced an exciting new methodology that can be called the iterative project development methodology (IPDM), which has a solid track record of success. IPDM will support projects in a variety of business areas and technical environments. It supports mainframe, client/server, open systems, and distributed systems to name a few. This methodology was presented in two levels of detail. Level 1 was an overview consisting of fifteen processes. Level 2 provided more detail per process, including input and output deliverables.

Project Resourcing— Roles, Responsibilities, and Monitoring

8

OVERVIEW

In this chapter the reader will learn about:

- Project resourcing
- Roles and responsibilities
- Estimation
- Project reporting
- Staffing projects
- Project monitoring

This chapter deals with understanding the resource requirements for completing a project on time and within budget. It focuses on the human side of project management and deals with the roles and responsibilities of the project manager, project team, and either stakeholders who are responsible for approving the project at various stages or stakeholders who are impacted by the results of the completed project. The roles and responsibilities of key players in project development are also described.

A project is an organized effort with clearly defined objectives, scope, and strategy to complete the deliverables. To achieve these deliverables in a timely manner, a project requires resources. Depending on the specific requirements of a project, these resources may be available internally. If the required resources and skillsets are not available internally, external resources may be required. The internal staff is typically obtained from the systems department. External resources can be obtained from a variety of sources, including consulting companies, outsourcing companies providing systems integration services, or individual fee-for-service consultants.

The project team has a variety of roles and responsibilities. These roles may be tied to specific project deliverables or they may occur throughout the life of the project. There are a number of attributes of a successful project. Most projects involve teamwork to achieve the desired results. Teamwork covers a number of elements including:

☐ A project manager with the right leadership, management, and technical skills
☐ A project manager who can identify issues, communicate them effectively, and resolve them in a timely manner
☐ A project team that can work together under the direction of the project manager
☐ A project team committed to deliverables and deadlines
☐ A project team where members learn from each other and contribute to an improved quality end result
☐ A project team focused on results
☐ A project team that understands the business processes and respects users' concerns

The project manager is typically either from the systems department or interfaces with the systems department to complete the project. The primary role of the systems department is to ensure that projects are delivered in accordance with user requirements.

ORGANIZATION

Project organization deals with a project manager and the team members responsible for the delivery of the project. The project manager has the overall responsibility for attaining the project goals on schedule, within cost, and in accordance with the requirements and expectations set out by the project sponsor. Typically, the project will involve staff from the systems department and representative staff from the user departments. For example, if the project is to develop a human resources information system, the project team may be comprised of:

- ☐ A project manager, usually from the systems department.
- ☐ Several analysts from the systems department, including systems analyst, data analyst, programmer analyst, and programmers. The roles and responsibilities of these positions are described in more detail later in this chapter.
- ☐ External consultants for specific skillsets, such as software package selection and evaluation, integration testing, and conversion.
- ☐ User analysts from human resources department with the expertise in the business of planning and managing human resources.

Consequently, most projects do not follow the typical hierarchical or functional organization structure, but rather, follow a matrix organizational structure. In a matrix organizational structure, a project team cuts across several functional units to get the appropriate mix of team members whose contribution is essential to the success of the project. The team members report directly to the project manager for project related work. In addition, each of the project team members from user departments continues reporting to his or her functional manager for department specific tasks. At the completion of the project, the respective team members return to their home departments.

Figure 8.1 shows the reporting relationship between the project manager and the team members.

RESOURCING

An integral part of managing projects is to have a clear understanding of resources required to complete the project, including developing a budget to plan and manage the resources. Budgetary items include salary and related benefits, equipment and supplies, travel, and consulting dollars. Examples of resources include:

- ☐ Salary and related benefits associated with project team members

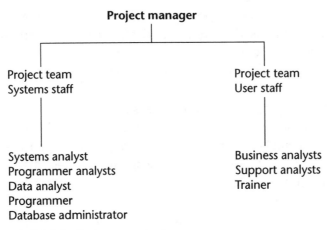

FIGURE 8.1 Project organization.

☐ Hardware and software tools to enable the project team members to complete their tasks in an effective and efficient manner
☐ Travel and related expenses for the project
☐ Availability of physical facilities, such as space for offices and meeting rooms
☐ Time commitment of the project sponsor
☐ Acquisition of appropriate project management tools and methodology (if not already available) to guide the development and implementation of the project

Project resources are directly related to completing projects in a timely manner, in conjunction with other factors (Figure 8.2).

The provision of project resources is fundamental to the successful delivery of the project. However, to determine resource requirements for a project requires experience in both managing similar projects and a diverse range of projects. Lack of resources will typically have an impact on the quality and timeliness of the project. But how does the project manager determine the size of the project team and the right mix of skillsets required for the project? For instance, how many analysts, programmers, data architects, and so on are required, and will they be required on a part-time or full-time basis to get the job done in a timely and cost-effective manner?

Several estimating approaches are available to the project manager,

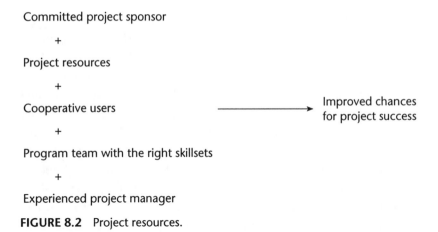

Committed project sponsor

+

Project resources

+

Cooperative users   ⟶   Improved chances for project success

+

Program team with the right skillsets

+

Experienced project manager

FIGURE 8.2 Project resources.

depending on the complexity of the project, the quality of resources available, and the commitment of the project sponsor. Typically, estimating techniques include the following:

1. Project estimation based on prior experience of working with projects of similar size and complexity. Under this approach, the project manager is estimating the costing requirements based on his or her past experience in working with similar projects. The key advantage of this approach is that the cost estimation process can be approximated rather quickly, based on the project manager's knowledge base. The project manager would have typically normalized the estimates to ensure that the project complexity and the project environment are comparable to the present environment.

   The disadvantage of this approach is that all variables may not have been considered and may result in underestimating the effort required to complete the project. In addition, the project manager may not be in a position to fully assess the strengths and weaknesses of the current project team and the expectations of the project sponsor. Consequently, it is possible that there could be significant deviations between the estimated cost and the actual costs.

   However, this technique may be quite appropriate for smaller projects entailing lower cost and limited project complexity, and may be also relevant for determining order of magnitude costing estimates.

2. Project estimation based on a detailed breakdown of tasks and estimation of resources required to complete those tasks. This approach requires a good understanding of the detailed tasks required to complete a project, as well as availability of the appropriate skillsets of the project team to complete the deliverables. Under this approach, a detailed spreadsheet could be developed for each team member, detailing the tasks and the time and costs required to complete those tasks. Allowance for coordination and monitoring of these activities, time for administrative tasks such as attending department meetings, vacation, and sickness allowance should be also included in the overall estimates. After developing these detailed estimates, the project manager can still apply his or her judgment and experience to validate and finetune the figures.

    This approach is typically used by consulting companies and systems integrators who are involved in fixed price application development projects. It can also be used for managing in-house projects.

3. Project estimation based on in-house standards. As an organization gets more experience in completing projects, a database of projects could be developed identifying the key project attributes and defining complexity in a quantifiable manner. Such a database of projects could help an organization in developing standards for project estimation based on project and organizational characteristics. Some of the elements for developing an in-house project database are:

    ☐ Number of project tasks
    ☐ Number of business functions and processes addressed by the application
    ☐ Project complexity (e.g., determined on a scale of 1 to 10, where 1 = not complex and 10 = very complex)
    ☐ Number of screens developed for conducting various functions and tasks
    ☐ Number and size of programs (e.g., lines of code)

- ☐ Number of data elements and number of records, files, and tables
- ☐ Number of hard-copy and soft-copy reports
- ☐ Methodology and tools used (e.g., use of computer-aided software engineering tools, tools for developing prototypes, and rapid application development techniques)
- ☐ Type of technology environment (e.g., legacy application or client-server application)
- ☐ Number of project team members
- ☐ Number of changes to the original requirements specifications

A database of projects could be helpful in establishing benchmarks when a new project is undertaken. In addition, the project manager can still exercise his or her judgment to ensure that the project estimates are realistic and incorporate new project characteristics.

ROLES AND RESPONSIBILITIES

The primary role of the systems department is to provide information technology services in support of business goals and objectives. These services include, but are not limited to:

- ☐ Preparing, coordinating, and maintaining information technology strategic, tactical, and operational plans
- ☐ Providing and maintaining hardware, software, and communications infrastructure to capture, process, and retrieve information
- ☐ Developing, maintaining, and supporting computer applications to enable better delivery of business functions and processes
- ☐ Developing and maintaining standards for developing applications in stand-alone and multiuser environments
- ☐ Acquiring hardware and software products in accordance with the standards
- ☐ Developing and administering data management practices to facilitate capture, store, and retrieval in a timely, secure, and reliable manner
- ☐ Providing computer technology training to organizational users
- ☐ Managing computer professionals in the delivery and support of information technology services

❑ Managing vendors of computer products and services to ensure that timely and cost effective services are received

In the project management context, the systems department is responsible for managing systems resources, facilitating projects by working in partnership with the user departments, and providing coordination and support for the timely delivery of projects.

Depending on the size, scope, and complexity of projects, a number of stakeholders are involved in the progress of the project and its successful outcome. Descriptions follow of some of the formal structures that can provide guidance to the project team and monitor the progress of the project so that it meets the stated goals and objectives.

Executive Committee

This committee is comprised of senior management of the organization, and has an overall responsibility for accepting and approving the project initiatives outlined in the information technology strategic plan, including funding and prioritization of projects before they are initiated.

Project Steering Committee

This committee provides general business direction to the application development project, and reviews and accepts deliverables. The steering committee is typically chaired by a user manager/director with the system director functioning in an advisory role on the committee. The project manager is part of this committee and receives input regarding project direction, priorities, and project funding. The steering committee usually provides a mechanism for reconciling conflicts between different user groups.

Project Manager

The project manager is directly responsible for the successful delivery of the project. The project manager reports to the steering committee on the status of the project and seeks advice from the committee on a variety of project related issues including direction, scope, and funding.

After the project manager has been assigned to the project, one of his or her primary tasks is to select the team members who will be responsible for completing the project deliverables. The project manager may be offered several resources from other departments; however, he or she should be careful in accepting these resources. The primary purpose of resource allocation is to ensure that there is a fit between the tasks to be completed and the corresponding skillsets to achieve the tasks. It should not be the project manager's responsibility to accept staff surplus from other departments. Utilizing staff without the appropriate skillsets is bound to impact the quality and timeliness of the project. If the project manager cannot find sufficient internal resources, then external resources with the appropriate skillsets should be acquired.

A project manager provides the glue linking a number of players, including project sponsor, stakeholders, project team, and user groups. Depending on the size and complexity of the project, the extent of the project manager's involvement may vary. For instance, for larger projects, project coordinators may be required to manage specific subsystems and in ensuring that the subsystems are integrated.

Typically, the responsibilities of the project manager include the following:

- Clarifying the scope of the project, including technologies to be used and interfaces to existing systems.
- Defining system functions to support the business functions, generating technology options, developing implementation strategies, and preparing an implementation plan.
- Identifying the business functions and processes requiring either change or improvement through automation, and identifying new or changed information needs.
- Obtaining approvals from the steering committee in accordance with the project plan.
- Working with the project team to identify/refine and prioritize project tasks and the responsibilities for the timely completion of those tasks.

☐ Monitoring the project and communicating the status to the steering committee on a regular basis. Regular project reporting provides a vehicle to communicate the project status to the steering committee. Regular reporting also tends to diffuse any communication problems that may have surfaced and require attention of the steering committee. Such problems could include change in system specifications, changes in the hardware or software environment, a change in business direction due to mergers, loss of certain key project team personnel, and lack of funding.

With the above responsibilities, the project manager must continually operate by building relationships with the project team and winning their respect. There will be situations where the project manager is required to negotiate terms with the team members and motivate them to accept the new arrangement and responsibilities. The project manager is a key influencer and consequently must have superb communications and interpersonal skills to manage a team with diverse skills. Wherever possible, the project manager should use influence and persuasion instead of authority to get results from the project team.

Project Team

The project team members report to the project manager. The project team has responsibility for completing the project tasks and in ensuring that the deliverables are completed in a timely and effective manner.

In addition to specific technical skills, the project team requires a good understanding of various business skills to enhance the chances of project success. Some of these business skills include, but are not limited to:

☐ Understanding of the business. This means that if the project is concerned with a financial services industry such as a bank or an insurance company, it is essential that the project manager and some of the analysts have competence in that business sector. Analysts need a good grasp of the business and technical skills in order to deliver the project.

□ Communication skills. A project involves teamwork. Usually, a variety of ideas and alternatives are discussed before formulating a plan of action. Communication skills include the ability to capture and analyze data, document the results, and provide feedback to the clients to ensure that there is right understanding of the tasks.

□ Technical skills. There is no substitute for technical skills. For instance, if programming skills are required for developing applications in an Oracle database environment, it is necessary that the programmer have experience in working under that environment. Sometimes, programming skills under a specific operating system environment, such as UNIX, may be required to streamline and expedite the application development process.

□ Analytical and problem-solving skills. A new project involves change. The project team members must be proficient in anticipating and responding to change and developing change management practices and procedures to ease client concerns.

□ Team-building and team player skills. A project involves a multidisciplinary team to complete the tasks and deliverables. Consequently, a high level of coordination and communication is required to minimize misunderstanding. Typically, a project will produce results in a timely manner if the team's efforts are synergistic. Conversely, with a technically proficient team having little team building and team player skills, the results will likely be less than successful.

The following list provides a brief description of a representative project team's functions and responsibilities for developing a client/server application using relational database management technology. The typical roles and responsibilities of the project team members are described. For each of the project team positions, a detailed job description may be required so that the relevant skillsets are obtained to work on the project.

Programmer/Analyst

Roles and Responsibilities

□ Assist in the definition, analysis, and refinement of application requirements

□ Provide input to estimates for work plans

☐ Develop, test, and document programs/modules as per specifications

☐ Review application performance to ensure that it meets the expectations

Skills

☐ Detailed knowledge of programming languages and database products

☐ Good knowledge of user interface tools and utilities

☐ Good knowledge of CASE tools

☐ Ability to work in individual and team environments and produce deliverables

Systems Analyst

Roles and Responsibilities

☐ Define, analyze, and refine requirements

☐ Provide input to estimates for work plans

☐ Prepare program and module specifications

☐ Test program modules to achieve the specified objectives

☐ Set up user test plans

Skills

☐ Analytical and problem-solving skills

☐ Good experience in the use and applications of database software

☐ Knowledge of graphical user interface (GUI) tools for screen design and navigation and prototyping

☐ Good communication skills

Database Analyst/Administrator

Roles and Responsibilities

☐ Install and maintain the database management system

☐ Conduct physical design of the database

☐ Maintain system files

☐ Communicate physical database changes to project team

☐ Conduct performance tuning on the database management system
☐ Review and document the physical schema
☐ Adhere to systems development standards and procedures
☐ Adhere to security standards and procedures

Skills

☐ In-depth knowledge of the database
☐ Solid knowledge of access language
☐ Good knowledge of the client/server operating systems and networks
☐ Good communication skills

Technical Analyst

Roles and Responsibilities

☐ Investigate and address technical problems
☐ Identify hardware and software elements and define the technology environment
☐ Determine system configurations based on application's planned requirements
☐ Provide solutions to data transport and internetworking issues
☐ Resolve hardware, software, and network issues

Skills

☐ Excellent knowledge of current and planned technology
☐ Ability to resolve problems in timely manner
☐ Good communications and interpersonal skills

Business Analyst

Roles and Responsibilities

☐ Identify key business functions and processes
☐ Provide relationships between these functions
☐ Provide input to project team regarding processes, procedures, and expected results
☐ Provide feedback to project team based on its analysis
☐ Assist the data and systems analysts with data attributes

Skills

- ☐ Excellent knowledge of business processes and planned direction
- ☐ Good problem-solving skills
- ☐ Good communication skills
- ☐ Working knowledge of technology tools
- ☐ Ability to work well in individual and team environments

Data Analyst

Roles and Responsibilities

- ☐ Provide input to data standards and procedures
- ☐ Interact with business and technical analysts
- ☐ Define data and their attributes based on the requirements
- ☐ Prepare, update, and maintain the data integrity matrix—i.e., create, read, update, and delete
- ☐ Translate functional requirement specifications and produce conceptual and logical data models
- ☐ Resolve conflicts pertaining to logical data elements

Skills

- ☐ Good knowledge of CASE tools
- ☐ In-depth expertise in developing data models and logical designs
- ☐ Good problem-solving and communication skills
- ☐ Ability to represent data properties independent of system constraints

Job Description Form   Figure 8.3 shows a form that can be used for preparing a detailed job description for each project team member, to define and document each project team member's role and responsibility. This job description can be used as a basis to discuss the specific skills of the team member and seek appropriate budgetary approvals.

TYPES OF APPLICATION DEVELOPMENT

The previous section detailed a full suite of roles along with their appropriate deliverables and skill requirements. The composition and

```
Organization:                          Position Number:

Project Name:                          Position Name:

Project Number:                        Project Effective Date:

Client Contact:                        Planned Completion Date:

Project Manager:

Project Description:

Deliverables:


_____                _____

Prepared by:                           Approved by:
```

FIGURE 8.3 Job description form.

timing of the use of those resources will depend in part on the nature of the development effort, the technology in use, and the business being automated. Most application development efforts will fall into one of three broad categories:

1. Automating new business practices
2. Replacing a legacy system
3. Benefiting from a new technology

Though a core set of resources are needed across each of the preceding examples, some exceptions do occur. One such example is a client/server application that seeks to replace small portions of a legacy system.

Automating New Business Practices

This type of development effort typically draws upon a standard set of development tools, standards, and methodology (although the use of a methodology such as the IPDM discussed in Chapter 7 provides a faster and more focused path to implementation).

A standard team structure for development projects is provided in Table 8.1

TABLE 8.1 Team structure automation of new business practices

Title	Involvement	Details
Project manager	All	Manages project from inception to post implementation.
Senior architect	All	Ensures that there is a balance between application and technology architectures.
Business analyst	All	Takes conceptual design down to detail requirements.
Technical analyst	Analysis Design	Verifies technical architecture's ability to support application.
Systems analyst	Design Coding	Converts detail requirements to design specifications.
Programmer analyst	Design Coding	Designs algorithms, libraries, object classes, and constructs.
Programmer	Coding	Constructs as per specifications.
Database administrator	Analysis Design	Designs database environment, database tables, and rules.
Data analyst	Analysis Design	Manages data and standards from corporate perspective.

The project manager is ultimately responsible for the success of every project. In this particular development effort, the areas of exposure lie in the business environment. The successful design and implementation of such a project hardly stops at the point at which code has been written and the software finds itself into the hands of the users. The project manager must ensure that the appropriate business practice documents have been developed and accepted by the user community. This is especially critical in instances where a new business is being automated.

As a final note, the automation of a new business practice is sometimes viewed as an opportunity to introduce new technology into an organization. This is a risky combination, as many new variables are introduced into an organization. A new technology brings with it a host of uncertainties that must be managed in a separate project. If a need has been identified (through some justification process) to implement a new technology (whether it be a tool set or an infrastructure) while designing a new business system, a great deal of care must be taken to stagger the work effort to allow time for the new technology to be incorporated into the infrastructure of an organization prior to the implementation of a new application.

Replacing a Legacy System

The design of an application aimed at replacing a legacy system requires details on the functionality of the existing system, as well as some knowledge of the evolution of the system. At times, the business processes automated by many legacy systems are modified to fit the limitations of the technology available at the time. The level of sophistication of the development tools today is far greater that those of ten or even five years ago.

As in the previous example, a great deal of emphasis will be placed in the business planning stage where the business processes are modeled. The replacement of legacy systems has typically presented opportunities for reengineering. This will again place additional stress on the business planning resources from both the development team and the business community. The team structure for such a design will look similar to that of Table 8.1 except for minor additions (see Table 8.2).

Two key differences worth noting at this point are in the areas of business planning and technology planning. The information architect will work closely with the business analyst and the user team to do workflow analysis. The primary purpose of this exercise is to verify the existing business processes and look for ways to introduce improvements. The technical analyst will concentrate on the technology infrastructure and its ability to support the new business processes. Statistically, the redesign of legacy systems has also meant the migra-

TABLE 8.2 Team structure—replacing a legacy system

Title	Involvement	Details
Project manager	All	Manages project from inception to post implementation.
Information architect	Planning	Will review business workflow and recommend reengineering opportunities.
Senior architect	All	Ensures that there is a balance between application and technology architectures.
Business analyst	All	Takes conceptual design down to detail requirements.
Technical analyst	Analysis Design	Verifies technical architecture's ability to support application.
Systems analyst	Design Coding	Converts detail requirements to design specifications.
Programmer analyst	Design Coding	Designs algorithms, libraries, object classes, and constructs.
Programmer	Coding	Constructs as per specifications.
Database administrator	Analysis Design	Designs database environment, database tables, and rules.
Data analyst	Analysis Design	Manages data and standards from corporate perspective.

tion of an application to another platform. A typical path is from a mainframe or mini to a micro/LAN architecture. This activity requires careful analysis and capacity planning. The technical architect has a tough task at hand in trying to translate the MIPS and DASD over to 80x86 and Megabytes.

Benefiting from a New Technology

Though there are numerous examples of this type of development, the client/server technology will be profiled in this section because of its relevance to real-world applications. Moving to client/server architecture involves a number of key issues, as shown in the following list:

☐ Evaluation and selection of an appropriate development tool set
☐ Design of an integrated development environment for the development team
☐ Design of a technology infrastructure able to support client server applications
☐ Appropriate training for both staff and clients to be able to undertake the design and support of a new technology

Although the preceding activities can easily be separate projects, they can be designed in phases with the appropriate settle-in time allowed for each major phase. An example of this is the design of a Wide Area Network (using routers) to enable the distributing of business processes across some geographic. This is clearly a strength of client/server (C/S) and the WAN will basically provide the supporting platform for this to happen.

In undertaking such a project, it is typically wise to do the following:

☐ Bring in consulting services to fast-track the development work. Also, establish a knowledge transfer protocol so that internal staff can benefit from the consulting services.
☐ Use a three-tiered approach to mustering the team. First, equip the team with the appropriate resources to design and implement the application. This team will typically consist of a number of consulting resources in order to bring in the new technology expertise.

Second, have a separate team charged with the mandate of being the support group for the application once it goes into production. This team will essentially be training and learning as the project evolves. Last and from a corporate perspective, it is wise to prepare a few staff for the next undertaking of this type of development. There are a number of good reasons for this; the key ones include the fact that with new technology, there will be staff turnovers. This is a fact of life and should be accommodated. Also, while the first team is still tied down with the post-implementation issues of the first application, it likely will be necessary to fire up a second application in your organization. With the people already trained, it will be a matter of simply moving the staff over to the next area of development.

Table 8.3 outlines a typical team structure for this type of development. The role of the technical analyst will be crucial. This individual will have to come up with a measurable technical solution for a proposed business problem. Further, this technical solution will have to fit into the overall infrastructure of the organization and be able to support future developments.

The role of the business analyst will become more complex in that the business process can now be distributed across the business environment. This will in turn lead to the distribution of data across the business infrastructure. This is a key advantage to be attained by client server technology.

MONITORING AND REPORTING

After the project has been launched, it is important to keep track of its progress and to communicate its status on a regular basis to the project sponsor and the stakeholders. The project manager is concerned with the quality and performance of the project—this means that the progress of the team members is monitored and appropriate feedback provided to them so that the team is properly aligned and working in unison to achieve the project goals.

The purpose of project monitoring is twofold. First, to describe the project progress to the project sponsor and the stakeholders, and sec-

TABLE 8.3   Team Structure—Benefiting from a new technology

Title	Involvement	Details
Project manager	All	Manages project from inception to post implementation.
Business analyst	All	Takes conceptual design down to detail requirements. With C/S technology, BA will also look into distributing business processes across business environment.
Senior architect	All	Ensures that there is a balance between application and technology architectures.
Technical analyst	Analysis Design	Profiles new technology. Provides capacity planning and ensures application is supportable on new technology.
Systems analyst	Design Coding	Converts detail requirements to design specifications.
Programmer analyst	Design Coding	Designs algorithms, libraries, object classes, and constructs.
Programmer	Coding	Constructs as per specifications.
Database administrator	Analysis Design	Designs database environment, database tables, and rules.
Data analyst	Analysis Design	Manages data and standards from corporate perspective.

ond, to use regular reporting concerning project progress as a means to obtain consensus among stakeholders and also to better manage their expectations and seek their support. Depending on the audience, the details regarding project monitoring and reporting may vary. The steering committee may be only interested in a monthly status report as outlined in Appendix C, but a detailed report indicating the progress by specific business function and subsystems may be of more interest to the user groups directly impacted by the project.

Typically, for larger projects, the project is monitored in accordance with the methodology used by an organization. For instance, the methodology may require that before proceeding to the next task, the analyst must ensure that the work is reviewed by the project manager or the data architect. If team members have encountered problems with given tasks, regular project meetings may provide an opportunity to address these problems and understand their implications on other tasks. In addition, the use of tools such as an electronic bulletin board for the project and electronic mail to communicate with members of the project team may also be effective in communicating problems and seeking ideas for possible solutions.

Project reviews are usually undertaken in one of the following ways:

1. Periodic project review. This type of review is driven by time, and typically conducted on a weekly or monthly basis. For instance, the monthly status report is an example of a time-driven review to communicate status and report on progress and obstacles, if any. The project manager can use reviews on a periodic basis to deal with specific problems, including issues related to the project team, changing specifications, problems with obtaining user consensus, or resources.

   Project reviews provide opportunities for the project manager to find timely and acceptable solutions. Reviews also help the project manager to stay on schedule and prevent future problems. We have found that project review meetings help the project team to clarify its expectations and requirements. Periodically, meetings should be conducted by the project manager with user and management groups to keep them informed about project progress and issues.

2. Deliverable-based review. Typically, this type of review is based on the completion of deliverables, including: review of documented user requirements, review of the application prototype, review of the documented functional specification, and review of the documented detailed design.

At the completion of each deliverable, the project manager reviews the progress with the project team and the appropriate user groups. It may be necessary to review key deliverables with senior management to ensure that key issues are communicated to and accepted by them.

3. Technical reviews. These are peer reviews undertaken by project team members, such as programmers and analysts, with the objective of reducing errors and improving the overall quality of design and code. These reviews could be undertaken periodically—either weekly or monthly or based on completion of specific tasks, such as testing the logic of a program module. The project manager usually participates in some of these reviews and provides advice regarding approach and use of quality assurance tools and techniques such as structured walkthroughs.

Standardized project management forms are typically used to monitor projects on a consistent and effective basis and communicate both with the project team and various user and management groups. Samples of various forms are provided in Appendix E to monitor and track project activities. Each of these forms can be customized to specific environments, conducive to the type of project and the nature of the organization. As a result, these forms should be used as a guideline.

SUMMARY

This chapter has described the resources required for completing projects and techniques for managing and monitoring projects. The roles and responsibilities of key players in project development were also described to give the reader a better understanding of the skills required to complete the project. In an organization, senior managers rely on project managers to execute projects in accordance with the business objectives of the organization. The project manager relies on the project team to deliver the deliverables and tasks in a timely and cost-effective manner. Project management discipline is based on a team approach and consequently requires delegation, effective communication for followup and feedback, and delegation of tasks to the appropriate team members.

If a project is staffed appropriately and provided with adequate resources, it will have a better chance for success. Staffing could be either internal or external depending on the availability of expertise. Internal staff are typically obtained from the systems department. External resources can be obtained from a variety of sources including consulting companies, outsourcing companies providing systems integration services, or individual fee-for-service consultants. In assembling the project team, the skills and the expertise should be of paramount concern. Use of surplus staff from other departments is not a good practice to achieve resourcing requirements.

Appendix E contains a variety of forms that can be used for describing and monitoring projects.

Outsourcing of Information Technology Projects

9

OVERVIEW

In this chapter the reader will learn about:

- A definition of project outsourcing
- Advantages and disadvantages of outsourcing
- Modes of delivery
- A methodology for evaluating outsourcing providers
- Outsourcing case studies

Outsourcing can be defined as a method of acquiring services from an external organization or company instead of using internal resources. In our day-to-day lives, we use outsourcing or contracting to acquire services of tradespeople such as plumbers, carpenters, and auto mechanics to meet our requirements. Outsourcing is also used to meet organizations' requirements. The alternative to outsourcing is delivering the required services with in-house personnel. Although it might be appealing for some organizations to rely mainly on in-house staff, it may not be economical and practical to keep them busy and gainfully occupied after a project is implemented.

With the benefits of economies of scale, outsourcing enables vendors to provide services at a competitive price. Outsourcing also implies

195

that another organization can provide similar or better services at a lower cost compared to using in-house personnel. External services are usually acquired for one or more of the following reasons:

- ☐ The outsourcing vendor has the required specialty to provide services more cost effectively than in-house personnel
- ☐ In-house personnel lack flexibility and expertise to keep abreast of changes in the marketplace and implement solutions requiring new and perhaps unproven technologies
- ☐ The outsourcing vendor can use economies of scale to serve its clientele and build up skillsets to meet needs in a timely manner
- ☐ The outsourcing vendor can provide services on an as-required basis consistent with the needs of the organization
- ☐ Using outsourcing services provides organizations with an opportunity to focus on their core business

Typically, the external vendors can be regarded as specialists and wholesalers of information technology services to the marketplace. Over the past ten years, there has been a gradual shift to outsourcing services. Some of the services normally provided by in-house company staff have moved to outsourcing vendors, including cafeteria services, printing and publication services, legal services, check printing and distribution services, cleaning and maintenance services, property management services, and of course, information technology services.

The primary issue in outsourcing is whether the required service is part of the core business. If the answer is no, then cost-effective alternatives to acquiring these services should be considered. It may make business sense to retain a small staff to provide the coordination role and basic services, but any significant requirements should be supplemented with resources from the outsourcing vendor.

In the information technology sector, with downsizing and the pressures to remain competitive in the global economy, many organizations have streamlined their operations and focused their attention on their core business by outsourcing services that do not add value directly to the organization. The information technology departments are becoming more vulnerable to a combination of budget cuts and the need for greater services, and consequently are looking at outsourcing as a viable way of delivering services to the organization. As the information technology function continues to mature, it makes business sense to consider outsourcing as a viable option to in-house systems services.

Outsourcing is about partnerships between providers and recipients of services and how these services can be delivered effectively to meet the business goals of the organization. If this partnership approach is going to be successful, the outsourcing vendor has to know the organizations it services and strive to continuously provide added value. Figure 9.1 outlines the elements of the outsourcing environment and the linkages.

Since the early 1980s, organizations have explored and considered outsourcing opportunities with the objective of achieving the following benefits:

☐ Reducing overall information technology costs without sacrificing service levels

☐ Achieving flexibility and responsiveness in acquiring services based on the needs of the organization

☐ Dealing with a vendor who is an "expert" in the field and manages diverse and changing technologies instead of hiring in-house staff

In-house services

- Building/construction
- Components manufacturing
- Equipment maintenance
- Information technology management—hardware/software, telecommunications
- Computer applications development

Outsourcing vendor

- Building/construction
- Components manufacturing
- Equipment maintenance
- Information technology management—hardware/software, telecommunications
- Computer applications development on a turnkey basis

Linkages

- Manage vendors
- Provide coordination role
- Retain flexibility
- Use vendors on pay-as-you-go or fixed-price basis
- Ensure quality

FIGURE 9.1 Outsourcing environment.

☐ Driving business needs by requirements instead of being constrained by existing hardware and software environments

☐ Focusing on managing the core business—using information technology to complement the core business without using internal staff

☐ Capitalizing on significant cost savings through the economies of scale achieved by outsourcing vendors

Outsourcing is based on a fundamental premise that an outsourcing vendor can provide equivalent or better services to an organization at a lower cost and increased flexibility. Outsourcing can be acquired in various forms ranging from complete outsourcing of information technology functions to selective outsourcing on a project by project basis depending on business requirements.

OUTSOURCING INFORMATION TECHNOLOGY FUNCTIONS

There are a number of opportunity areas for outsourcing information technology services. These range from complete outsourcing of the information technology function to specific outsourcing projects, depending on the requirements of the organization. The following list shows technology functions that can be provided in-house versus functions that could be outsourced; use this list as a guide, because the specific outsourcing activities will be dependent on the objectives and needs of the organization.

Functions Provided In-house

☐ Project coordination between the user and the outsourcing vendor

☐ Quality assurance throughout the system's development lifecycle— e.g., from project initiation to project implementation

☐ Determination of functional requirements

☐ Development of a logical design for an application

☐ Selection of an application software package—e.g., selection of a database management system software for the enterprise

☐ Outsourcing vendor management

Functions Provided by the Outsourcing Vendor

- □ System construction
- □ System implementation
- □ Application testing, including unit and integration testing
- □ Application training
- □ System and user documentation
- □ System maintenance and enhancement
- □ Any overload-related functions of the information technology department
- □ Complete system integration and turnkey application development

ADVANTAGES AND DISADVANTAGES OF OUTSOURCING

Outsourcing should be viewed as one of the modes of managing services required in an organization, and driven by specific business needs. It is not a panacea and may not be suited for all organizations. Some of the advantages and disadvantages of outsourcing follow.

Advantages

If properly planned and managed, outsourcing offers several advantages to an organization:

1. Costs can be predicted and fixed over a period of time. Outsourcing services can be defined and measured. It is easier to predict fixed costs with the outsourcing vendor over time. For instance, the outsourcing vendor can provide a fixed price estimate for developing and implementing a computer application, servicing 2,000 users by managing a Help Desk, or providing a performance uptime guarantee for a computer network.

2. The client organization has an opportunity to focus on the core business. If the organization's business is to manufacture products such as office furniture, it may not be critical to have another vendor manage its information technology requirements. In such a situation, the role of the organization would change from providing

information technology services with in-house personnel to managing the outsourcing vendor to ensure that performance and service levels are delivered in a timely and cost-effective manner.

3. Workload can be better managed—service levels can be monitored on a regular basis. If the organization's workload is seasonal or requires greater flexibility due to changes in the marketplace, the outsourcing vendor can satisfy the need by offering services on a demand or as-required basis.

4. No increase in staff will be needed if the workload increases. Having an outsourcing vendor provides flexibility to an organization to pass on the extra work if there is an increase in business activity. A partnership approach with the outsourcing vendor provides an opportunity to transfer more workload over time, if there is an acceptable level of service at a competitive price. For non-core business functions, it may be prudent to expand the business without expanding the staffing levels.

5. Service agreements can be reviewed frequently—for example, every year or every two years. The contract expiration date with the outsourcing vendor provides a logical point to review the types and value of services acquired. The duration of the contract is dependent on a number of factors, including the type of services acquired, value of total services, cost and risk associated with changing an outsourcing vendor, service responsiveness from the vendor, viability of the outsourcing vendor, reliability of the vendor, and ability to meet deliverables when promised.

   For instance, a contract duration of two years with a one-year extension may be appropriate to monitor the service levels with the vendor. A microcomputer maintenance agreement to service microcomputers and peripherals throughout the country could be for two years with an option to renew for one year. On the other hand, a service agreement to manage a computer center and telecommunications services could be for a longer time period, say, up to five years, because the vendor may have to make capital investments in hardware and software to deliver the service and performance levels.

6. Accountability can be tied to performance and service levels; unacceptable performance could be subject to financial penalty. An outsourcing vendor is in the business of providing services at a

competitive price. As these services are distinct and measurable, it is important that service levels are monitored and reported. Typical measures of service levels are:

☐ Timeliness of service. If a microcomputer maintenance agreement requires service within 4 hours of placing a telephone call to the vendor, then this activity can be measured and reported. If the service level is not met, financial penalties may be imposed provided that they are specified in the service agreement.

☐ Availability of service. If the computer center is required to be available 24 hours a day, 7 days a week, the service availability can be measured and monitored. Again, there could be financial penalties associated with lack of availability.

☐ Response time of the computer system. This is a visible factor for determining the effectiveness of a computer system. A subsecond response time for 95 percent of the transactions is the normal expectation of the user. Again, this measurable indicator could be an integral part of the service agreement.

☐ Quality of service. Although quality is difficult to measure, it can be experienced by the users of the service. Quality can include responsiveness to a request, ability to meet deadlines when promised, preparing the users for a change of software release before it is implemented, testing a product before it is released, providing support services for problem resolution, and so on. Quality of service could be measured by customer surveys, for example, once a year, to determine some of the problem areas and ensure that they are addressed adequately.

Disadvantages

There are several disadvantages to outsourcing if it is not properly managed, including:

☐ Outsourcing may be costly in the longer term—after the outsourcing vendor has acquired the understanding of the client organization, both unit costs and total costs may increase as the outsourcing vendor seeks additional revenue-generating opportunities.

☐ Requirements that were not anticipated would be contingent on the availability of funds—the vendor can demand additional funding to incorporate these unanticipated requirements.

☐ Limited skills transfer may occur from the outsourcing vendor to the client—the vendor may not be cooperative in skills transfer to the client organization.

☐ Difficulty may arise in measuring and managing quality.

☐ Staff morale at the client organization may be impacted—with a greater amount work being transferred to the outsourcing vendor, the more interesting work could be potentially outsourced.

☐ The outsourcing vendor retains control over the ultimate level and quality of services provided.

☐ A higher level of risk is incurred if there are changes at the outsourcing vendor organization.

☐ Typically, a higher price results when the client organization decides to change the outsourcing vendor—e.g., conversion and migration costs, training costs, greater coordination, and risk of downtime.

OUTSOURCING—MODES OF DELIVERY

There are several delivery models for managing outsourcing services. The two distinguishing characteristics between these delivery models are the level of control over the service and the amount of risk the organization is prepared to take with the outsourcing vendor. Figure 9.2 depicts the relationship between the various outsourcing factors.

To acquire outsourcing services, there are primarily three modes of delivery.

In-house Project Delivery

This delivery model includes the provision of services by in-house staff, based on the priorities and requirements of the internal client within the organization. The degree of responsiveness and the associated allocation of resources could be driven by priorities set by senior management of the organization, or alternatively, based on internal pricing to recover costs and overhead.

```
Key Constraints

Greater exposure to risk
(e.g., security risk, lack of
data integrity)

Limited degree of control

Difficulty in measuring
performance and service levels

Limited control over costs
and quality

Limited understanding of
the client's business and priorities
```

FIGURE 9.2 Key constraints.

Of the three modes of delivery, the in-house project delivery model is typically the most expensive but most effective. Depending on the requirements of the organization, it might make business sense to deliver high-priority services by in-house staff and acquire less critical services from the outsourcing vendor.

Use of Supplementary Consultants and Systems Integrators

This delivery model includes the selective use of consultants and systems integrators on an as-required basis. Typical examples of using consultants and systems integrators would include developing computer applications; maintaining computer applications; implementing computer systems; and acquiring a complete turnkey system, including hardware and software.

This model is effective for specific project-related activities where the scope and deliverables are clearly understood. Many organizations use consultants when acquiring specific skillsets that are not readily available in the client organization. Sometimes consultants are also used to supplement in-house resources to get the job done in a timely manner. This mode of acquiring outsourcing services would also include using services to jumpstart support capabilities, followed by skills transfer to in-house staff.

Systems integrators are used when there is a need to acquire specific solutions for the client organization. For instance, systems integrators may be considered for vertical market applications such as systems for the dental office, insurance broker, property management office, or advertising office.

Complete Outsourcing of Projects

This delivery model includes the provision of all designated services by the outsourcing vendor, at a predictable cost. In-house systems provide a coordinating function. The nature and scope of services are determined by the senior management of the company in accordance with the requirements of the organization. Service parameters would include cost, quality, and timeliness of services.

Request for Proposal (RFP)

Outsourcing services are usually acquired on a competitive basis. Depending on the size and complexity of the services required from the outsourcing vendor, a Request for Proposal (RFP) document is prepared to outline the business and systems requirements of the client organization. An RFP is a formal document sent to a list of qualified vendors, inviting them to propose a cost-effective system solution to meet the client's requirements. Identical copies of the RFP are sent to vendors so that all the vendors are responding to similar requirements. The RFP process typically involves the following steps:

1. The client organization prepares a Request for Proposal including a description of the company's background, a description of how the RFP process will be conducted, and a description of its current information technology environment. In addition, the RFP will

include a description of hardware, software, network, and services which the client organization intends to acquire as part of the RFP process. The RFP provides a detailed listing of mandatory and desirable items for the proposed goods and services. A description of how the vendor proposals will be evaluated is also provided for the vendors.

2. A list of qualified vendors is prepared.
3. The RFP is distributed to the qualified vendors. Vendors are usually allowed 10 to 20 business days to respond.
4. Vendors submit their proposals to the client organization.
5. The client organization evaluates these proposals based on an evaluation methodology.
6. The successful vendor proposal is determined and the vendor advised.
7. A contract is negotiated between the vendor and the client to finalize the arrangements between the two parties.
8. The vendor provides information technology goods and services in accordance with the contract.

EVALUATION CRITERIA

Some of the key factors to be considered when acquiring the services from an outsourcing vendor follow.

1. Overall cost to the client organization. The overall cost to the client organization can be determined on a yearly basis for a minimum of three years. Understanding the costs over a three-year period provides a better understanding of the cost variables and their relationship to time. Wherever appropriate, cost factors should be tied to specific services required from the outsourcing vendor. Unit costs should also be clearly understood by the client organization to assess the cost variation with volume.
2. Level of risk. Outsourcing projects requires greater coordination, especially if parts of the project are assigned to different vendors. In addition, projects developed by one vendor require maintenance changes that are implemented by another vendor. It is

important to plan the outsourcing projects so that the deliverables are distinct and manageable as such. It may also make sense to deal with a limited number of outsourcing vendors to enhance consistency of standards and integration between systems.

Outsourcing projects also involve financial risks to the client organization in terms of cost overruns due to incomplete or unclear specifications. If the system specifications are clearly and adequately defined, the outsourcing vendor would assume the financial risk of delivering the system at a fixed cost and time. The information technology organization would be responsible for ensuring that the outsourcing vendor can actually deliver the system as originally proposed.

3. Performance measurement. Vendor management is an important function to ensure that systems that are delivered meet well defined performance criteria. Performance criteria include response time of the application, the ability to process a minimum number of transaction volumes as per specifications, user-friendly applications including GUI design principles, and an intuitive application that facilitates efficient navigation throughout the application.

4. Flexibility and responsiveness. Outsourcing vendors are an extension of the services provided by the in-house information technology organization. Consequently, it is easier to manage the information technology workload with increased flexibility and responsiveness by partnering with an outsourcing vendor. By supplementing resources with the outsourcing vendors, in-house client requirements can be met in a more timely manner.

5. Accountability. The ultimate responsibility for the definition, design, and delivery of systems rests with the information technology organization. Accountability includes the costs and benefits of implementing information technology and in ensuring client acceptance for the completed applications.

6. Skills and knowledge transfer. As part of vendor management, skills and knowledge transfer should be an integral part of vendor responsibility. Skills transfer includes supporting documentation, user and system training, and ongoing communication of system problems and how they were resolved.

A METHODOLOGY FOR EVALUATING OUTSOURCING VENDOR PROPOSALS

When evaluating different vendor proposals, it is useful to have an approach that is defensible and fair to vendors. Such a methodology also helps the evaluation team to obtain consensus from their management and the project stakeholders before undertaking a detailed evaluation.

The key elements of an evaluation methodology follow.

1. Evaluation team. A team is usually established to evaluate the proposals submitted by the vendors in response to the RFP for acquiring hardware, software, and services. Depending on the size and complexity of the project, additional team members may be required. The team is typically comprised of a project manager, a business analyst, and a systems manager. The primary responsibility of the evaluation team is to evaluate each proposal and make final recommendations to the steering committee.

2. Vendor qualification. The evaluation team evaluates each of the proposals submitted, and can use the criteria outlined in this section to prepare a short list of proposals that qualify for further evaluation.

3. Vendor viability. The vendor proposal provides details on stability and viability. Proposals can be disqualified because

   (a) the company has been in relevant business for less than three years; (b) the company is financially unstable, based on analysis of data in the vendor-supplied annual report. The company is deemed to be financially unstable if it reported a loss for each of the last three fiscal years. If annual reports are not available, analysis may be performed based on vendor-supplied financial statements. (c) There is a lack of demonstrated experience in similar-sized accounts.

4. Mandatory requirements. The vendor's proposal must meet the requirements outlined in the RFP. The evaluation team must be satisfied that the proposed solution meets all the mandatory requirements. If any of these requirements are not met, the vendor's proposal is rejected.

5. Viability of implementation and operation. The project team will evaluate the viability of the implementation and operation of the vendor-proposed solution. Information relating to the analysis can be obtained from a number of sources including, but not limited to, client references, published research reports, and performance data. The evaluation team will assess the vendor's ability to meet the requirements as outlined in the Request for Proposal. Proposals will be disqualified if, in the opinion of the evaluation team, the recommended solution is not viable from an implementation or operational point of view, or for organizational, environmental, or technological reasons, or if the proposed solution cannot be implemented in a reasonable time frame.

6. Credibility and quality of proposals. The proposed solution will be accompanied by models or statements of experience in similar-sized accounts, which will demonstrate that the proposed solution has been configured in a manner that will meet the workload and performance requirements of the client organization. Should the supporting documentation not support the workload and performance requirements, the vendor proposal is disqualified.

7. Contractual compliance. Each vendor is requested to indicate compliance with the terms and conditions outlined in the RFP. All contract modifications requested by the vendor may be assessed to ensure that the long term interests of the client organization are served.

8. Detailed evaluation of vendor proposals.

   (a) References. Typically, vendors are requested to submit three to five references, depending on the project. Reference checks are usually conducted for qualified vendors based on a detailed evaluation of their proposals. Reference checks performed by the evaluation team will not be necessarily restricted to the supplied references. Proposals will be penalized for the following reasons:
       (1) References provided are not being served by the vendor in any manner similar to the approach proposed by the client organization
       (2) Service and support has not been provided recently by the vendor at the referenced client

(3) A claim made in the vendor proposal is found to be inaccurate

(4) The vendor has been unable to fulfill commitments made to the client, whether initial or during the term of the contract.

References will be evaluated based on response to a series of questions relating to vendor's performance and service levels. References will be scored on a scale of 1 to 10. The average score will be determined; if the score is less than 90, a penalty of up to 15 percent of the total evaluated cost of the vendor's proposal will be assigned. Some of the sample reference check questions are included in Figure 9.3.

Reference Check Questions

1. How long have you been using the vendor's services?
2. Briefly explain the nature of services provided by the vendor.
3. Please indicate the level of satisfaction experienced in using these services.

1	2	3	4	5	6	7	8	9	10
Poor		Marginal		Acceptable		Good			Excellent

4. Service   Rating

   a) Overall vendor service (responsiveness and cooperation in servicing requests, _____
      staff attitude)
   b) Consulting service (enhancements, consulting, etc.)   _____
   c) Maintenance of hardware, network, and application software for currency _____
   d) On-call service for resolution of system and application problems _____
   e) Optimization of the performance and throughput of the application _____
   f) Service re: software additions, changes, upgrades _____
   g) Application availability and reliability _____
   h) Application security _____
   i) Online response time performance _____
5. In addition to the above, indicate the key strengths and weaknesses of the vendor's products.
   a) Strengths
   b) Weaknesses
6. Would you use the current vendor for another application? Explain.

FIGURE 9.3 Reference check questions.

(b) Evaluation period. The evaluation team will evaluate proposals for the duration of the contract, for example, over 24 or 36 months.

(c) Financial factors. The evaluation team may consider using financial factors such as net present value (NPV) or the internal rate of return (IRR) to allow for the time value of money.

(d) Evaluated cost. The evaluated cost of each proposal will include the following components:

    (1) Charges proposed by the vendor, as adjusted by the evaluation team. This includes all hardware, software, support, and maintenance charges.

    (2) Charges related to installation, upgrade, or hardware relocation charges.

    (3) All charges incurred directly by the client during the implementation of vendor proposal. For example, conversion costs and telecommunications costs for the network.

    (4) Application of any other credits or charges, as provided in the proposal. For instance, the vendor proposal may include the provision of 100 training hours to the client at no extra cost.

    (5) Cost for all desirable items requested by the client and proposed by the vendor. Vendor proposals will not be disqualified for failing to respond to desirable items. The number of desirable items met, and those included in the standard price, will be determined for each proposal during evaluation. For vendor proposals that do not include desirable items, the evaluation team will assign an evaluated cost to the vendor's proposal.

    (6) Business risks associated with implementation. A potential cost associated with implementation includes disruption of the client's business operations if the implementation is incomplete and/or results in unanticipated delays due to resolution of problems. The depth of a vendor organization represents an asset to the client in meeting unanticipated requirements during the term of the contract. Alternatively, the lack of depth in an organization may restrict the client's capability to request additional service from the successful vendor. The evaluation team will

assess business risk and assign a quantifiable figure which will be included in the evaluated cost of the vendor proposal.

9. Determination of the successful proposal. After identification and inclusion of all costs as identified in this section, the best proposal—i.e., the proposal with the lowest evaluated cost that has met all other criteria as indicated above—will be designated as the successful proposal. The successful proposal can then be presented to the steering committee for approval.

OUTSOURCING—CASE STUDIES

A Consumer Products Company

A large, diversified consumer products company was considering whether to continue managing its system department as it had done in the past, that is, to provide virtually all services using in-house personnel from its systems department. The organization was going through a restructuring exercise and looking for ways to streamline its business processes and practices by focusing on its core business.

As part of the focusing exercise and after adequate deliberations, the senior management team decided that it would be worthwhile to review alternative ways of delivering information technology services to support its business. Outsourcing of some or most of the information technology services would be another viable way of providing services.

Some of the key issues in considering whether to outsource included:

☐ A growing number of users who required support in the use of productivity tools such as e-mail, word processing, and spreadsheets
☐ An increasing number of requests for application development ranging from building local databases to managing business functions and processes
☐ A greater demand on end users of computer technologies to be more productive through improved coordination and integration of activities between departments

☐ Rapid advances in the information technology marketplace placing more demands on company's systems staff to stay abreast of these developments and deploy these solutions in a cost-effective and standardized manner throughout the organization

☐ Increasing demands placed on systems staff to find solutions that are stable and work well in a production environment

☐ Demands on the systems department to cut costs and provide improved services to a growing number of users

Faced with these issues, the company decided that it would be prudent to achieve its objectives through outsourcing of several key services, including Help Desk, maintenance of its microcomputer servers and peripherals, and application development. The company finalized agreements with an outsource, after a competitive selection and evaluation process, to provide these services for a period of three years. Most of the company staff involved in application development would be absorbed by the outsourcing vendor as part of the outsourcing agreement.

The net impact of this move to an outsourcing vendor was an immediate savings of 25 percent per year for three years. The application development portfolio was agreed as part of the agreement, including maintenance of all existing applications. Outsourcing vendor management and the coordination of all their work would still be the responsibility of the systems department.

The company staff is now busy analyzing the key business processes that have an impact on the core business, preparing recommendations and solution strategies in areas they never had time to approach, and providing more timely services to their users. The staff have more time to look at high payoff areas and assess where their efforts will have the greatest value to the company.

The company is prepared to try this arrangement for three years. It recognizes that there are risks associated with outsourcing, but the management has come to the conclusion that given their objectives, such risks do not pose a major threat to the company. The contractual arrangement includes a monthly review at two levels—a performance review between the operational managers of the company and the outsourcing vendor, and a review with senior management. The company also has the option to terminate the contract if the performance measures are not achieved. The performance measures include actual time to respond to and resolve a problem, application development times for each application, software assurance, levels of system and application testing, and user acceptance criteria.

A Public Sector Agency

A large public sector agency was processing its batch and online applications on a usage-sensitive basis by acquiring computer processing services from an outsourcing vendor. The agency was faced with increasing pressures to streamline its business processes and deploy information technologies wherever appropriate, to provide a more responsive service to the public, and to reduce the total computer processing and network management costs.

With changing market and business conditions, the agency had an opportunity to explore all service alternatives to ensure that it receives an excellent return on technology investment as well as improved service levels. The agency considered using facility management services employed by several organizations, including acquiring computer services at a fixed and predictable operating cost.

The agency was determined to move to acquiring services on a fixed-price basis depending on anticipated resource utilization on the host computer and related network usage based on the following objectives:

☐ To reduce and contain costs
☐ To provide timely, affordable, and easy-to-use host services to users
☐ To retain flexibility to accommodate changes in the computer processing workload
☐ To deliver improved services to agency staff by offering additional tools and applications aimed at enhancing staff productivity

Based on a competitive acquisition process, the agency acquired all host processing services from the outsourcing vendor, including computer processing, disk and tape storage, backup and recovery services, contingency planning and disaster recovery, province-wide Help Desk support through a toll-free number, and all network management functions. As a result of this process, the agency reduced its processing and network management costs by 20 percent in the first two years, and capped its costs for the third year despite an increase in processing and network workload.

OUTSOURCING IN THE 1990s

Outsourcing will continue to be a viable option in managing the information processing workload in organizations as pressures to rationalize service offerings continue. Outsourcing will provide organizations with the flexibility of managing information processing requirements with a modicum of staff, adapting from mainframe-centric to distributed-centric operating styles, and maintaining or improving service throughout this transition. We believe that in most organizations, outsourcing services will become an integral part of the information technology operating budget. Organizations are already utilizing selective outsourcing such as training, computer application development, maintenance of computer applications, and maintenance of the computer center to meet their resourcing requirements at a manageable and predictable cost.

Based on an organization's specific requirements, outsourcing of computer services will continue to focus on the following objectives:

☐ To predict, control, and contain costs
☐ To provide timely, affordable, and easy-to-use computer services to users
☐ To retain flexibility to accommodate changes in the computer processing workload at a least cost, should business requirements or technology change
☐ To enable the organizations to focus on their core services and use information technology to support those core services
☐ To deliver improved services to the organization by offering additional tools and applications aimed at enhancing staff productivity

A proactive outsourcing strategy will become an integral part of the delivery of total information technology services in organizations and will include developing processes for identifying outsourcing services; managing outsourcing vendors; ensuring that outsourcing contracts include performance factors and skills transfer to in-house staff, where appropriate; and to maintain continuity and a nonthreatening work environment. Outsourcing projects will become successful if they are managed in a partnership mode between vendor staff and in-house staff.

SUMMARY

This chapter has described the importance of outsourcing to an organization. With the downsizing of organizations and rapid changes in technology, outsourcing is here to stay and will evolve over time. Outsourcing is a partnership between the provider of services and the recipient of services—both parties have to understand and work together to make it work effectively. Where services are outsourced, there is a distinct change in role for the organization from a doer to a coordinator of vendor services. Vendor management becomes another job function with its associated risks and accountability.

There will be continued pressure on information technology departments to provide value to the organization, and outsourcing will be one of the ways to achieve that objective. Outsourcing is not a panacea—it requires a solid understanding of the business by the vendor and the commitment to deliver results at a competitive price.

10

Introduction to Microsoft Project 4

This chapter introduces the project manager to Microsoft Project's planning system, and its tools to facilitate task scheduling, managing and assigning of resources, monitoring costs, and generating reports for analysis and presentation.

In its simplest form project management involves planning, organizing, and managing tasks and resources to accomplish an objective, usually with the constraints of time and finances.

Microsoft Project 4 is an effective product for planning, organizing, and managing all tasks and resources as well as for communicating information about the projects effectively. This application combines the power of the critical path method (CPM), PERT charts, and Gantt charts to produce project scheduling and monitoring reports in a graphical environment.

FIGURE 10.1 Microsoft Project icon.

For individuals new to Project 4, the tutorial, online Help facility, and Cue Cards make it easy for users to become familiar and proficient with Microsoft Project.

This chapter covers all the finer points to creating an effective, informative, and eye-catching presentation. Detailed instructions and accompanying screens and examples are presented for users to follow. The chapter will take the reader through the steps of creating, saving, and modifying a project plan. The section will focus on two examples: reviewing a DBMS product and designing a software video game.

INSTALLING MICROSOFT PROJECT

The following steps are required to install Microsoft Project on a stand-alone workstation running Windows. Microsoft Project has a Setup program that checks your computer's physical system and offers a series of options for installing the software. The setup program automatically decompresses the files on the program disks.

1. Initiate Microsoft Windows
2. Insert Setup Disk 1 in drive A or B.
3. Go to Program Manager in Windows, select **File** and **Run** (Figure 10.2).
4. In the command line enter **a:\setup**. Select **OK** (Figure 10.3).
5. Follow the Microsoft Project interactive instructions on your screen.

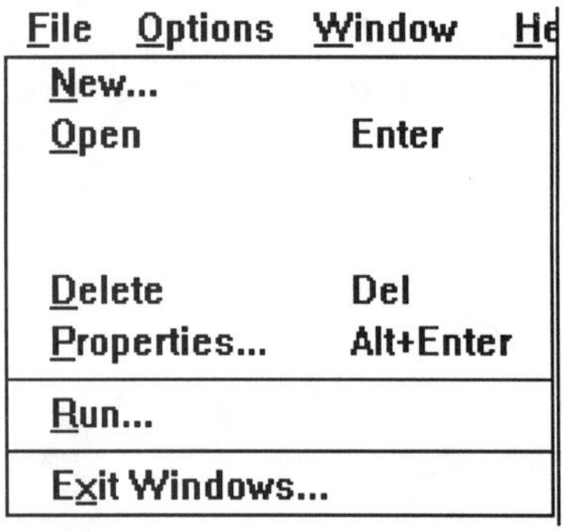

File	Options	Window	He
New...			
Open		Enter	
Delete		Del	
Properties...		Alt+Enter	
Run...			
Exit Windows...			

FIGURE 10.2 File Run.

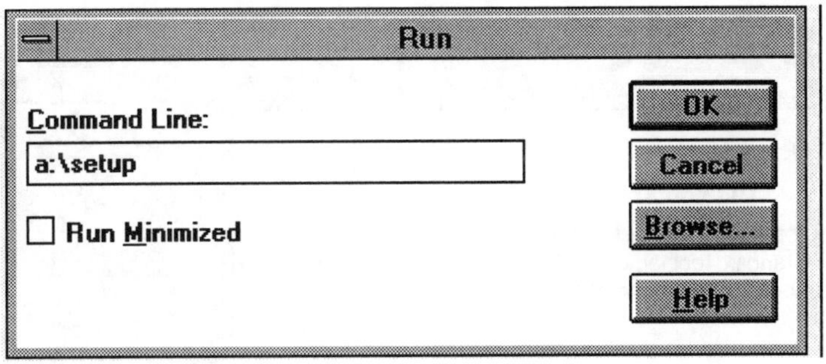

FIGURE 10.3 Run.

6. Once the installation is completed, you will be prompted to restart Windows. When Windows is reinitiated all the Microsoft Project icons will be displayed.

You are now ready to use Microsoft Project.

STARTING WITH MICROSOFT PROJECT

1. Double-click on the Microsoft Project icon.
2. Select **OK** to get rid of the Tip of the Day dialog box (Figure 10.4).

The Main Screen is displayed, ready for input.

> *Note: The Tip of the Day screen can be set up by the user so that it is never displayed again. At the bottom lefthand corner, click on the box to suppress the Tip from being displayed during the startup process.*

NAVIGATION IN WINDOWS APPLICATIONS

In a nutshell, Windows is an operating system that allows users to run more than one application at the same time. It also allows information

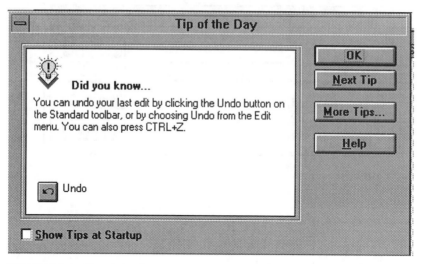

FIGURE 10.4 Tip of the day.

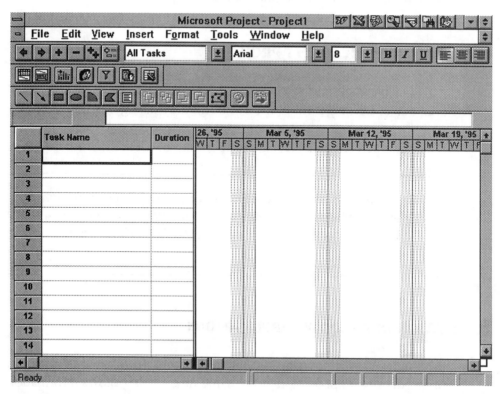

FIGURE 10.5 Project tasks.

to be transferred between applications. Fully compatible with DOS, Windows allows DOS applications to be accessed through it.

Navigation in Microsoft project is made easy through the use of the mouse as well as by keystroke combination(s). It is possible to toggle back and forth with other Windows applications using the standard Microsoft command keys.

Using the Mouse

Using the mouse is a faster alternative to the keyboard and keystrokes. However, users should access whichever is most comfortable for them. MS Project is fully functional with both the mouse and keystrokes—all the options/features can be accessed either way.

For users who are not entirely familiar with the mouse, the following is a brief description of the various mouse techniques.

There are typically two buttons on a mouse, although some older models may have three buttons. For the two-button mouse, the left mouse button acts like the Enter key on the keyboard: use it to invoke a command or position the cursor. The right mouse button allows access to pulldown menus and features for the particular area you are in without having to move the mouse to Toolbars and button bars. The three-button units perform in the same manner, but the middle button serves as a cancel option.

There are four mouse movements, namely pointing, dragging, clicking, and double-clicking.

Pointing The mouse controls the pointer on the screen. In MS Project the pointer appears either as an arrow or a plus sign, depending on the current location in the application. Moving the pointer to any position on the screen involves moving the mouse in the desired direction. Remember, the mouse is as fast as your hand movements.

Dragging Dragging allows the user to select a portion of the screen for editing or deletion, and it also allows the user to move objects around on the screen. Dragging involves holding the left mouse button down while moving the pointer. To drag on the screen, move the mouse pointer on top of the object, press and hold the left mouse button, and move in the desired direction.

Clicking This allows the user to select a feature or object in the application. Clicking refers to the process where the user points to an object or option and clicks on the left mouse button very quickly.

Double-Clicking Double-clicking means pointing to an object and clicking twice very quickly on the left mouse button. This technique is used primarily for exiting an application, or for calling up submenus.

Using Keys

The user can use the keyboard to access the menu options in the application. By pressing the Alt key and then the <u>underlined</u> letter of the desired option, any selections and pulldown menu can be accessed.

By selecting the Enter key the user accepts any command; the Esc key cancels the current command, and in some cases takes the user back to the previous menu.

TOOLBARS

A toolbar is a series of buttons or features of Microsoft Project that provide command shortcuts within the application. In most instances, the Toolbar buttons are usually faster than choosing a command using the keyboard and pulldown menus. Toolbars are a very important and convenient feature of Microsoft Project. By default, the standard toolbar and the formatting toolbars are displayed once MS Project is installed.

The standard toolbar displays the most commonly used features and is consistent with the standard toolbars of other Microsoft products.

While the standard toolbar is displayed, Microsoft Project allows the user the option to customize and assign any command or specialized function that is used frequently.

FIGURE 10.6 Toolbar.

TABLE 10.1 Modifying Toolbar Options

To do this . . .	*Do these actions . . .*
Move the toolbar to a new location	Point mouse on the toolbar, and drag to new location
Create a new toolbar	Hold Ctrl+Shift keys, and drag a button from the toolbar. A new toolbar is automatically created with this button in the first position.
Move button to another new location	Hold Shift key and drag the button to its location
Delete a button	Hold the Shift key and drag the button from the toolbar into non toolbar area
Insert space between toolbars	Hold Shift key and drag one of the toolbar buttons towards the right, but not off the toolbar

GETTING ONLINE HELP

Microsoft Project comes equipped with a complete set of online documentation. There is an online tutorial, help, technical information, and Cue Cards, containing a large percentage of the software information.

Cue Cards/Tutorial

For users new to project planning or unfamiliar with Microsoft Project, this tutorial provides an introduction to both Microsoft Project and project management techniques.

FIGURE 10.7 Help icon.

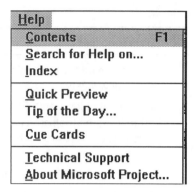

FIGURE 10.8 Help options.

Select the Help option from the status bar to access the tutorial. Press the down arrow until Cue Cards is highlighted. Press Enter.

Another way to access the online tutorial is by performing the above step and then selecting the option Up and Running Tutorial.

Microsoft Project's online Cue Cards are an excellent tool for individuals new to project management. They replace the standard tutorial

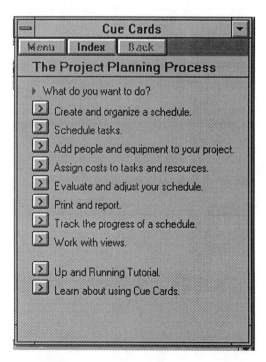

FIGURE 10.9 Cue Cards button.

that requires the user to follow an inflexible, sequential path. These Cue Cards provide step-by-step instructions for basic as well as advanced project management procedures. The Cue Cards sit above the project window, and remain visible until you close the window.

To use the Cue Cards, select Cue Cards from the Help Menu, or click on the Cue Card button from the toolbar. The Cue Card menu lists all the available options.

The following are a few pointers to remember when using the Cue Cards in MS Project.

☐ Cue Cards will only work with the use of a mouse—they cannot be accessed by using the keyboard
☐ Click the menu button on the Cue Card to see the Cue Card Main Menu
☐ To view the online index, click on the Index button
☐ To return to the previous cue card, click on the Back button

Online Files

Technical information is also available through a group of online files.

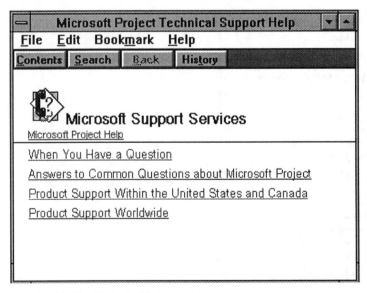

FIGURE 10.10 Technical Information.

☐ From Help menu, select Contents.

☐ Click on Reference Information, and then click on Technical Information. The following information is displayed.

SETUP OPTIONS

By defining the Setup options in Microsoft Project before starting the project plans, the user is assured that all settings and desired options are consistent, and will not change unless the setup options again modified.

There are nine options, or tabs, that can be customized according to user specifications. The following is a description of these tabs and the options that can be customized by the user.

1. At the Tools menu select Options.
   -or-
   Hold the Alt key down and press T, arrow down to Options until it is highlighted, and press Enter (Figure 10.11).
2. A list of tabs is displayed. Click on the desired tab and make the necessary changes.

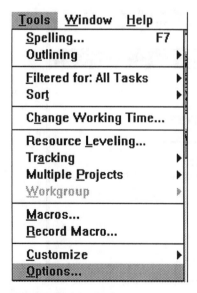

FIGURE 10.11 Tools.

Note: You should not forget to press OK to confirm your changes, otherwise click on Cancel (to discard the changes).

TABS

View Tab

This tab allows the user to customize the manner in which MS Project displays project information.

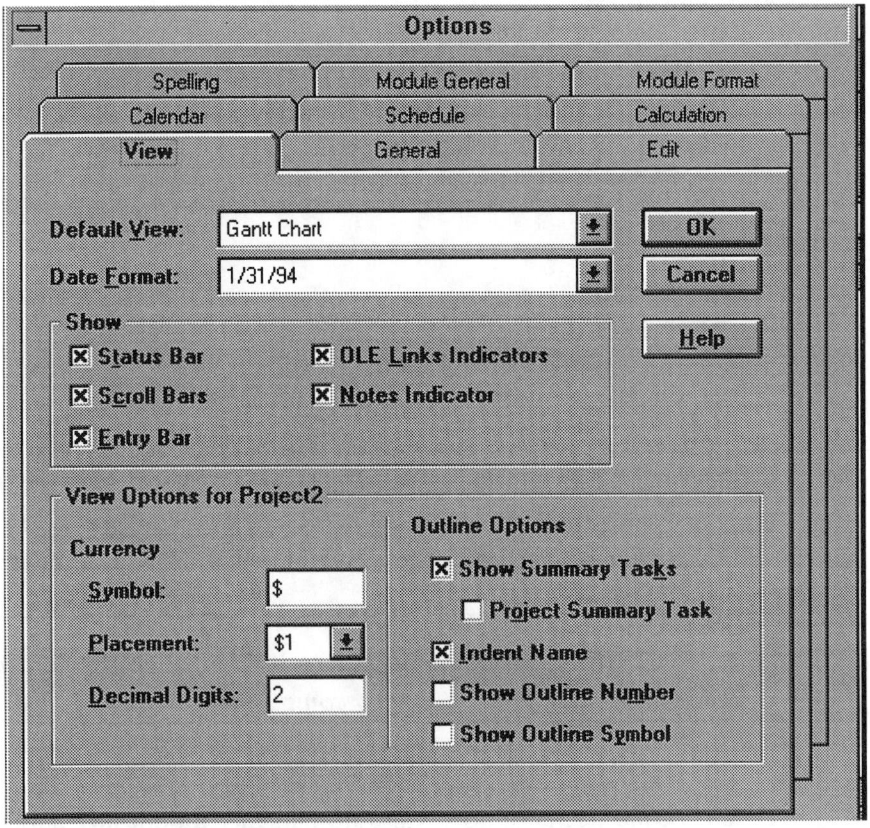

FIGURE 10.12 View tab.

Default View Select the desired view that you want displayed upon startup of Microsoft Project. In our example we have chosen the Gantt View.

Date Format Click on the down arrow and select the desired date format for your project plans.

Show Click on the Show boxes to select the default items to be displayed, such as the scroll bars, status bar, and so on. Select OLE Indicator to display the indicator for any linked objects in the project plan. Select the Notes Indicator to display the notes indicator for tasks and resources that have attached notes.

Currency Click on this to specify the currency symbol and the position it occupies.

1. In the Symbol box, enter the currency symbol that you want to use.
2. In the Placement box select the example that shows where the currency symbol is to be placed.
3. In the Decimal Digits box, enter the number of decimal points to be used.

Outline Options This option allows the user to select the information that MS Project displays at the startup of each application. The following options can be selected by the user:

Show Summary Tasks   This option allows the user to display all the summary tasks in a project plan. Click on the box to display the summary tasks. To hide the summary tasks, click on the box again. The [x] will disappear, and the summary task information will be hidden.

> *Note: When the summary tasks are hidden, the user will not be able to use any of the Outlining commands.*

Indent Name   This option will automatically indent any subtasks that the user may enter in the Name column.

Show Outline Number This option displays the outline number to the left of each task name that is entered.

Show Outline Symbol This option displays the symbol denoting whether a task is a summary or subtask.

General Tab

This tab allows the user to specify an operating preference for the general operation of Microsoft Project. The settings, once specified, become global.

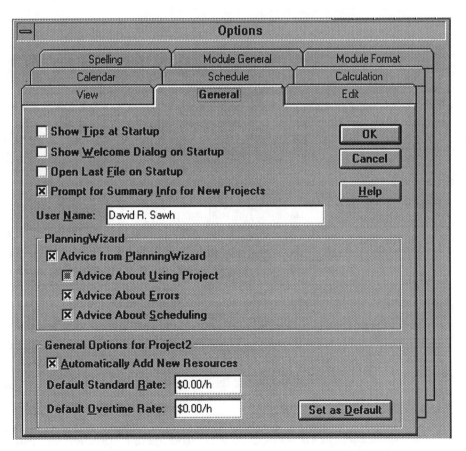

FIGURE 10.13 General tab.

Select Options from the Tools menu and click on the General tab.

The following settings are available on the General tab:

Show Tips at Startup Selecting this feature allows the user to have a Tip of the Day dialog box, displayed each time MS Project is invoked. For users not very familiar with the product, this option is wonderful for startup tips.

Welcome Dialog on Startup With this option users get a quick walk-through of MS project and the use of Cue Cards.

Prompt for Summary Info on New Projects This option prompts the user each time a new project is created.

> *Note: All of the above options can be removed by clearing the [x] from the boxes.*

User Name With this option the user can enter the name of the person who is using MS Project. The name can be changed at any time.

Planning Wizard Planning Wizard is a feature in MS Project that serves as a guide for users. This feature prompts the user by pointing out problems or inconsistencies in the project plan, as well as providing assistance and suggestions to improve the plan. There are five advisors in the Wizard feature, all of which scan the project plan and look for inconsistencies.

Advice from the Planning Wizard By selecting this option, Wizard will display advice as specified by the remaining settings in the groups.

Advice about Using Project This option identifies faster ways of using MS Project.

Advice about Errors Wizard alerts the users to problems that may arise during the creation of the project plan.

Advice about Scheduling In instances where the project manager inadvertently schedules work on holidays or weekends, Wizard will inform the user and provide options for resolving the problem.

Automatically Add New Resources With this option, a new resource is automatically assigned the default Resource information as defined by MS Project. If you want to be prompted to enter your own resource information, clear the [x] in the option.

Default Standard Rate In situations where the project manager wants to track and control standard or overtime rates, this option can be selected. MS Project will then assign a standard pay rate.

Default Overtime Rate To assign overtime pay rates to resources, select this option. Note that this option can be overridden at any time.

Set as Default To accept all the current settings that you have defined as the default settings, select this option by clicking on the left mouse button or highlighting the option and pressing Enter.

Edit Tab

By defining the settings in this tab, users can specify how MS Project should allow them to edit the data that is entered into the project plans.

From the Tools menu, select Options and choose the Edit tab (see Figure 10.14).

Allow Cell Drag and Drop By selecting this option users can use the mouse to drag, drop, and move rows, columns, and fields to new locations.

Move Selection After Enter Choose this option to move one line down after pressing Enter. If this option is not selected, the Enter key may not be able to move to another line.

Ask to Update Automatic Links In situations where the project plan has linked objects, any changes to the links will be automatically updated, once this option is selected.

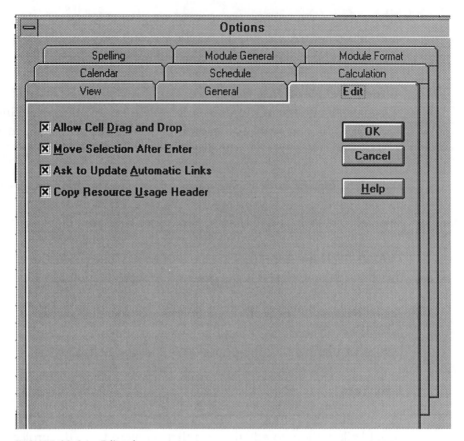

FIGURE 10.14   Edit tab.

Copy Resource Usage Header Selecting this option will automatically include column headings whenever the Copy command is used in the Resource Usage View.

Once all the settings are selected, click on OK to accept the changes.

Calendar Tab

Using this tab allows the user to define the calendar (dates and times) settings for his or her project plan. Once the definitions are set, each time the calendar is selected the defined settings are maintained.

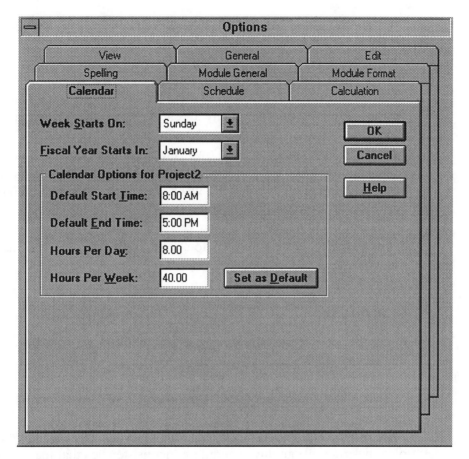

FIGURE 10.15 Calendar tab.

From the Tools menu select Options, and click on the Calendar tab.

The following options will be displayed, allowing the user to define the settings.

Week Starts On Depending on user preferences, some project managers may prefer the week to begin either on a Sunday or a Monday. Select the first day of the week.

Fiscal Year Starts In Using this option, users can specify the starting month of their particular fiscal year. MS Project is aware that organizations have different timescales for defining their fiscal periods, and allows this time to be defined.

Default Start and End Time Defining the default start time allows the user to specify a start time for all assigned tasks. The default end time option allows the user to specify an end time for all assigned tasks.

Hours Per Day This option allows the user to enter the number of hours that are to be assigned to a task per week. By default MS Project enters a duration of 40 hours per week. To change this option enter the appropriate number of hours.

Set as Default Click on this box to accept all the changes you made in the window.

Schedule Tab

Using this option will allow the user the ability to dictate how his or her project will be scheduled.

From the Tools menu select Options, and click on the Schedule tab.

Show Scheduling Messages Click on this option to have MS Project display messages about any scheduling inconsistencies that may occur as you schedule tasks, such as incompatible start and finish task dates.

New Tasks Start On With this option users can define the start dates for the tasks in the project plan.

Project Start Date This option starts the new tasks on the start date for the project.

Current Date This option uses the current date as the start date for new tasks that are entered.

Default Duration Type MS Project allows users to customize their task durations by the use of two options, resource driven and fixed duration.

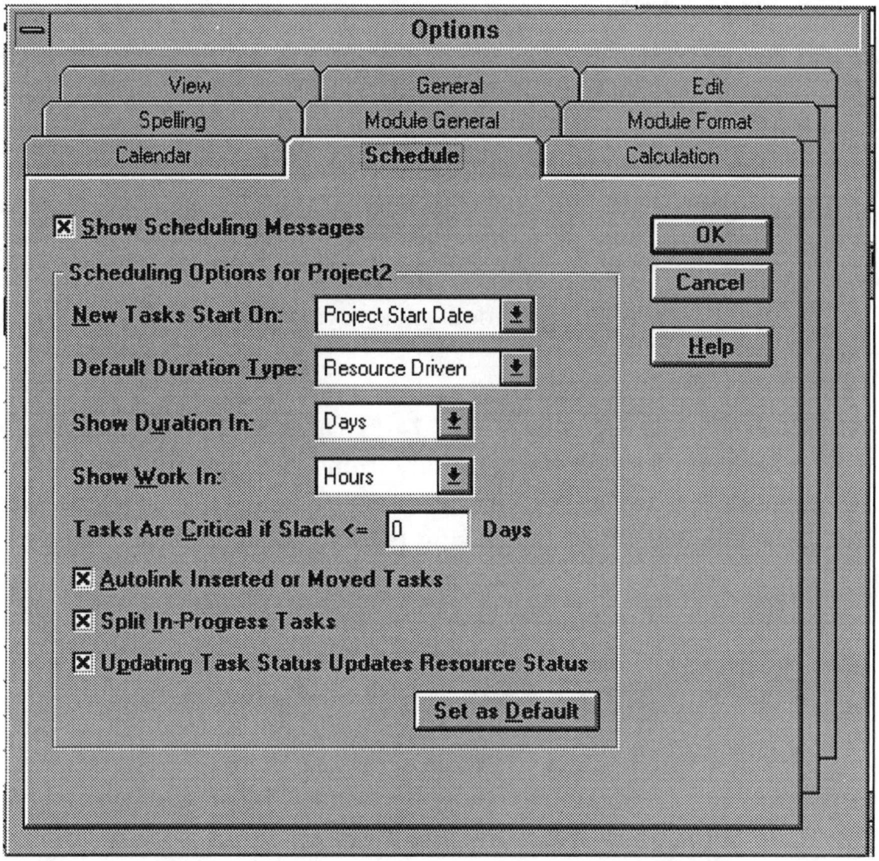

FIGURE 10.16 Schedule tab.

Resource Driven MS Project calculates the duration and dates of the tasks based solely on the number of resources assigned to the task.

Fixed Duration   With this option selected, MS Project determines the duration of the task solely on the data entered by the user.

Show Duration In This option allows the user to select the unit of time (minutes, hours, days, or weeks) that will be used in the duration field. MS Project uses this time if no unit is entered when the user is entering the duration for a task.

Show Work In By selecting the unit of time, whether it is in minutes, hours, days, or weeks, MS Project uses this selected unit whenever the user is assigning times to a project plan.

Tasks Are Critical if Slack < = With this option the user can specify the number of slack days for a particular task. Determining the number of slack days will allow MS project to calculate the critical nature of the task. For instance, if the number of slack days are less than or equal to the number of specified slack days then the task is considered critical.

Autolink Inserted or Moved Tasks During the course of a project the manager may find it necessary to move or insert tasks. In such situations it is helpful to have a utility that would keep all the linked task relationships without having to redo them. By selecting this option, MS Project will automatically link any of the tasks that have been edited.

Split In-Progress Tasks By selecting this option, MS Project will automatically reschedule the remaining task schedules in the instance where one particular task slips, or has fallen behind schedule.

Updating Task Status Updates Resource Status To automatically calculate the actual and remaining work load and cost for the resources once they are entered by the user, select this option.

To save all the settings listed above as the default, click on the Set as Default box.

Calculation Tab

Defining this option will allow MS project to perform calculations according to the user specifications.

Select the Calculation tab from Options.

Select Automatic to have MS Project automatically calculate schedules whenever information is entered. Manual recalculates only when the

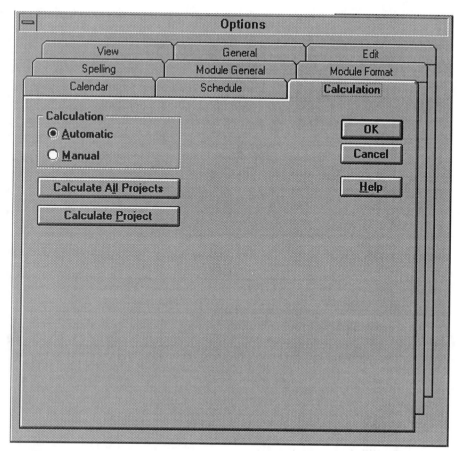

FIGURE 10.17 Calculation tab.

user selects the options Calculate All Projects or the Calculate Project Button.

Spelling Tab

This option once selected will specify all the spell-checking parameters for the Spelling command.

Fields to Check Enter Yes in the entry bar to have MS Project spell check all the fields each time you invoke the spellchecker. Enter No if you do

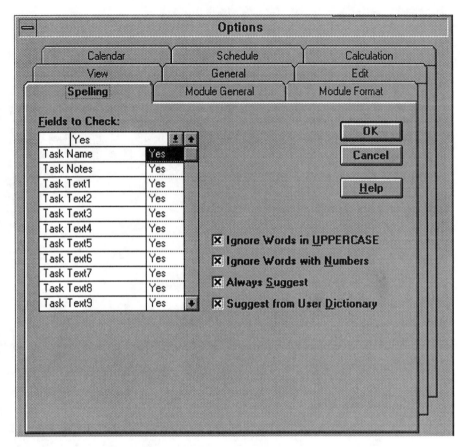

FIGURE 10.18 Spelling tab.

not want the fields checked. You can also define whether to spell check words in UPPERCASE, or words that contain numbers.

Always Suggest Select this option to have MS Project check the dictionary and suggest possible alternatives for those words not found in the dictionary. Select the Suggest from User Dictionary to allow MS Project to set up a user dictionary, so that the user can add words not found in the standard dictionary into the user dictionary.

11

Creating the Project Plan Using Microsoft Project 4

OVERVIEW

This chapter will focus on how project managers can utilize the power of Microsoft Project to schedule, manage, and communicate project information. All the steps, from initiation to implementation, used by managers when planning and managing a project will be illustrated in an example project.

By following the example project, the reader will learn how to organize and create a project schedule. The reader will learn how to:

- Define the business requirements and activities
- Define project environment
- Identify project tasks
- Determine the task relationships
- Assign resources to the tasks
- Monitor the schedule

DEFINING THE PROJECT ENVIRONMENT

The project environment will vary for each individual project. Therefore, the project manager, before beginning to define tasks and resources, should set up the project environment for the particular project.

Project management generally involves three phases. The first phase can be called creating the project. In this phase, the project manager defines the tasks and their relationships, durations, resources, and various other project elements that will be dealt with later in this chapter. In other words, this phase establishes the project environment. The second phase is managing the project, which involves the coordination of the project on an ongoing basis, from the project plan initiation to its completion. The third phase can be referred to as reporting. In this phase the manager provides informative reports to various departments and individuals detailing the status of the project at various stages.

Click on the MS Project icon to initiate MS Project.

SETTING THE BASE CALENDAR

A base calendar is best described as a standard calendar that is defined by the Project Manager to account for all the working and nonworking days of a project.

By default, MS Project uses the standard calendar for all the resources in the project. MS Project takes weekends and holidays into account when scheduling. The calendar defines working days and

FIGURE 11.1 Microsoft icon.

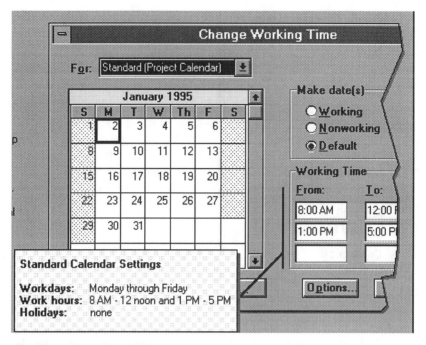

FIGURE 11.2 Base calendar.

hours as Monday to Friday, 8:00 AM to 5:00 PM. The user can make modifications to the calendar by performing the following steps.

1. Click on the Tool menu, and select Change Working Time, as shown in Figure 11.3.
2. Enter the resource whose calendar you want to change in the For box. Select the Working, Nonworking, or Default option box.
3. Enter the new working hours in the From and To boxes.
4. Click on OK once the options have been selected to save the changes.

SETTING THE WORKING ENVIRONMENT

Page Setups

Using the Page Setup option, you can change your project schedule to look visually more appealing. By selecting Page Setup you can make the following changes or enhancements to your project plan:

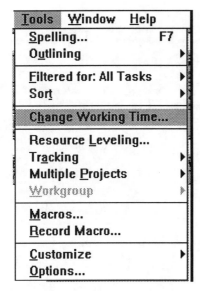

FIGURE 11.3 Tool menu.

☐ Change the orientation of the plan to either portrait or landscape. By default, MS Project orients the page for landscape printing.
☐ Reduce the view so that it can fit on a specified number of pages.
☐ Change the margin widths, according to the user specifications.
☐ Add borders around the plan for all or specific pages of the project.
☐ Insert headers or footers on one or all printed pages.
☐ Insert or remove page breaks.
☐ Add legends on Gantt and/or PERT charts, or even print on separate pages, if the user wishes.
☐ Print only the visible columns or all columns.
☐ Print a specific number of columns of a sheet on every page.

Each of these is described in more detail in this chapter.

Page Orientation

By default, MS Project displays and prints to a landscape orientation. For small project plans, the user may choose to work, print, and view his or her project plan in a portrait orientation.

1. Select File, Page Setup and select Enter, or use the left mouse button.
2. Using the mouse click on the desired option and then select OK.
3. The page dialog box will be displayed.

Page Margins

1. Select File, Page Setup and click on the Margins tab.
2. Change the margins according to your preference and click on OK.
3. The Border option can also be invoked at this point. This option would place a border around your project plan.

File	Edit	View	Insert	Format	Tools	W

New	Ctrl+N
Open...	Ctrl+O
Close	
Save	Ctrl+S
Save As...	
Save Workspace...	
Find File...	
Summary Info...	
Page Setup...	
Print Preview	
Print...	Ctrl+P
Send...	
Add Routing Slip...	
1 \WPWIN60\WPDOCS\VENA\MSPROJ.MPP	
2 \...\VENA\EVALUATE.MPP	
3 \...\VENA\C_SERVER.MPP	
4 C_SERVER.MPP	
Exit	

FIGURE 11.5   File page setup.

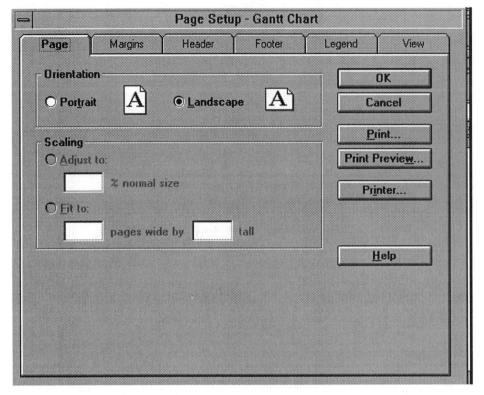

FIGURE 11.6 Page setup.

Headers and Footers

Adding a header or footer to the project plan enhances the appearance of a document and gives it a more professional look. Project managers may take this opportunity to enter personal/company information about the project for presentation or filing purposes. Users can enter up to three lines of text in a Header, and one line in a Footer.

1. Select Page Setup and click on the Header tab.
2. In the Left, Center, Right tab box, click on the alignment and enter the text for your Header. If you selected Center, all text you enter will be centered at the top of the project plan.

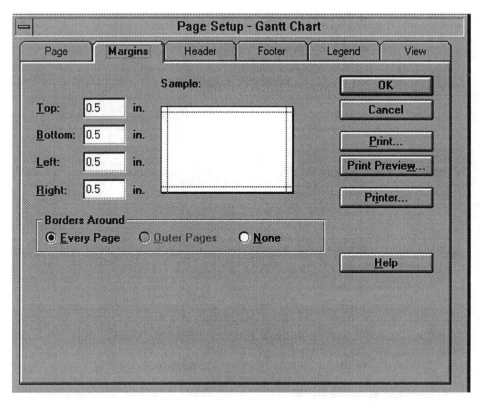

FIGURE 11.7 Margins.

3. To enter additional information, such as company name or date, click on the box below the Left, Center, Right tab, and click the mouse pointer on the arrow. A list of options is displayed. Select an option by double-clicking on it.

Footers

Footers can be defined in the same manner as the headers (see Figure 11.10).

1. Select File, Page Setup and choose the Footers tab.
2. Enter the information for the footer in the Left, Center, Right tab box. To add other information to the footer, click on the arrow key at the bottom of the Left, Center, Right tab box.

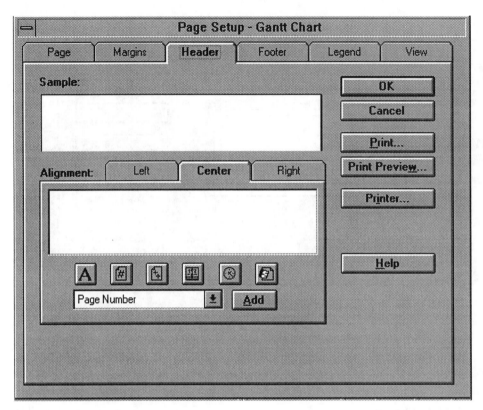

FIGURE 11.8 Header.

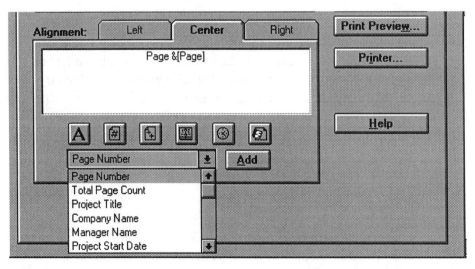

FIGURE 11.9 Options.

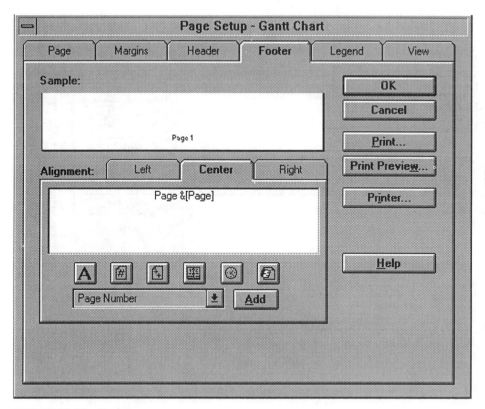

FIGURE 11.10   Footer.

Legends

1. Select File, Page Setup and select the Legend tab.
2. Enter the required information and click on OK.

Selecting Font Types and Attributes

By default MS Project uses Arial 8pt as the default font and size. If this font is not to your liking, you can change it on your project plan.

From the main menu.

1. Click on the Format menu option, or use Alt O.
2. Select Font, and choose a selection from the list.
   -or-

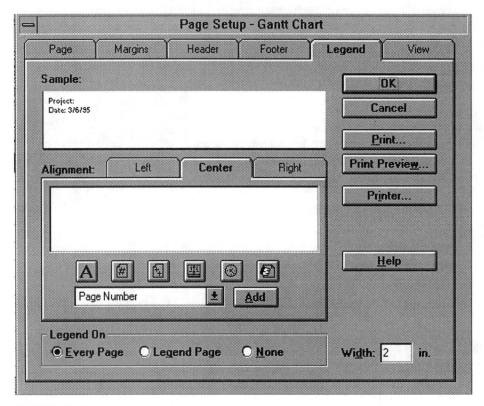

FIGURE 11.11 Legend.

3. Click on the Font button on the MS Project button bar. A list of installed fonts will be displayed.
4. Select the desired font.
5. To change the size of the font, click on the size button on the menu bar.
6. Select the desired size, as shown in Figure 11.13.

Once the font and size have been selected, you may wish to make some text distinct from the rest. This can be done by the use of **bold**, *italics*, or underlined. These options can be accessed from either the button bar or from the keyboard. Use the buttons on the righthand corner by clicking on the desired button.

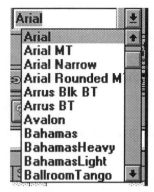

FIGURE 11.12   Font pulldown.

To access the same options using the keystrokes, simply hold the Ctrl key and the accompanying letter, as shown in Figure 11.14.

Ctrl +B - **Bolds the text**

Ctrl +I - *Italicizes the text*

Ctrl +U - <u>Underlines the text</u>

To cancel the option, simply press the Ctrl and the letter keys again, and the option will be turned off.

Users also have the option of changing the justification of their text from the button bar. These buttons appear on the top right side of the screen, and allow the user to Left Align, Center, and Right Align. To

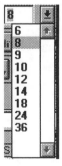

FIGURE 11.13   Size pulldown.

FIGURE 11.14 Bold buttons.

access these options, block the text and click on the desired justification button.

OUTLINING FEATURES

In this section, the focus will be on building the project plan, or outlining the project schedule. Outlining ensures that the project plan is presented in an organized manner, thereby making the schedule easier to manage. Utilizing the outlining option in MS project, the user can

1. Use a hierarchical structure to arrange tasks and subtasks by either demoting or promoting the tasks
2. Identify the major phases of the project with summary information
3. Display the project using a task numbering system called a work breakdown structure
4. Identify dependencies, thereby allowing the user to manage tasks that can be worked on in parallel.
5. Manage both planned and actual resource efforts through flexible calendar features.
6. Use different project views (i.e., PERT) to identify, display, and manipulate tasks for the purpose of optimizing the project workflow
7. Allow users numerous presentation features to enhance the visual aspect of the project plan

FIGURE 11.15 Alignment buttons.

FIGURE 11.16 Outlining buttons.

8. Create reports that include or exclude subtasks, summary tasks, or both.

Defining Summary and Subtasks

A summary task can be defined as a broad task or a major heading under which there are several components or subtasks. MS Project allows the project manager to visually depict these tasks. The summary tasks are outdented and bolded while the subtasks are indented in the Gantt chart. In our example the summary and the subtasks are clearly displayed.

Indenting a Task

1. From the View menu select Gantt chart.
2. Highlight the task that is to be demoted to a subtask.
3. Select the Tools menu, choose Outline, and selectIndent

> *Note: Using the mouse button, highlight the task to be indented and click on the Indent button on the Format Toolbar. The selected task will be indented.*

FIGURE 11.17 Indent button.

Outdenting a Task

By selecting this button a task can be outdented, thereby denoting it as a summary task.

1. From the View menu select Gantt chart.
2. Highlight the task that is to be promoted to a Summary Task.
3. Select the Tools menu, choose Outline, and select Outdent.

Note: Using the mouse button, highlight the task to be outdented and click on the Outdent button on the Format Toolbar. The selected task will be outdented.

Collapsing the Project Plan

By collapsing the project plan, the user can hide or display the subtasks of summary tasks. For reporting purposes, managers may want to display certain tasks and hide others. You also have the option of collapsing and expanding specific parts of the outline, highlighting or hiding the tasks, groups, or groups of tasks you want.

1. From the View menu, select the Gantt chart.
2. Select the tasks of the outline that you want to collapse.
3. From the Tools menu, choose Outlining, and then select Hide Subtasks.

More experienced users can save time by highlighting the tasks and clicking on the collapse button on the formatting toolbar.

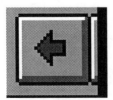

FIGURE 11.18 Outdent button.

SETTING THE PRINT ENVIRONMENT

Before printing your project plan you should ensure that you are connected to a printer.

1. From the File menu, select Print tab, and then select Printer tab.
2. A Printer Setup dialog box will be displayed. Ensure that the printer that is displayed is the printer to which you are physically or logically (LAN connection) connected.

MS Project allows the user to preview the pages of the plan before they are actually sent to the printer. This gives the manager an opportunity to check the page margins, headers, footers, and layout.

1. From the File menu select Page Setup and click on the Print tab.
2. Select the Print Range, or select All to print all the pages of the plan.
3. Once all your options are selected, click on the OK button, and the plan will be queued up to the printer.
4. To preview the chart instead of printing it, click on the Print Preview button, and the plan will be displayed.

Printing the plan can also be invoked by the following:

Select the File Menu and click on Print.

The same screens will appear as described above.

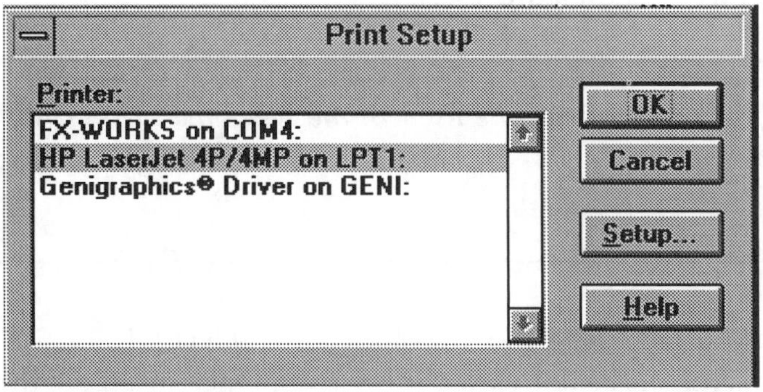

FIGURE 11.19 Printer setup.

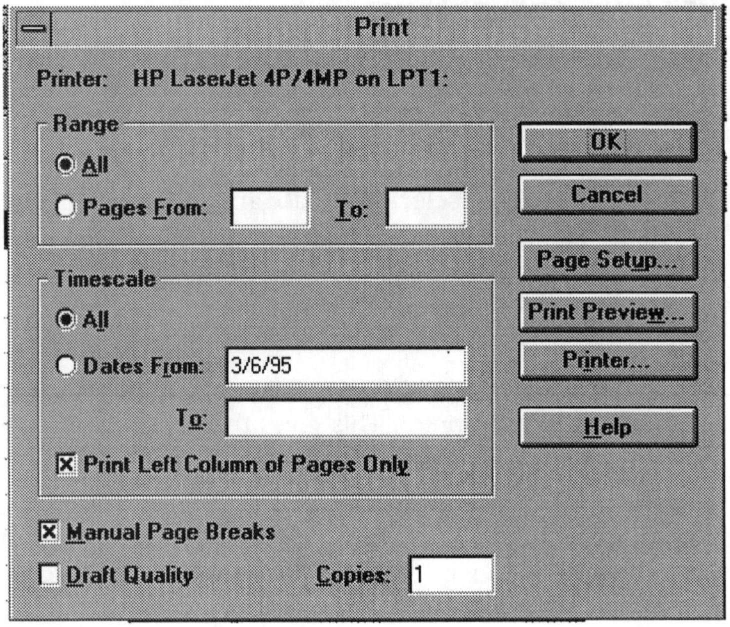

```
┌─────────────────────────────────────────────────────────────┐
│ ⊖                            Print                           │
├─────────────────────────────────────────────────────────────┤
│  Printer:   HP LaserJet 4P/4MP on LPT1:                      │
│  ┌─Range────────────────────────────┐  ┌───────────────┐    │
│  │ ⊙ All                            │  │      OK       │    │
│  │ ○ Pages From: [      ]  To: [    ]│  └───────────────┘    │
│  │                                  │  ┌───────────────┐    │
│  └──────────────────────────────────┘  │    Cancel     │    │
│                                         └───────────────┘    │
│  ┌─Timescale────────────────────────┐  ┌───────────────┐    │
│  │ ⊙ All                            │  │  Page Setup... │    │
│  │ ○ Dates From: [3/6/95          ] │  ┌───────────────┐    │
│  │                                  │  │ Print Preview...│    │
│  │           To: [               ]  │  ┌───────────────┐    │
│  │ ☒ Print Left Column of Pages Only│  │   Printer...   │    │
│  └──────────────────────────────────┘  ┌───────────────┐    │
│                                         │     Help      │    │
│  ☒ Manual Page Breaks                   └───────────────┘    │
│  ☐ Draft Quality      Copies: [1    ]                       │
└─────────────────────────────────────────────────────────────┘
```

FIGURE 11.20   Print menu.

DEFINING THE PROJECT VIEW

Once the project environment has been defined and established, the project manager must define all the tasks for the project.

1. At Program Manager in Windows, double-click on the Microsoft Project icon (see Figure 11.1).

> *Note: If you are a first time user, in the Welcome to Microsoft Project dialog box, click on the Start With A Blank Project option button.*

2. Once you have read the Tip of the Day, select OK.
3. The Microsoft default view is displayed. Once installed, the default view is always the Gantt chart.

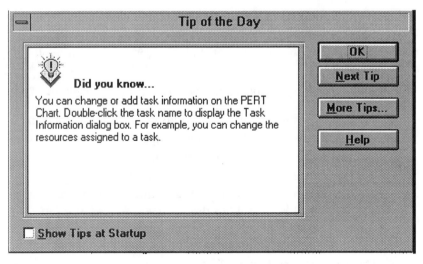

FIGURE 11.21 Tip of the Day.

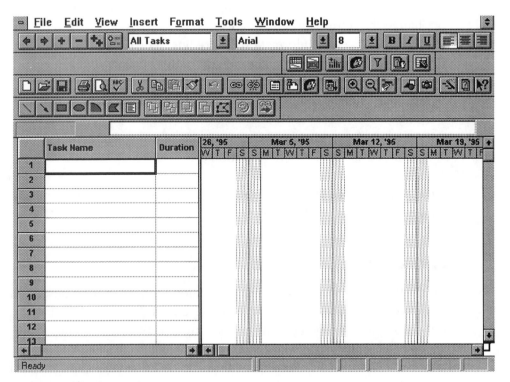

FIGURE 11.22 Gantt chart.

Gantt charts allow projects to be viewed in a graphical manner. Like bar charts, these graphical representations allow the users to view the progress and duration of projects, as well as start and end dates on a timescale.

Using the Gantt charts you can do the following:

☐ Create a project by entering tasks and their durations.
☐ Establish sequential relationships between tasks—this allows managers to determine how changes in the task durations affect the start and finish dates of other tasks.
☐ Track progress by comparing planned and actual start and finish dates and by checking the percentage complete of each task.

Customizing the Gantt Chart

Project managers may want to customize their Gantt charts to reflect the following changes:

☐ Change the information that is displayed
☐ Emphasize specific information by bolding, italicizing, or underlining
☐ Distinguish information categories from other tasks
☐ Change the units of time displayed
☐ Add text, change colors or patterns, or assign symbols to a task category
☐ Display, hide, or change the appearance of nonworking time
☐ Add labels or charts to the Gantt chart

Once the Gantt chart has been saved, the options for the customized view will be saved with the project file.

PERT Charts

PERT (Program Evaluation Review Technique) charts can be described as network diagrams or flowcharts. PERT charts display tasks and their relationships by showing a line connecting two boxes. The lines represent the relationship between the tasks. By default, the PERT chart displays one diagonal line through a task that is in progress and crossed diagonal lines through a completed task. PERT charts can be used to:

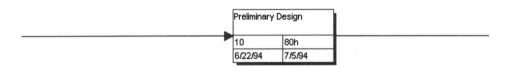

FIGURE 11.23   PERT chart.

☐ Create and finetune your schedule
☐ Link tasks to specify the task sequence as well as determine start and finish times
☐ Display completed, in-progress, and not yet started tasks graphically
☐ Assign resources to specific tasks

Like Gantt charts, PERT charts can be customized according to the users specifications, such as the following examples:

☐ Display in each PERT box the most important task information
☐ Assign a different border style to tasks of a certain type
☐ Change the line appearance
☐ Format information categories to distinguish information
☐ Change the PERT view to display fewer or more boxes
☐ Align PERT boxes to give them an orderly appearance

An example of a PERT chart is shown in Figure 11.23.

DEFINING PROJECT TASKS

Preliminaries

Now that the environment has been defined, you are ready to define the project tasks.

1. To start MS Project double-click on the MS Project icon from Windows.
2. After reading Tip of the Day, click on OK.
3. From the File Menu, select either NEW or Summary Information (See Figure 11.24).
4. Click on the Project Information tab, and enter all the relevant information (Figure 11.25).
5. Once all the information has been entered about the project, click on OK.

To enter information on the document:

6. Click on the Document tab, and enter the appropriate project information (Figure 11.26).

File	Edit	View	Insert	Format	Tools	W
New					Ctrl+N	
Open...					Ctrl+O	
Close						
Save					Ctrl+S	
Save As...						
Save Workspace...						
Find File...						
Summary Info...						
Page Setup...						
Print Preview						
Print...					Ctrl+P	
Send...						
Add Routing Slip...						
1 SOFTDEV.MPT						
2 \WPWIN60\WPDOCS\VENA\MSPROJ.MPP						
3 \...\VENA\EVALUATE.MPP						
4 \...\VENA\C_SERVER.MPP						
Exit						

FIGURE 11.24 File summary information.

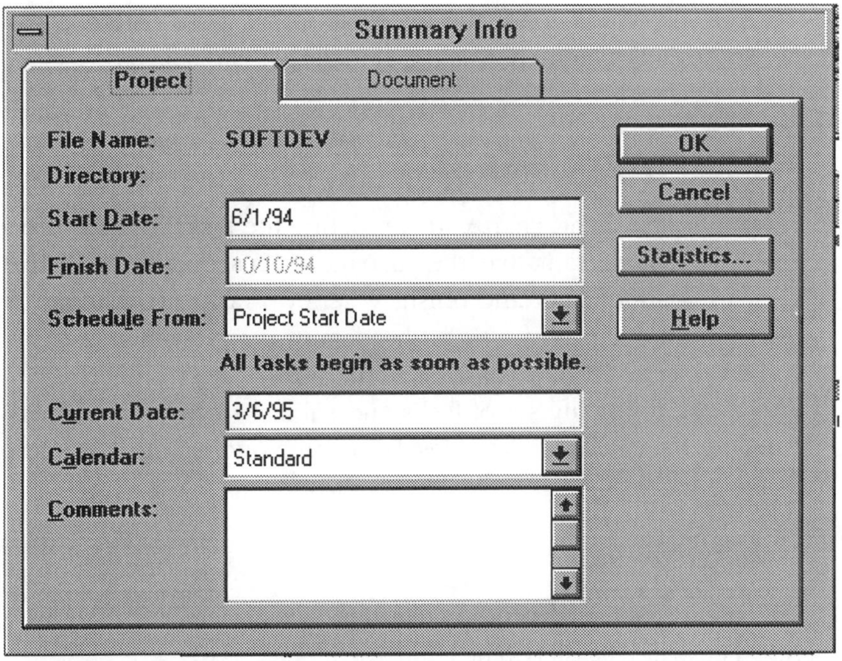

FIGURE 11.25 Project information.

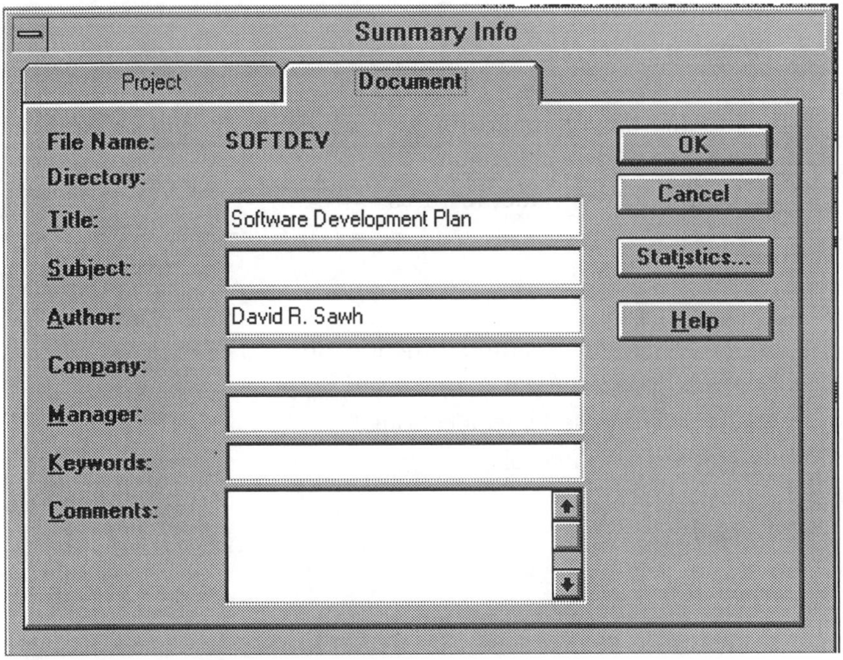

FIGURE 11.26 Document information.

7. Click on OK, once the information has been entered.
8. A blank Gantt chart is the screen that is displayed.

Actual Task Definition

Once in the Gantt chart you can define the tasks for a project.

It is important that the manager focus on the tasks that have a clearly defined start and finish. Whenever tasks are entered in MS Project, it automatically assigns the default duration of one day (1d), and the project start dates as well as the finish date.

The following set of tasks and subtasks has been defined, according to their business activities, by a company that designs and produces video games.

Market Research

☐ Identify existing product features
☐ Perform feasibility study
☐ Identify market niche

Planning

☐ Identify new game features
☐ Prepare high level design
☐ Verify niche product features

Analysis

N Model product features/functionality
☐ Model process/data
☐ Prepare detailed specifications
☐ Prepare resource plan

Design

☐ Design schematic
☐ Optimize design using CAD/CAM tools

☐ Design integrated circuit board
☐ Prototype product

Development

☐ Build screens
☐ Build database
☐ Build code
☐ Test

Prepare Promotional Strategy

☐ Use promotional media
☐ Establish timing
☐ Target audience

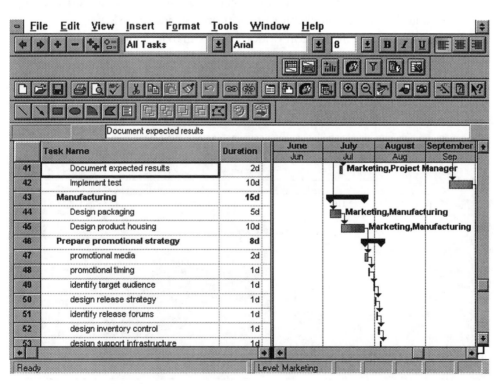

FIGURE 11.27 Project plan.

Release Strategy

☐ Use distribution forums
☐ Establish inventory control
☐ Build support infrastructure

Task Entry

1. Select a project plan in which the tasks are to be entered.
2. In the Task Name Field enter the task name.
3. Tab over and enter the duration of the task.

Detailed Task Information

In many instances, project managers may want to enter and require detailed information about one or more particular task(s).

The Task Information option allows managers to enter information on a task, for reference at any time, by selecting a tab.

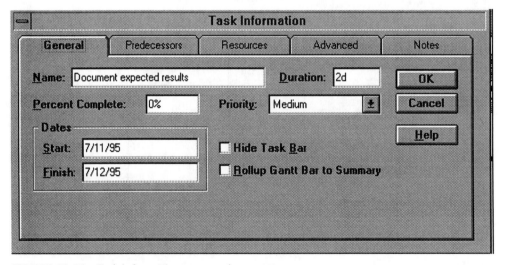

FIGURE 11.28   Task information—general.

Basic Task Information

MS Project defaults on the General tab. This option specifies basic information about the selected task. In our example we selected "identify existing product features" task. Figure 11.28 shows the basic information about the task.

1. From the Insert menu select Task Information.
2. The General tab will be displayed.

Predecessors Tab

This option specifies information about the selected tasks' relationships (if any).

From the Task Information option select Predecessor tab.

ID—This refers to the predecessor's id. If you do not know the id, type the name of the task in the Task Name column.

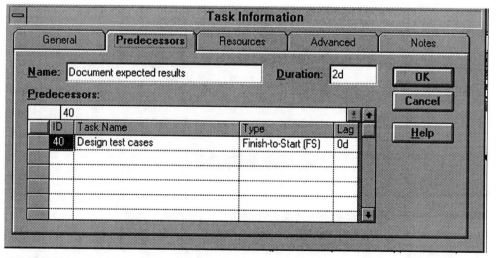

FIGURE 11.29 Task information—predecessor.

Type—This option lets the user define the task relationship. The relationships are entered by using one of the following two-letter combinations:

FS—Finish to Start

FF—Finish to Finish

SS—Start to Start

SF—Start to Finish

Lag—Refers to the lead or lag time that may occur between tasks. In the Lag column, enter any lead time with a negative number, and lag time with a positive number.

Resources Tab

This tab specifies information about the resources that have been assigned to the selected task.

1. From the Task Information option select Resources tab.
2. Select OK when the information has been entered.

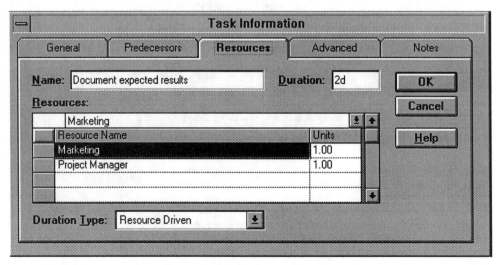

FIGURE 11.30 Task information—resources.

Resource Name Enter the name of the resource that has been assigned to that particular task.

Units Refers to the amount of resource units being allocated to the task. In our example, John Crabtree has been assigned 1 unit.

Advanced Tab

The Advanced tab option allows the manager to specify additional information about the selected task.

1. From the Task Information option select Advanced tab (Figure 11.31).
2. Select OK when the information has been entered.

In the Advanced option, managers can use Type to specify any restrictions on the start or finish dates for the tasks. One constraint per task can be assigned.

    If a constraint is marked As Soon As Possible, MS Project calculates

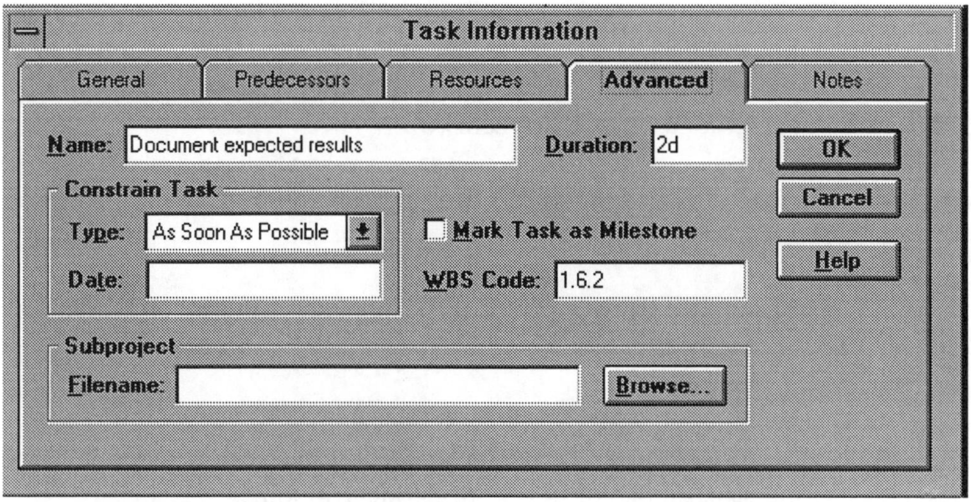

FIGURE 11.31 Task information—advanced.

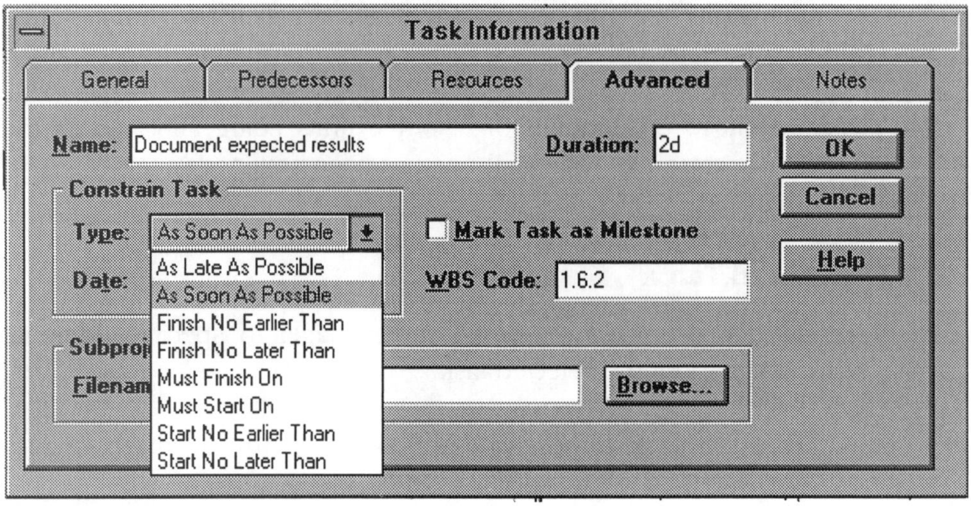

FIGURE 11.32 Task information—advanced options.

the earliest possible start and finish dates for the task, and vice versa for the latest possible start and finish dates.

Mark Task as Milestone Milestones can be defined as tasks that have a duration of zero. This would mean that the task has been completed, and indicates that it was a significant and important step for the completion of the project. By default all milestones appear as diamonds in MS Project's Gantt chart. Any task can be denoted as a milestone by simply entering a duration of zero (0).

-or-

At the Advanced tab of the Task Information box, select the option Mark Task as Milestone.

A milestone in a project plan can be enhanced by either bolding or changing the color for contrast.

1. From Format menu, select Text Styles.
2. Click on Item to Change, select Milestone Tasks, and select the font, size, and color of the milestone symbol.

WBS Code (Work Breakdown Structure) By default, MS Project uses the tasks outline number as the WBS Code. The WBS code appears when the WBS field is displayed.

Notes Tab

The Notes tab option allows you to type or review notes for a selected task.

1. Select Task Notes from the Insert menu, or select Task Information command and select Notes.
2. Select OK when the note has been completed.

DEFINING RESOURCES

A resource can be defined as either the people or the equipment—including cost, schedule, work information—or any related notes or

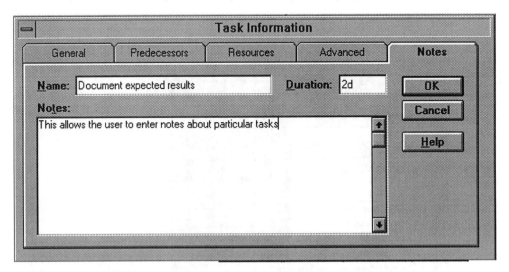

FIGURE 11.33 Task information—notes.

FIGURE 11.34 Resources icon.

objects needed to complete a task in a project. In situations where the project involves more than a few people, project managers may find it useful to assign specific individuals to work on each task.

To assign a resource to a task, do the following:

1. From the Gantt chart select the task that is to be assigned a resource.
2. Click on the Resource Assignment button on the standalone toolbar, or select Resource Assignment from the Insert menu.
3. In the name field, enter the name of the resource that is to be assigned.
4. Select the Assign button.
5. Once all the resources have been assigned, select the Close button.

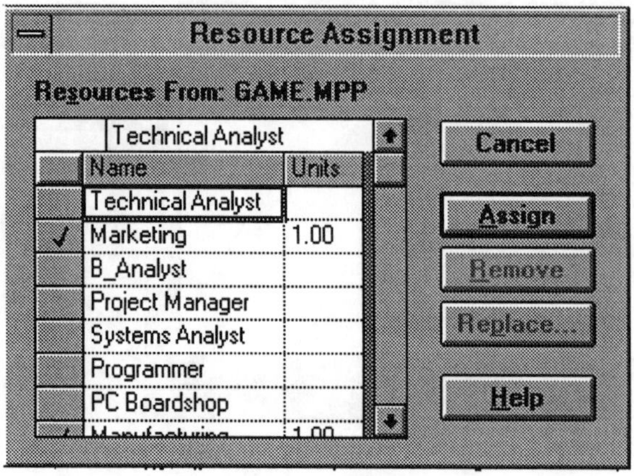

FIGURE 11.35 Resource assignment.

> Note: Once a resource has been assigned to a task, the name of the assigned resource is displayed to the right of the Gantt bar.

Additional information can be entered in the Resource Assignment dialog box; also, details on particular resources can be entered in the Resource Information dialog box.

Resource Information

1. Click on the Resource Assignment button on the toolbar. Or select Resource Assignment from the Insert menu.
2. Double-click on the resource in the Name field.
3. In the Resource Information dialog box, enter the additional information you want for the selected resource.
4. Select OK.
5. Select Cancel when you have entered all the relevant information.
6. To view the resource list, select View and choose the Resource Sheet.
7. When you have finished looking at the resource list, select Gantt chart from the View Menu.

Notes

This feature allows the user to enter notes for any task or resource in the project plan. In many instances project managers may find that it is help-

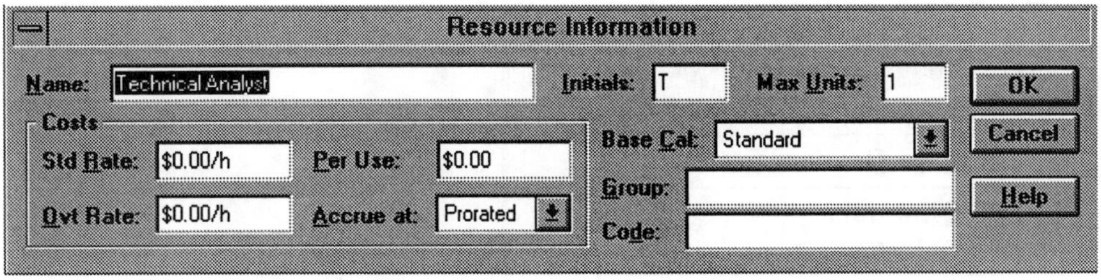

FIGURE 11.36 Resource information.

FIGURE 11.37 Notes icon.

ful to enter detailed information (notes) about a project or a resource, whether it be about the duration, function, or any personal data on the resource or task. Notes can be used in the Task and Resource options.

Task Notes The Task Notes feature allows the user to enter or review notes for a selected task.

The Notes option can be accessed from either the standard toolbar or from the Task Information option on the Insert pulldown menu.

From the toolbar the Notes facility can be accessed by double-clicking on the Notes icon, shown in Figure 11.37.

-or-

1. From the Insert menu, select Task Notes (see Figure 11.38).
2. Click on the Notes tab and enter the information.

Insert	Format	Tools	Window
Insert Task			Ins
Insert Recurring Task...			
Insert Column...			
Task Information...			Shift+F2
Task Notes...			
Resource Assignment...			Alt+F8
Page Break			
Drawing...			
Object...			

FIGURE 11.38 Insert menu—task notes.

3. The name of the selected task is displayed in the Name box. Enter the note for the task.

 If no task is selected, the Name box will be blank.

In the instance where the manager wants to enter notes about the project instead of a specific task, the Summary Info command from the File menu will allow Notes to be entered about the project.

Resource Notes Resource Notes, like Task Notes, allow the user to enter notes about a particular resource or all the resources in the project plan.

 The Resource note option can be accessed from the standard toolbar by selecting the Note icon with the mouse.

 Using keystrokes to access the Resource Notes:

1. Select the View menu, and choose Resource Usage (Figure 11.40).
2. The Resource Usage view is displayed (Figure 11.41).
3. Click on the Notes icon and enter any notes for that particular resource (Figure 11.42).
4. Once the note has been entered, a Note icon is displayed to the left of the resource.
5. Select OK when the note you entered is completed.

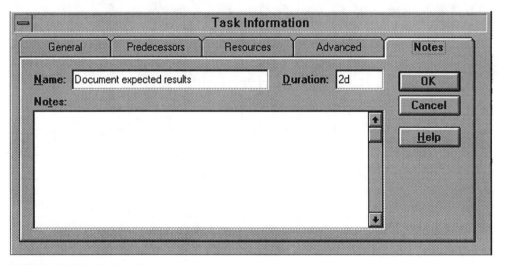

FIGURE 11.39   Notes tab.

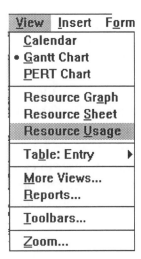

FIGURE 11.40 View—Resource Usage.

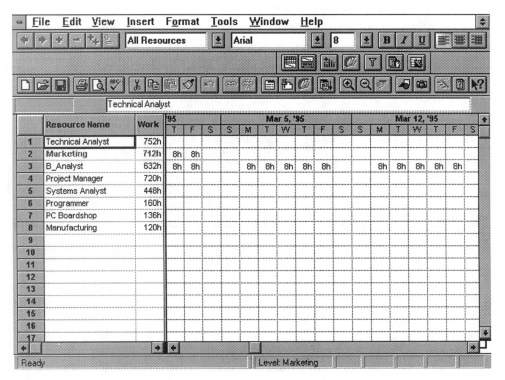

FIGURE 11.41 Resource Usage View.

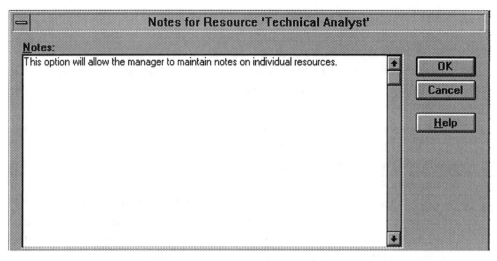

FIGURE 11.42 Resource notes.

6. The resource with the note added will have a little Note icon displayed to the left of the resource name (see Figure 11.43).

MANAGING RESOURCES

Project management includes management of resources and involves the managing of tasks, schedules, durations, and budgets in a coordinated manner. Resources are managed and controlled within the project environment in order to do the following:

☐ Monitor and track the amount of work completed by the resource
☐ Clearly define task and resource responsibilities and relationships—this enhances accountability for project reporting

	Resource Name	Work	95				
			T	F	S	S	M
1	Technical Analyst	752h					
2	Marketing	712h	8h	8h			
3	B_Analyst	632h	8h	8h			8h

FIGURE 11.43 Note icon.

□ Allow for greater flexibility in the resource planning and assigning functions

□ Track and control the resource costs

□ Allow resources to be reassigned, in situations where there are too many or too few resources assigned

Microsoft Project allows for all the above attributes to be monitored, tracked, and controlled. Once resources, durations, and their costs (if entered) are entered into a plan, MS Project will calculate the costs for the tasks and the resources.

MS Project suggests (to enhance productivity and manageability) that a resource list be created before tasks are assigned. This resource list would include information such as names of resources, associated costs, and the manner in which costs are accrued.

Creating a Resource List

The assigning of resources in a project is a very important facet of project management. In a successful project management plan, managers create a resource list for a various number of reasons, some of which are

□ To track the amount of work done by the resource, whether equipment or people

□ To have greater flexibility in planning task durations and start and finish dates

□ To monitor resources that may be either overworked or underworked

□ To track and account for resource costs

□ The ability to produce ad hoc reports and others

To create a resource list, do one of the following:

1. From the View menu, select Table and click on the Entry option (see Figure 11.44).
2. At the View menu, double-click on the Resource Sheet, as shown in Figure 11.45.

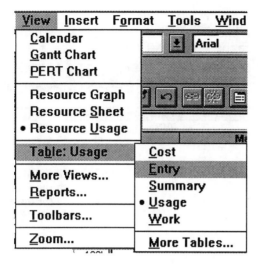

FIGURE 11.44 View—Table: Entry.

The View changes and a blank resource sheet is displayed (shown in Figure 11.46).

3. In the Resource Name column enter the resource name for your project in any of the blank columns.

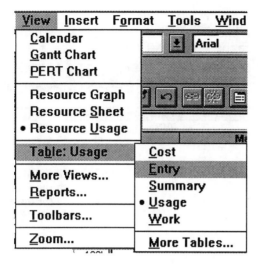

FIGURE 11.45 View—Resource Sheet.

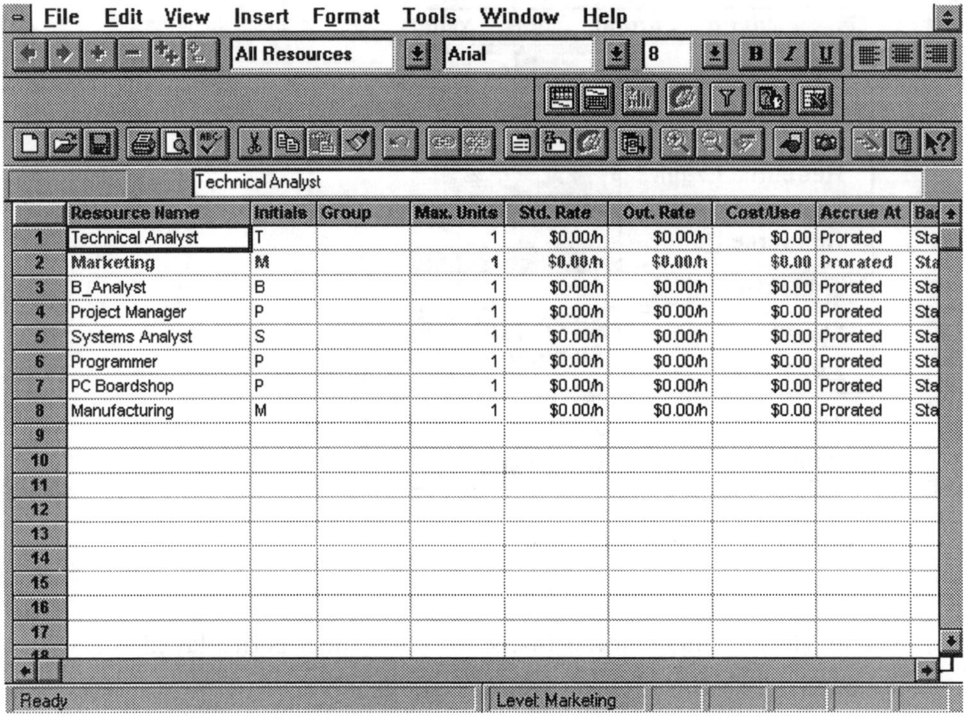

	Resource Name	Initials	Group	Max. Units	Std. Rate	Ovt. Rate	Cost/Use	Accrue At	Ba
1	Technical Analyst	T		1	$0.00/h	$0.00/h	$0.00	Prorated	Sta
2	Marketing	M		1	$0.00/h	$0.00/h	$0.00	Prorated	Sta
3	B_Analyst	B		1	$0.00/h	$0.00/h	$0.00	Prorated	Sta
4	Project Manager	P		1	$0.00/h	$0.00/h	$0.00	Prorated	Sta
5	Systems Analyst	S		1	$0.00/h	$0.00/h	$0.00	Prorated	Sta
6	Programmer	P		1	$0.00/h	$0.00/h	$0.00	Prorated	Sta
7	PC Boardshop	P		1	$0.00/h	$0.00/h	$0.00	Prorated	Sta
8	Manufacturing	M		1	$0.00/h	$0.00/h	$0.00	Prorated	Sta

FIGURE 11.46 Resource Sheet.

4. Enter the Group name if the resource belongs to a particular group. For example, if the resource Devin Chow is one of a number of programmers, you can enter in the group Programmer.

5. If a Group is defined, the user can enter the Max. Units. The Max. Units refer to the number of resource units available in this resource group.

6. To track the resource costs, the user can enter the information in the adjacent columns.

MS Project allows users to customize the Resource Sheet (as well as any other column view in any Views) to their specifications. The following steps are necessary to change a column definition:

1. At the column that needs to be changed double-click on the column name. A dialog box (shown in Figure 11.47) will be displayed.

2. Arrow down to the desired column definition and select OK.

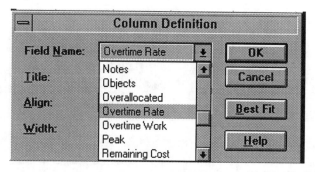

FIGURE 11.47   Column Definition.

Assigning a Resource

Project managers have the option of assigning resources to specific tasks. Resources can be assigned as full-time or part-time, multiple, or multiple units of a resource group to any task. Once the task is assigned the task name, the percentage of time that is allocated to the resource is displayed on the Gantt chart next to the bar (task) to which it is assigned.

1. From the View menu, click on the Gantt chart (see Figure 11.48).
2. Retrieve the project plan into the chart, and select the task that is to be assigned a resource, as shown in Figure 11.49.

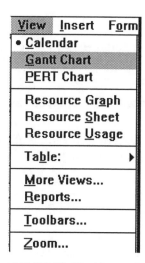

FIGURE 11.48   View—Gantt Chart.

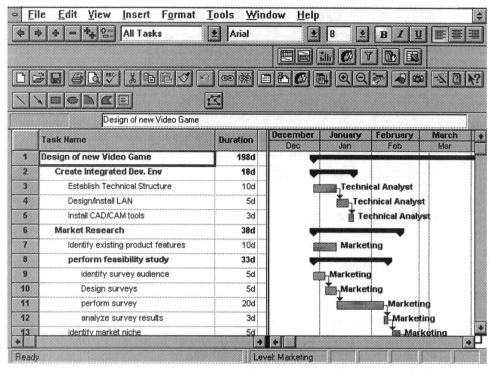

FIGURE 11.49 Gantt chart.

3. At the highlighted task, select from the Insert menu the Resource Assignment option (see Figure 11.50).

   -or-

   Click on the Resource Assignment icon (Figure 11.51) on the standard toolbar.

4. The Resource Assignment dialog box will be displayed, as shown in Figure 11.52.

5. Enter the name of the resource to be assigned, the units if known, and select Assign to assign the resource to the task.

A check mark is displayed indicating that the resource has been assigned.

6. Once the information is entered and the resource assigned, select the Close button to close the dialog box.

Insert	Format	Tools	Window
Insert Task			Ins
Insert Recurring Task...			
Insert Column...			
Task Information...			Shift+F2
Task Notes...			
Resource Assignment...			Alt+F8
Page Break			
Drawing...			
Object...			

FIGURE 11.50   Insert—Resource Assignment.

Note: To view a Resource Information Form double-click on the resource in the Resource Assignment dialog box. In this box all the information is displayed on the resource.

Removing/Replacing a Resource

1. From the Gantt Table, select a task.
2. Click on the Resource Assignment icon, or select the option from the Insert menu (see Figure 11.52).
3. Select the resource that is to be deleted.
4. Click on either the Remove or Replace button (see Figure 11.52). The resource will disappear.
5. To close the dialog box select the Close button.

FIGURE 11.51   Resource icon.

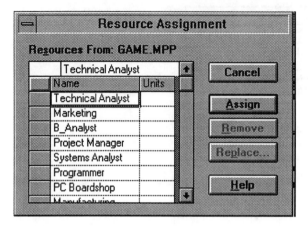

FIGURE 11.52 Resource Assignment.

USING RESOURCES

Now that the resources have been assigned to the appropriate tasks, the project manager now must track, use, and control elements of the project. The aim at this point, from the manager's perspective, is to be able to evaluate and adjust the project plan at any time. In an effort to maintain an accurate and up-to-date evaluation of the project at any time in the project lifetime, the manager must keep in mind the following points:

☐ The end date for the project schedule
☐ The manner in which resources are allocated
☐ The costing of the schedule

TABLE 11.1 Resource Assignment

To Assign . . .	Perform This Action . . .
Part-time resource	Enter a decimal or fraction in the unit field.
Several different resources	Select them
More than one of the same resource	Enter the number of resource units in the unit field

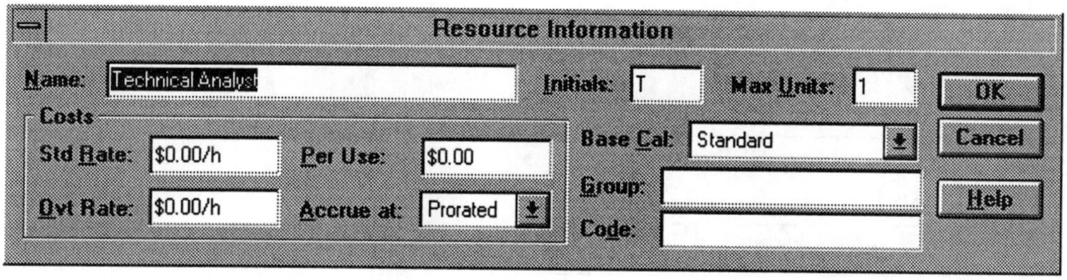

FIGURE 11.53 Resource Information.

MS Project makes tracking and controlling the project plan/schedule very easy. By using the critical path method, which calculates the total duration of the project based on individual task durations and all their interdependencies, managers can adjust the finish dates by altering the critical tasks.

In this section we will focus on strategies on how the project manager can alter the critical tasks by establishing tracking and scheduling tools, resolving any overallocated resources, and/or shortening or lengthening tasks.

In an effort to schedule and track resources, managers may find the resource calendar in MS Project an excellent tool to schedule vacations and any special working times or holidays that the resource may require. By using the resource calendar, MS project will not schedule any work for that resource for the time that the user has specified as having off.

Defining Working Hours and Days Off

Use this option to set the working hours and days off for a resource. Once this option has been defined, MS project uses this information in the calculation of the finish dates for the project.

1. From the Tools menu, select Change Working Time, as shown in Figure 11.54.
2. In the Change Working Time dialog box, click on the For box, and select the resource whose calendar is to be changed (see Figure 11.55).
3. Select the days that are to be changed on the calendar.

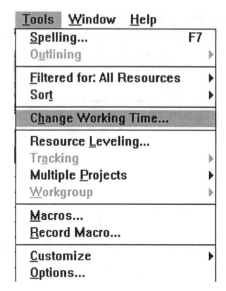

FIGURE 11.54 Tools menu.

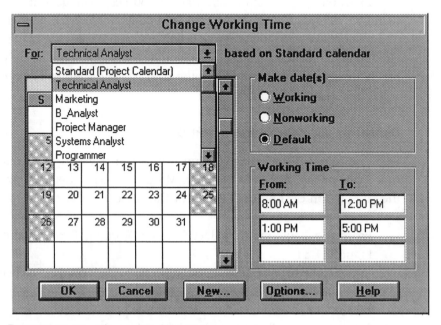

FIGURE 11.55 Change Working Time.

4. Click on the Working, Nonworking, or Default option buttons to define the days.
5. Enter the new time in the From box or To box.
6. Click on the OK button.

Assigning a Calendar to a Resource

Assigning a calendar to a resource serves as a tool to show the manager all the working and nonworking days for the resource.

To assign a calendar to a resource, perform the following actions:

1. From the View menu, select the Resource Sheet (Figure 11.56).
2. Select the resource that a calendar is to be assigned.

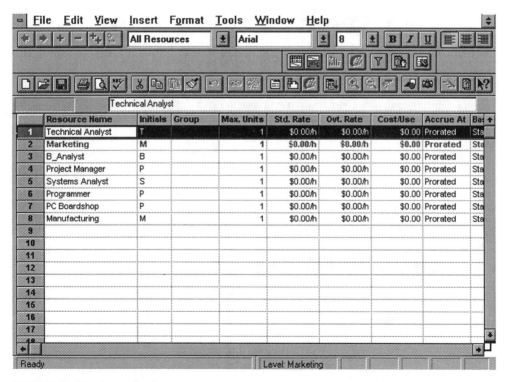

FIGURE 11.56 Resource sheet.

FIGURE 11.57 Resource information icon.

3. Click on the resource information icon on the standard toolbar (see Figure 11.57).

 -or-

 Select Resource Information from the Insert menu (see Figure 11.58).
4. The Resource Information dialog box will be displayed, as shown in Figure 11.59.
5. In the Base Cal box, select the calendar that you want to assign to the resource.
6. Select OK, once the option has been selected.

Changing the Work Schedule

Managers may find that they have to evaluate their schedules at some point and make changes to offset setbacks and delays in time,

<u>I</u>nsert	F<u>o</u>rmat	<u>T</u>ools	<u>W</u>indow
Insert <u>R</u>esource			**Ins**
Insert <u>R</u>ecurring Task...			
Insert <u>C</u>olumn...			
Resource Information... Shift+F2			
Resource <u>N</u>otes...			
Resource <u>A</u>ssignment...			Alt+F8
<u>P</u>age Break			
<u>D</u>rawing...			
<u>O</u>bject...			

FIGURE 11.58 Insert—Resource Information.

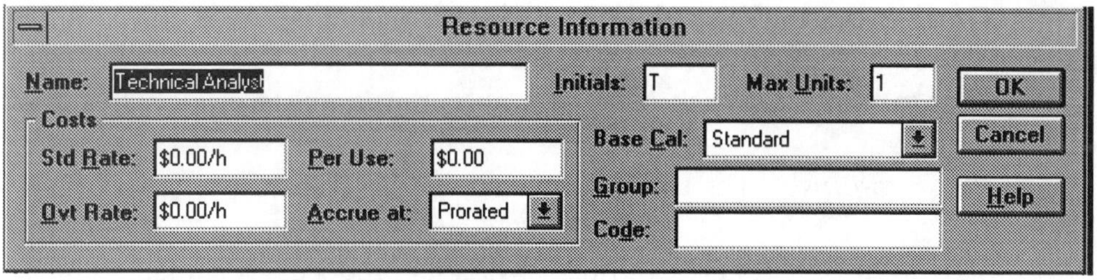

FIGURE 11.59 Resource Information dialog box.

resources, and costs. In most instances, managers who evaluate their projects are able to identify problem areas, for example:

☐ Task relationships and the critical path
☐ Slack time
☐ Constraints on tasks
☐ Overallocated resources
☐ Cost of the tasks

By identifying these areas, the manager can then make adjustments to the tasks, resources, and their allotted timeframes. This would ultimately result in reduced slack time (the amount of time in which a task can be delayed without actually delaying the finish date of the project. In evaluating and changing the work schedule, the manager should take into consideration the task relationships—whether the tasks are predecessor or successor tasks, and how they affect the other tasks.

Task Relationships

Predecessor Tasks These are tasks that must either start or finish before another task can begin.

Successor Tasks These tasks can be defined as those that depend on a previous (preceding) task to be started or finished, before it can begin.

Both the successor and predecessor tasks can be altered and adjusted to ensure that the project is completed on time. By utilizing the task relationships effectively, the work schedule can be changed to compensate for any lost time. The following task relationships can come up in the project schedule:

Finish-to-start   One task begins when another task ends.

Start-to-start   The task must start no earlier than its predecessor task.

Finish-to-finish   The task can finish no earlier than its predecessor task.

Start-to-finish   A task can finish when its predecessor starts.

Identifying Slack Time in the Workplan

In any project there may be instances when tasks may have to be delayed, either intentionally or unintentionally. In this situation the end date of the project can be affected. To avoid this situation, the astute project manager would look at his or her project plan and try to locate any free slack time in the tasks. By identifying this slack time, the project manager can at his or her discretion use the slack time during the critical periods of the project. This ensures that the finish date of the project is met. Free slack time can be defined as the period of time that a task can be delayed before it delays another task. Total slack time is the amount of time a task can be delayed before it affects the finish date of the project.

1. At the project chart, select the View menu.
2. Select Table and Schedule as shown in Figure 11.60.
3. Using the mouse, drag the divide bar over to the right, until the Free Slack and Total Slack Time is displayed, as shown in Figure 11.61.

Locating Overallocated Resources and Task Assignments

In addition to locating slack time in the project plan, project managers can also try to locate any overallocated or underallocated resources in their project plan to ensure that the finish date is met.

1. From the View menu select Toolbars (Figure 11.62).
2. Select Resource Management, from the menu that is displayed (Figure 11.63).

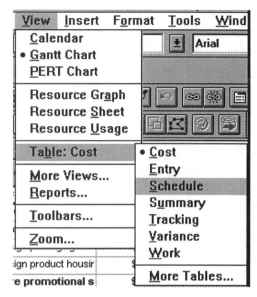

FIGURE 11.60 View—Schedule.

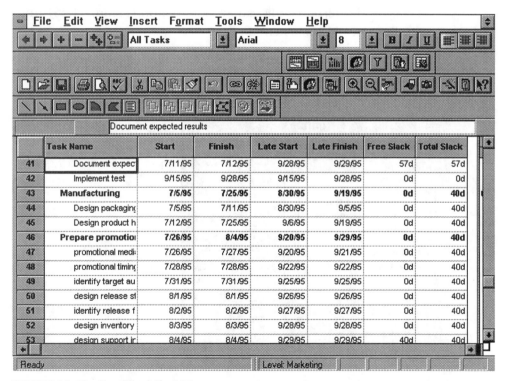

FIGURE 11.61 Free/Total Slack Time.

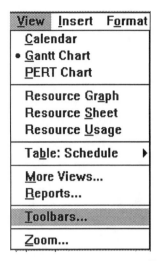

FIGURE 11.62 View—Toolbars.

3. On the left side of the project plan, the Resource Management button bar is displayed, as shown in Figure 11.64.

4. Click on the resource allocation view button (Figure 11.65) from the Resource Management toolbar.

The Resource Allocation screen will be displayed, as shown in Figure 11.66.

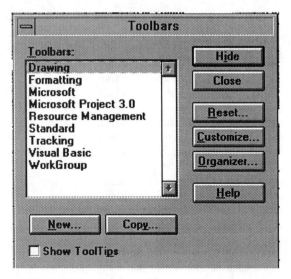

FIGURE 11.63 Toolbars—Resource Management.

		Start	June	July	August	September	October	Noven
			Jun	Jul	Aug	Sep	Oct	No
41		7/11/95		Marketing,Project Manager				
42		9/15/95				Marketing,Project		
43	Manufacturing	7/5/95						

Document expected results

FIGURE 11.64   Resource Management button bar.

FIGURE 11.65   Resource Allocation view button.

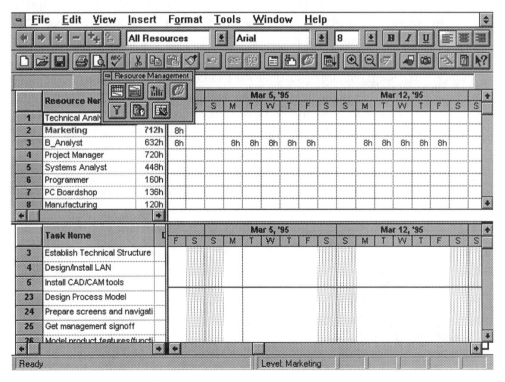

FIGURE 11.66   Resource Allocation screen.

5. In the Resource Name field, click on the Go to Overallocation button (Figure 11.67).

The overallocated hours of work assigned to the resource will be displayed.

Assigning Overtime Hours to Resources

Once the overallocated/underallocated resources have been identified, managers may now want to focus their attention on the finish date of the project and their ability or inability to adhere to this date. In instances when the finish date of the project date may be jeopardized, project managers may opt to have overtime hours assigned to resources.

Microsoft Project operates on a resource-driven schedule. Simply defined, this means that the task's duration in a project is calculated on the amount of work and the number of resources assigned to complete the work. By assigning overtime to a task, the project manager can shorten the duration of the task, thereby reaching the scheduled finish dates.

To assign overtime hours to resources, do the following:

1. From the View menu, select Gantt Chart.
2. Open the desired Gantt chart.
3. From the Window menu, select Split.
4. Click on the lower pane of the mouse.
5. From the Format menu, select the Details option, and then click on resource work.

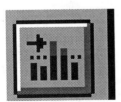

FIGURE 11.67   Go to overallocation button.

FIGURE 11.68 Window menu.

6. In the top window, select the task that is to be assigned the overtime hours.
7. In the bottom window, enter the number of hours that is to be assigned in the Ovt. Work column.
8. Click on OK when the hours have been entered.

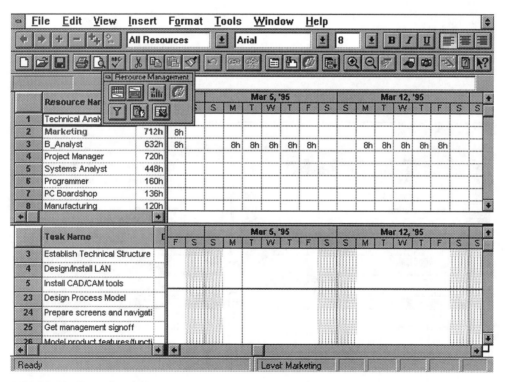

FIGURE 11.69 Split window.

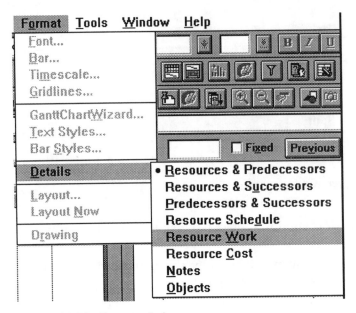

FIGURE 11.70 Format window.

FIGURE 11.71 Ovt. Work.

LEVELING RESOURCES

Once resources have been assigned and the project is well underway, project managers may find that the resources may be overallocated, such as when the work assigned to the resource is beyond the capacity and allotted timeframe. When such a situation arises, MS Project is sensitive enough to inform the project manager. A message is then displayed on the status bar advising that the resource is overallocated and that it should be leveled. Resource leveling can be defined as the process of evening out overallocated resources by delaying the start dates of the tasks that have been assigned to the resource.

It is important to note that the Leveling option has a few restrictions that affect its decision-making ability. Leveling should only be initialized after the project manager has entered everything that is known about the tasks/project. In addition, the use of constraint conditions should be kept to a minimum. The reasoning behind this is that these constraints can limit the decisions that MS Project makes with regard to leveling the resource.

Finally, leveling should not be used when scheduling from a finished date. By scheduling from a finished date, there is no room for MS Project to move slack time.

Identifying the Critical Path

Before the project manager or MS Project decides to level a project plan, the critical path has to be identified. The critical path can be defined as the duration of a series of consecutive tasks that must be completed in order for the project to be completed on time. These tasks are critical to the timely completion of the project. To identify these tasks the following steps can be followed:

1. Select Gantt View, and the plan that the critical path is to identify.
2. From the Format menu, select the option Text Styles, as shown in Figure 11.72.
3. Select the Item to Change field, click on the Critical Tasks option.
4. Click on the Color field and change the color to identify the critical tasks.
5. Click on the OK button.

FIGURE 11.72 Format—Text Styles.

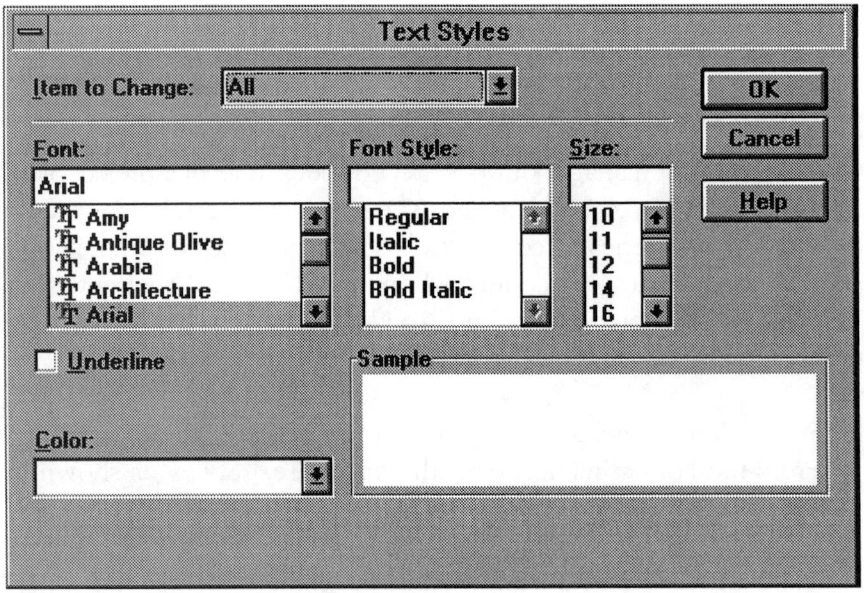

FIGURE 11.73 Text Styles.

In the Gantt chart, all the color-coded tasks are now identified as the critical tasks.

Once the critical path has been identified, the manager is faced with the objective of meeting his finish date. Microsoft Project will allow the user several avenues to shorten the schedule. The two ways that we will focus on are adding lead time and adding lag time.

Adding Lead or Lag Times

Once the critical path has been identified, the project manager now has to take steps to ensure that the finish date is met. To do this, the manager may add lead or lag time to the tasks.

Lead time describes the time where a task begins before its predecessor task is completed; that is, task 3 may begin before task 2 is completed. In Microsoft Project lead time is always indicated as a negative number.

Lag time can be used to delay the start of a task in order for the predecessor task to catch up. In Microsoft Project, lag time is always indicated by a positive number.

1. Select the task that is to be assigned lead or lag time.
2. Click on the Information icon (Figure 11.74).
     -or-
     From the Insert menu select the option Task Information.
3. Select the Predecessors tab.
4. In the Lag field, enter the lead or lag time, as well as the unit of lead or lag time. (Remember that lead times are negative numbers

FIGURE 11.74 Information icon.

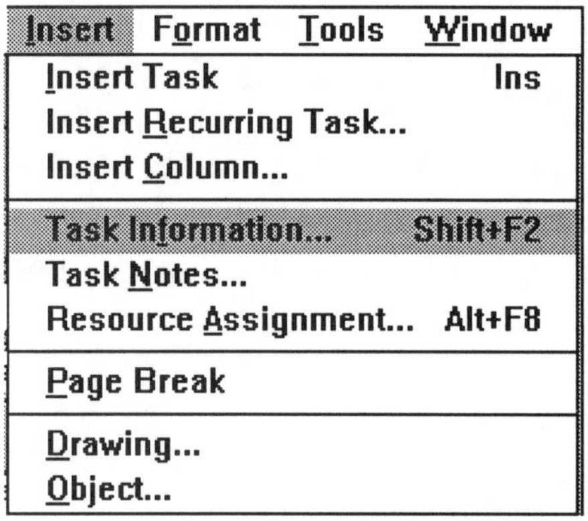

Insert	Format	Tools	Window	
Insert Task			Ins	
Insert Recurring Task...				
Insert Column...				
Task Information...			Shift+F2	
Task Notes...				
Resource Assignment...			Alt+F8	
Page Break				
Drawing...				
Object...				

FIGURE 11.75   Insert—Task Information.

and lag times are positive numbers). The Units can either be minutes (m), hours (h), days (d), or weeks (w).

5. Once the information is entered, click on the OK button.

Automatic Leveling by Microsoft Project

Once the critical path has been identified, the project manager may want to have any resource overallocation leveled. Leveling can be done either automatically by MS Project or by the manager.

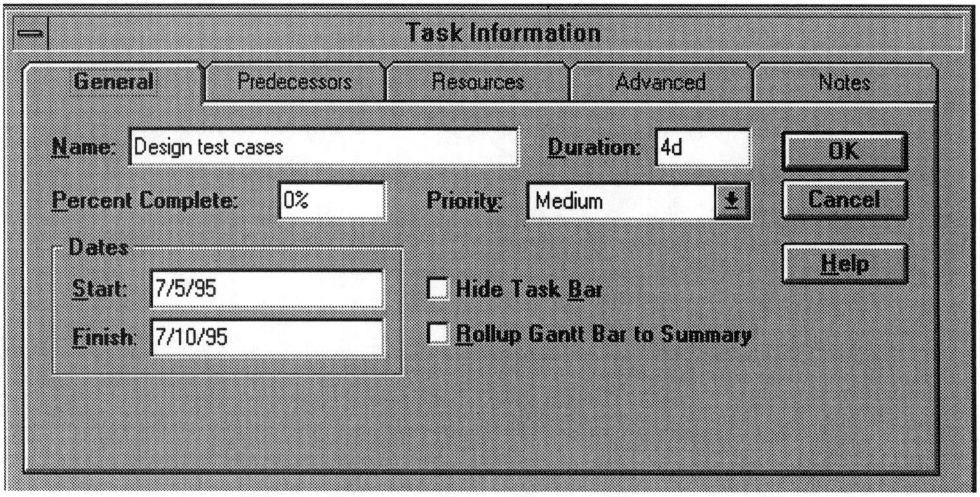

FIGURE 11.76   Task Information.

When MS Project automatically levels the project plan, it checks all task relationships and constraints, slack times, dates, and milestones before it decides to delay a task. If the automatic option is selected, project managers should ensure that they have analyzed, prioritized, and made any modifications to the project plan before they choose the automatic leveling.

Note: The automatic leveling option should not be used in instances where the project plan was calculated from the finish date of the project. The reason for this is that MS Project will delay overallocated tasks and resources as late as possible. If the project is calculated from the finish date, there will be no slack time in which the application can delay any of the tasks.

---

1. From the Tools menu, click on the Resource Leveling option (Figure 11.77).
2. Click on the Automatic option.
3. Select the Level Now option (Figure 11.78).

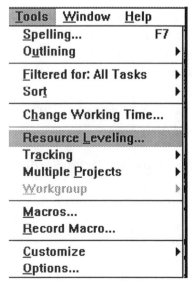

FIGURE 11.77   Tools—Resource Leveling.

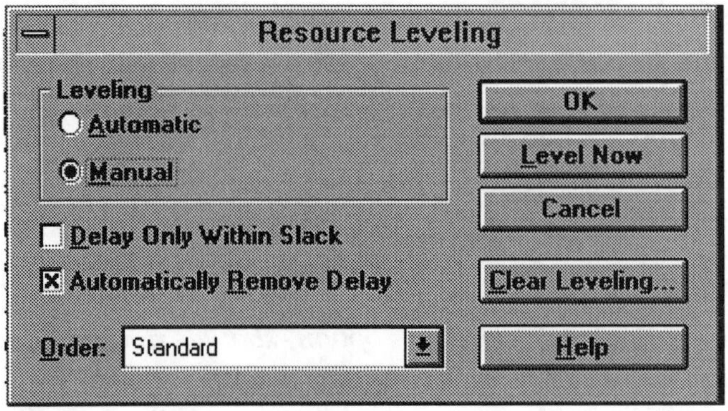

FIGURE 11.78 Resource Leveling.

To undo the leveling that was done by MS Project:

1. Select Resource Leveling from the Tools menu.
2. Click on the Clear Leveling button.

The effects of the leveling will be undone.

Manual Leveling

Manual leveling allows the project manager to resolve overallocations. In many instances, automatic leveling may not have the desired adjustments required by the manager. In these types of situations, the manager may be able to manually change the leveling to reflect the needs of the project.

To manually level the project plan, first select the plan that is to be leveled and follow the proceeding steps.

1. From the View Option, select toolbars (see Figure 11.79).

Select the Toolbar Resource Management.

2. Click the Resource Allocation View button from the Resource Management toolbar (see Figure 11.80).
3. The screen changes and a blank resource allocation view is displayed (Figure 11.81).

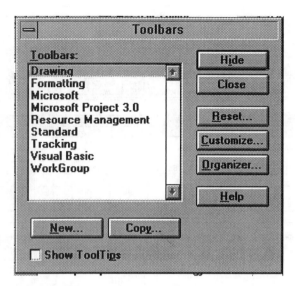

FIGURE 11.79 Toolbar—Resource Management.

4. In the bottom half of the screen, scroll (left) to the beginning of the row, then click on the Go to Resource Allocation button, as shown in Figure 11.82.
5. The overallocation dates and total time allocated will be displayed in the top half of the screen in red, if using a color monitor, or in bold for monochrome screens (Figure 11.83).
6. The manager can now resolve the overallocation by adjusting the timescale in the bottom half of the screen, as shown in Figure 11.84.

At this point tasks can be delayed, resources can be reassigned, and the amount of work allocated can be adjusted.

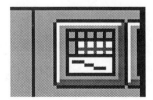

FIGURE 11.80 Resource allocation view button.

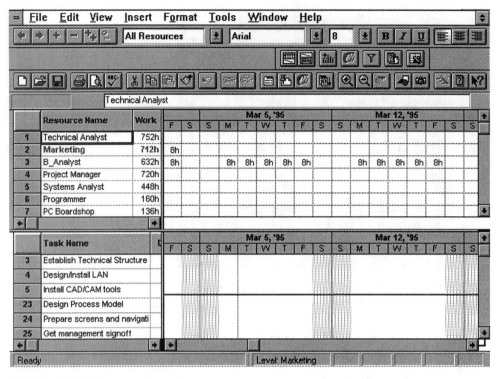

FIGURE 11.81 Resource allocation screen.

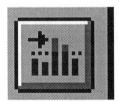

FIGURE 11.82 Go to Resource Overallocation button.

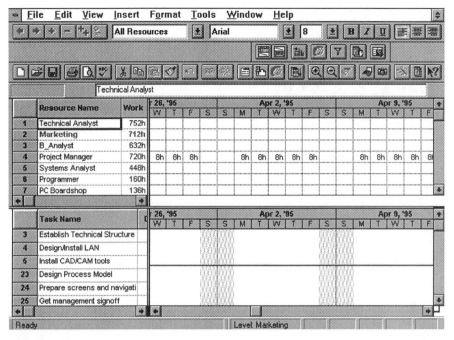

FIGURE 11.83 Overallocation screen.

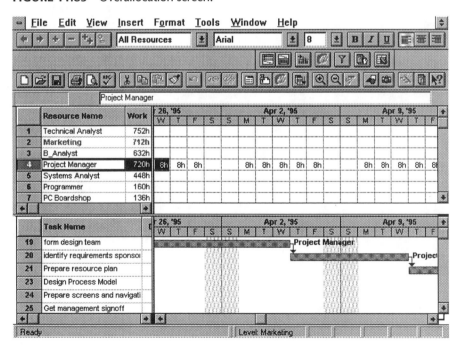

FIGURE 11.84 Resolved overallocation screen.

Reporting and Monitoring the Project Plan Using Project 4

12

Communicating the progress of the project every step of the way and the ability to produce ad hoc reports for presentations, for any variety of persons, are perhaps the most powerful functions of the project manager. This communication informs people that the project manager and the participants are well informed about the project, and it also allows the manager to be better able to make modifications in difficult situations.

Through MS Project, specific reports can be printed at various stages in the project. In addition, MS Project has a number of predefined formats, such as:

- Project Overview Information
- Task Information
- Resource Information
- Cost Information
- Tracking Information
- Object Linking and Embedding

PREDEFINED REPORTS

MS Project has several predefined reporting category structures in place. To access the predefined reports, perform the following actions:

1. From the View menu select the option Reports, as shown in Figure 12.1.
2. A dialog box with all the predefined reports will be displayed, as shown in Figure 12.2.
3. To access any one of the reports either double-click on the option, or click once on the option and click on the Select button.

Types of Reports

Overview This report, shown in Figure 12.3, displays information for the entire project. Within this option there are five different report types. Click on the options and then click on the Select button.

Project Summary By selecting this report, the manager obtains a summary of the project, including the tasks and resources numbers, status, start and finish dates.

View	**Insert**	**Form**
Calendar		
Gantt Chart		
PERT Chart		
Resource Gr**a**ph		
Resource **S**heet		
• Resource **U**sage		
Ta**b**le: Usage ▶		
More Views...		
Reports...		
Toolbars...		
Zoom...		

FIGURE 12.1 View—Reports.

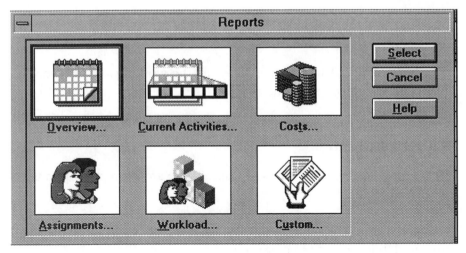

FIGURE 12.2   Reports icon.

Top Level Tasks   This report displays all the information for all the primary tasks in the project plan.

Critical Tasks   This option displays all the critical tasks in the project, as well as all the successor tasks and task notes.

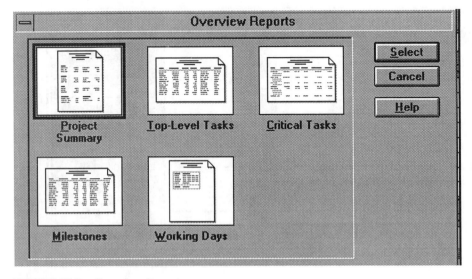

FIGURE 12.3   Overview Reports.

Milestones All project Milestones, including the summary tasks and task notes are displayed.

Working Days This option displays all the working and nonworking days during the course of the project.

Current Activities

This report contains the status of tasks. There are six report options, as shown in Figure 12.4.

Unstarted Tasks This option displays tasks that have been defined and assigned, but are not as yet started.

Tasks Starting Soon This report shows tasks that are to begin between specific dates.

Tasks in Progress This option displays in one-month periods all the tasks that are in progress for the entire project.

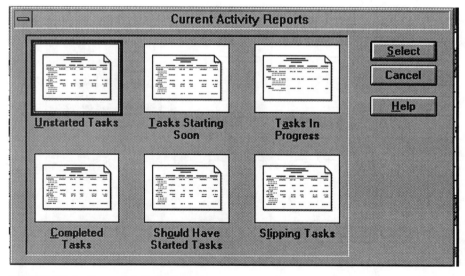

FIGURE 12.4 Current Activity Reports.

Completed Tasks This report displays the completed tasks in one-month periods.

Should Have Started Tasks This option displays tasks that should have started on a specified date.

Slipping Dates This report shows the tasks that are behind schedule, and includes all the summary tasks and task notes.

Costs

This report displays, shown in Figure 12.5, the cost information for the project. Information such as project budgets can be reported.

Weekly Cash Flow This option displays the costs per task, and is displayed in one-week intervals.

Budget This option shows the task budgets for the entire project.

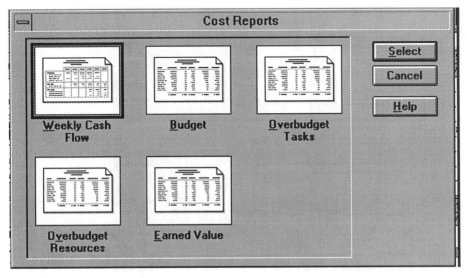

FIGURE 12.5 Cost Reports.

Overbudget Tasks This choice displays all the tasks that are over budget for the project.

Overbudget Resources This report shows all the overbudget resources in the project.

Earned Value This choice displays the earned-value information for the project.

Assignments

Assignment reports (Figure 12.6) display the assignments for resources and task schedules, as well as all overallocated resources.

Who Does What This option displays all the task schedules for the duration of the project.

Who Does What When This report displays all the task assignments and the work information.

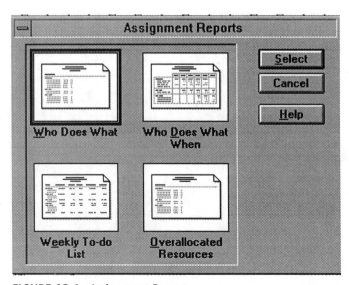

FIGURE 12.6 Assignment Reports.

Weekly To-do List This choice shows the tasks that resources are assigned on a weekly basis.

Overallocated Resources This option displays all the overallocated resources for the entire project. It also includes task schedule information and totals.

Workload

This type of report, shown in Figure 12.7, shows the task usage and resource usage.

Task Usage This report displays the resources that are assigned to tasks.

Resource Usage This report displays the tasks that have been assigned to resources.

Custom Reports

This option allows the manager to create a new report or customize existing ones.

The following options are available to the user, as shown in Figure 12.8.

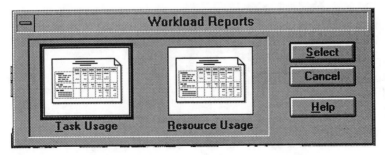

FIGURE 12.7 Workload Reports.

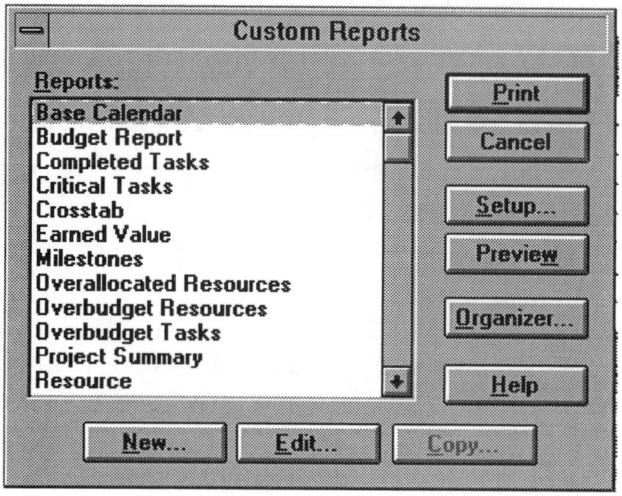

FIGURE 12.8 Custom Reports.

New Select this option to create a new report.

Edit, Copy In these dialog boxes, the user can change the fonts, sizes, bold, and underline characteristics of text.

Print The new report can be printed by selecting this box.

Setup This option displays the Page Setup for the report (see Figure 12.10).

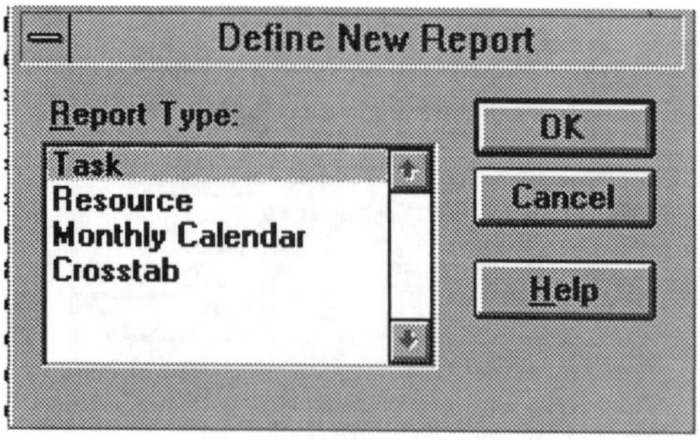

FIGURE 12.9 Define New Report.

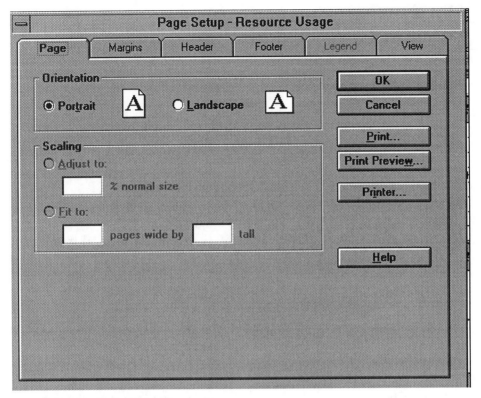

FIGURE 12.10 Page Setup.

Preview This choice allows the user to preview the report before it is printed.

Table 12.1 displays the various reports that can be printed by the project manager.

Note: For a more extensive discussion and table, please check the Microsoft Project User's Guide.

Printing a Custom Report

1. From the View menu select the Report option. Click on Custom, and then choose the Select button.

TABLE 12.1 Report Choices

Information Desired	Report to Select
The number of tasks and resources, project costs, amount of work, project start and finish dates	Select the Overview Reports (project summary)
List of highest summary tasks, showing start and finish dates	Select the Overview Reports (Top-Level Tasks)
List of milestone tasks, sorted by their start dates	Select the Overview Reports (Milestone Report)
Working and Nonworking time in the schedule	Overview Reports (Working Days Report)
A list of tasks showing assigned resources and amount of work assigned to each	Use the Workload reports (Task Usage)
A list of critical tasks	Use Overview reports (Critical Tasks)
A list of resources showing their assigned tasks, and the amount of work assigned to each resource	Assignment Report (Resource Report)
A resource's tasks, broken down by week	Assignment Reports (Week To-do list)
A list of overallocated resources and their tasks	Assignment Reports (Overallocated Reports)
The cost of each task per week, total costs of all tasks per week, total costs of each task	Cost Reports (Weekly Cash Flow)
Resource list whose costs are going to exceed the baseline cost	Cost Reports (Overbudget Resources)
Comparison of costs and tasks as they relate to where they are in the project	Cost Reports (Earned Value Report)
A list of tasks that are going to exceed the baseline cost	Cost Reports (Overbudget Tasks)

2. In the Reports box highlight the Task report and click on the Edit button (see Figure 12.11).

To display Summary Tasks and Gray Band checkboxes:

3. Click on the Definitions tab, and click in the Show Summary Tasks and Gray Band checkboxes (see Figure 12.12).

To print only specific tasks:

4. In the Definitions Tab, select the Filter box and choose the filter that is to be printed.

To show Task Notes and Resource Assignments:

5. Click on the Details tab, (shown in Figure 12.13) and then click on the appropriate boxes (e.g., Notes checkbox, Schedule, Cost, or Work checkbox)

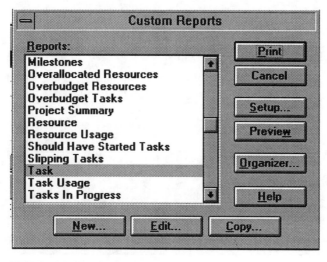

FIGURE 12.11 Custom Reports.

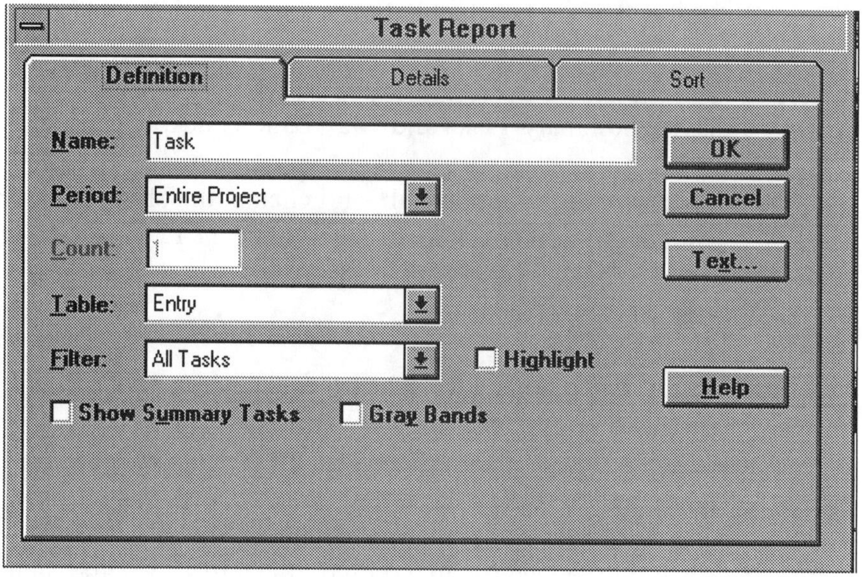

FIGURE 12.12 Task Report—Definition.

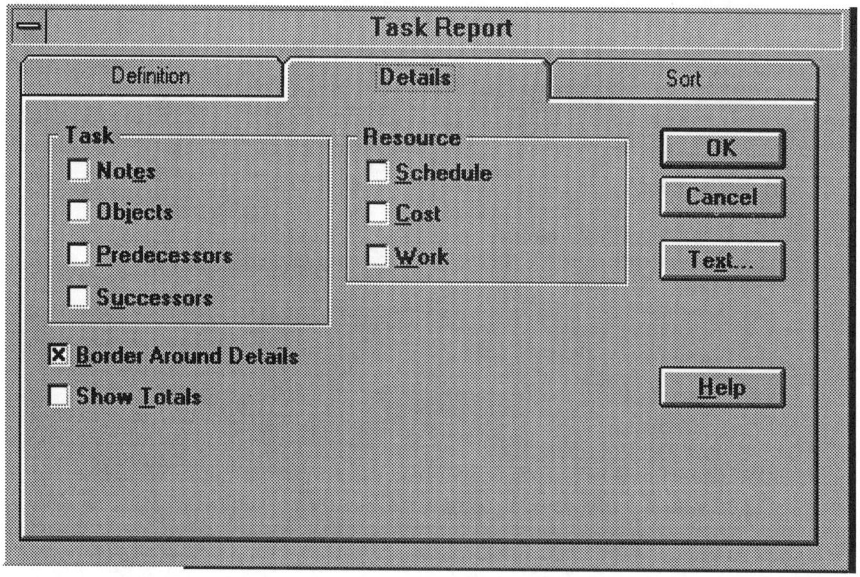

FIGURE 12.13 Task Report—Details.

To change the format of all the tasks in a category:

6. Click on the Text button. Select the Item to Change box, and select the formatting changes that are to be made.
7. Once all the changes have been made, click on the OK button and then select the Print option.

The customized report will now be printed. The same procedure can be carried out to print any type of custom report.

AVAILABLE VIEWS IN MICROSOFT PROJECT

For the purposes of presenting and communicating the project plan to a variety of users and clients, the Views option in MS Project is a wonderful tool. Using this tool will allow the project manager to present, organize, schedule tasks and resources, and change and display information in many different ways. Using View will allow the user the ability to

☐ Produce presentation quality charts and graphs
☐ Print and display customized project information
☐ Edit tasks and resource information
☐ Track the project

To access the View option:

1. From the View menu select the option More Views (see Figure 12.14).
2. A list of Views will be displayed, as shown in Figure 12.15. Select the View of your choice from the list.

The following are some of the available views in MS Project.

Note: For a more in-depth and comprehensive list, check the Microsoft Project User's Manual.

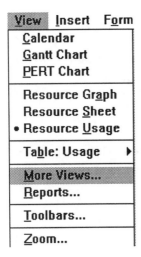

FIGURE 12.14 View—More Views.

TRACKING AND MONITORING PROJECT PROGRESS

Tracking and monitoring the progress of a project is yet another feature in MS Project to assist in successfully managing the project. With Microsoft Project almost every facet of the project can be tracked. Tracking the project will allow the manager to be well informed of the

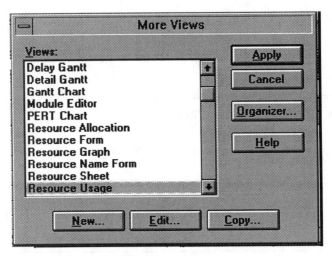

FIGURE 12.15 More Views.

TABLE 12.2   Some Available Views in MS Project

View	Description
Gantt Chart	A bar chart showing task and related project information. Can be used to enter and schedule a list of tasks.
PERT Chart	A network chart (much like an organizational chart) that displays tasks and related project information.
Calendar	A monthly calendar showing the tasks and their durations.
Task Form	A form that allows the project manager to enter and edit information about a specific task.
Task PERT Chart	A networked chart displaying all the predecessors and successors of one particular task.
Delay Gantt	A list of tasks and information about all task delays, as well as a bar chart showing the delay of the tasks during leveling.
Task Entry	A combination view of Gantt Chart (top) and Task Form (bottom). This view can be used to edit, add, and review detailed information about the task selected.
Resource Sheet	A list of resources showing the allocation, cost, or work information for each resource over a specified time.
Resource Form	A form to enter and edit specific information about a particular resource.
Resource Allocation	A combination view with the Resource Usage view on top and the Delay Gantt on the bottom. Useful to resolve overallocations.

project through every phase, and be able to produce status reports for update and presentation purposes. Managers will also be able to identify and resolve/accommodate any problems as they occur.

Tracking in Microsoft Project takes the form of a three-step process:

1. Create a baseline plan from the initial project plan.
2. Update the plan occasionally to reflect the changes in the project as they occur.
3. Compare the updated version to the baseline version, thereby tracking progress.

Types of Tracking

Tracking is done at the discretion of the manager; however, it is recommended for large-scale projects that there be some form of tracking. Information in the project plan can be tracked either minimally or in detail.

Minimal Tracking This type of tracking involves comparing and tracking the start and finish dates of the project to the dates in the baseline project.

Detailed Tracking Detailed tracking involves the tracking of tasks durations, task start and finish dates, percentage of each task that is complete, the cost of the project, individual tasks, and resources, as well as the specific hours of work that the resource has completed.

Establishing a Baseline Plan

Simply defined, a baseline plan is an initial project plan that is used by MS Project to compare costs, work, and scheduled dates as the project progresses. Once the baseline plan is set up, the project manager can modify it to reflect the changes. This new baseline is called an interim plan.

Setting the Baseline Plan

1. Click on the Tools menu and select the Tracking option (as shown in Figure 12.16).
2. Select the Save Baseline option, and click on OK (Figure 12.17).
3. Click on the option Entire Project (or make sure that it is selected).

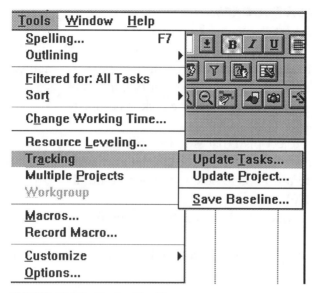

FIGURE 12.16 Tools—Tracking.

On the project plan screen, a new bar is displayed of a different color or shading, indicating that the plan has now been defined as a baseline plan.

Once the baseline plan is saved and the project manager makes any changes, the plan can be saved as an interim plan. To do this follow the steps defined above, except save the plan as an interim plan. MS Project will allow the user to save up to five interim plans.

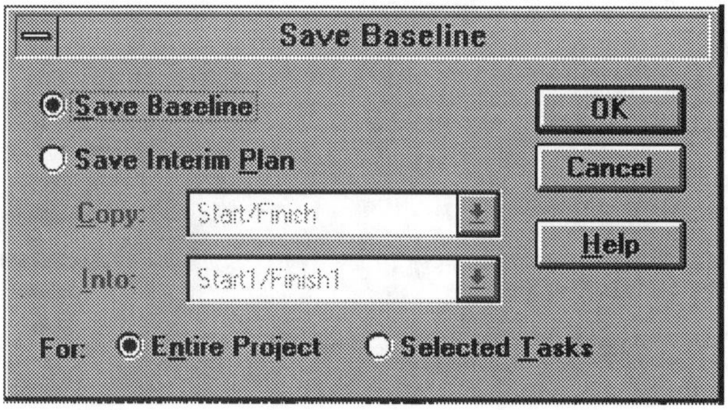

FIGURE 12.17 Save Baseline.

MEASURING THE TASK PROGRESS

In tracking the progress of the project, managers can also track the percentage of work done on tasks in the project. A percentage value of 0 (zero) indicates that the task has not yet begun, whereas a percentage value of 100% is an indicator that the task is complete.

1. Select the project plan that is to be updated.
2. Click on the Information button on the standard toolbar.
3. In the Percent Complete box, type a whole number between 0-100 (Figure 12.20).
4. Click on OK once the information is entered.

On your project plan screen, you will see the new percentage as defined (Figure 12.21).

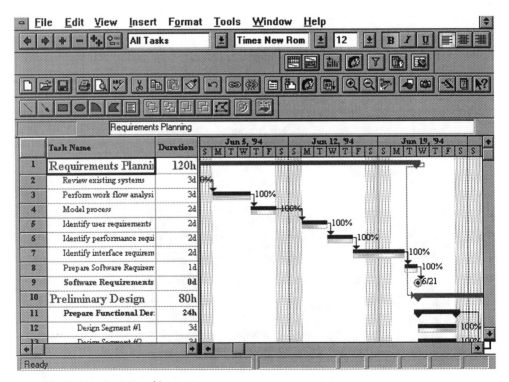

FIGURE 12.18   Gantt tracking.

FIGURE 12.19 Information button.

TRACKING TOOLBAR

On a final note, the Tracking toolbar is an added utility provided by MS Project to assist managers. This toolbar makes it convenient for the manager to view project information and update schedules.

To access the Tracking toolbar:

1. From the View menu, select the option Toolbars.
2. In the Toolbars list select the Tracking option, click on OK.

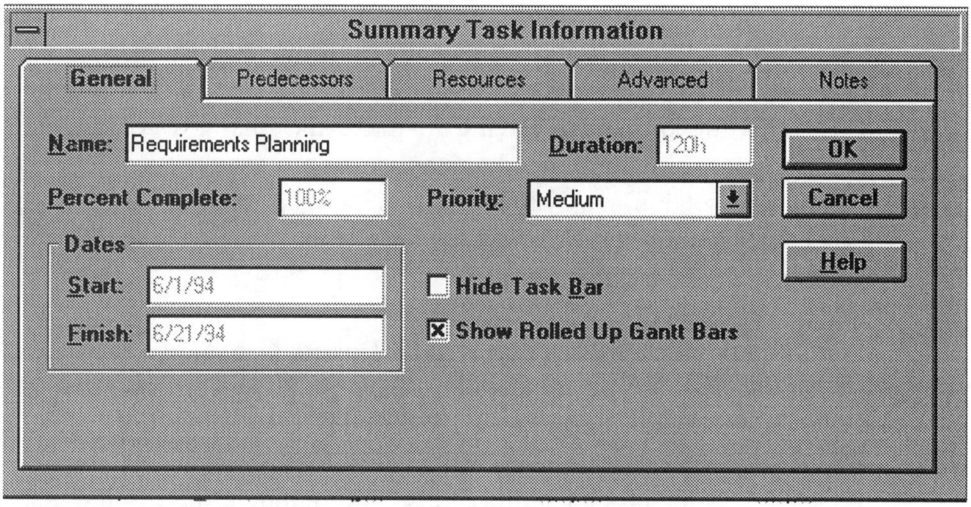

Summary Task Information

| General | Predecessors | Resources | Advanced | Notes |

Name: Requirements Planning   Duration: 120h   **OK**

Percent Complete: 100%   Priority: Medium   Cancel

Dates

Start: 6/1/94   ☐ Hide Task Bar   Help

Finish: 6/21/94   ☒ Show Rolled Up Gantt Bars

FIGURE 12.20 Task Information—General.

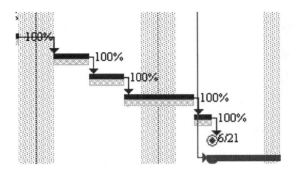

FIGURE 12.21 Percentage Complete.

LINKING AND EMBEDDING A MICROSOFT PROJECT CHART IN EXCEL

For reporting and presentation purposes, managers may find the OLE (Object Linking and Embedding) features in Windows-based applications very useful. In instances where managers need to have an exchange of information between MS Project and another Windows application, the concept of OLE comes into play. OLE allows the user to take a chart from MS Project and physically link it to another application document, such as in Excel or in Word. By linking the files, any time changes or modifications are made to the MS Project chart, it automatically updates the chart in every application with which it is linked. This saves the user from having to make the changes consistent in every application where the charts exist.

In this section we will link an MS Project chart into Microsoft Excel, and demonstrate the efficiency of this process. The following steps begin the link process:

1. Open the Project Plan that is to be Linked, from MS Project.
2. To select the entire project plan, click in the Top Left corner of the numbered column of the Plan (Figure 12.22).
   -or-
To select specific tasks, use the mouse and highlight the desired tasks.

	Task Name	Duration	Jun 5, '94	Jun 12, '94	Jun 19, '94
			S M T W T F S	S M T W T F S	S M T W T F S S
1	Requirements Planni	120			
2	Review existing systems	3d	0%		
3	Perform work flow analysi	3d	100%		
4	Model process	2d	100%		
		2d		100%	

FIGURE 12.22 Gantt chart.

3. Once the Plan is highlighted, click on the Edit menu and select the Copy option (Figure 12.23).
4. Swap out of MS project and open the application with which the project plan is to be linked.

In our example, we will object link our project plan to Microsoft Excel (see Figure 12.24).

5. In Excel, click on the Edit menu and select Paste Special (Figure 12.25).

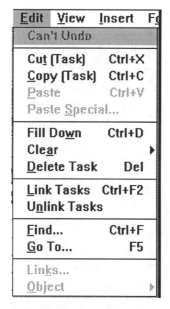

FIGURE 12.23 Edit—Copy.

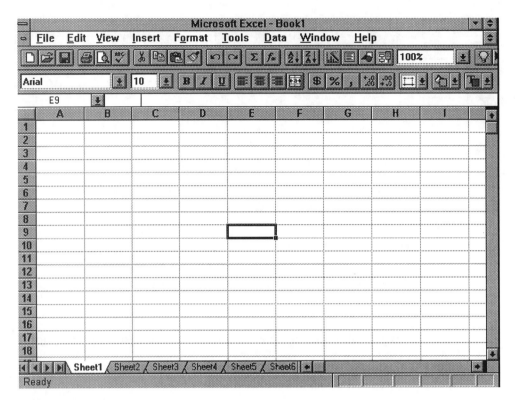

FIGURE 12.24 Microsoft Excel.

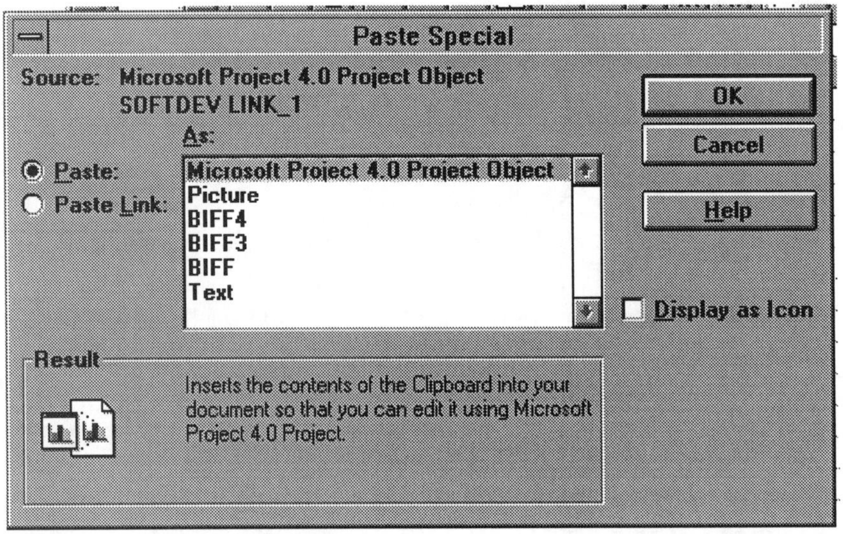

FIGURE 12.25 Paste Special.

6. In the Paste Special dialog box, click on the Paste Link option, making sure that Microsoft Project 4 Project Object is selected.
7. Click on OK.

You have now established a link between your project plan and your Excel spreadsheet. Any changes to this project plan will automatically be reflected in your Excel spreadsheet.

Note: The project plan you have just linked can be sized, shaped and formatted (lines, color, border, etc.)

Making Changes to Linked Objects

To make any changes to your project plan, there are two options. The first option is to double-click on the project plan object that is now embedded in Excel. This initiates the Microsoft Project application. Once initiated, the embedded project plan is automatically displayed, and made available for change. The second option is to swap (or exit, depending upon the memory capacity of your machine) out of Excel and into MS Project and then bring up your project plan.

Regardless of the manner in which any of the changes to the project plan are made, the next time you enter your linked Excel document, you will be prompted to re-establish (or refresh) the links to your document, as shown in Figure 12.26. This brings in all the changes that were last made to your project plan in Microsoft Project.

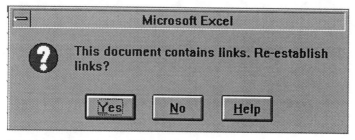

FIGURE 12.26 Re-establish Link.

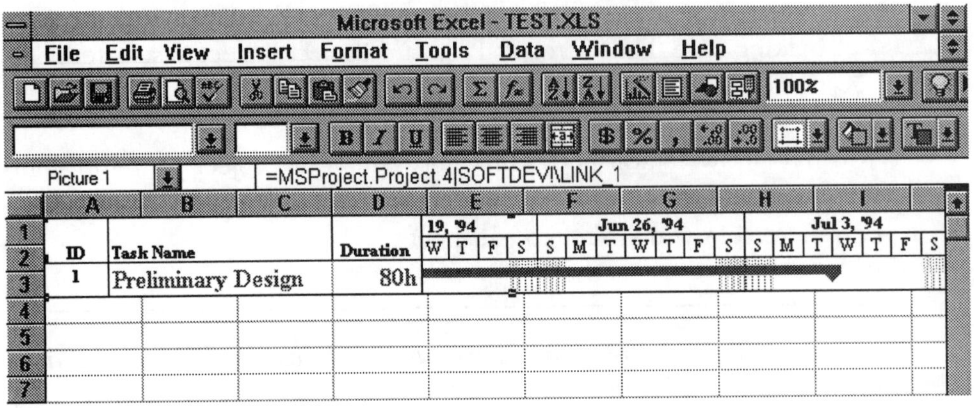

FIGURE 12.27 Linked MS Project.

In Figure 12.27, a Microsoft Project plan is linked into a Microsoft Excel spreadsheet. The link is dynamic and will be updated as the project plan changes. Also, as indicated above, updates can be launched from Excel as information regarding the server application (MS Project) is part of the link.

Sample Project Plans

REVIEWING A DBMS PRODUCT

The following project plan outlines the steps necessary in reviewing a relational database management system. The tasks are outlined and resources are identified. Further, relationships are identified between tasks. As this is not a typical development project, it lacks the familiar SDLC components. However, there are a number of key ideas such as:

- Entering tasks
- Identifying resources
- Showing relationships
- Showing subtasks
- Identifying milestones

The project plan that follows shows a Gantt view of the activities and relationships.

DESIGNING A VIDEO GAME

This sample project plan outlines the steps necessary to design and market a new video game. This example takes the reader through all the necessary steps, starting from the establishment of an integrated development environment through the release of the prod-

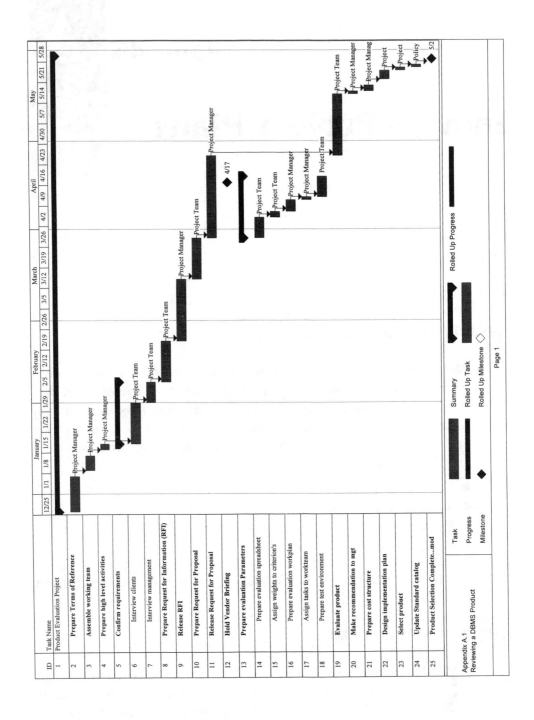

ID	Task Name
1	Product Evaluation Project
2	**Prepare Terms of Reference**
3	Assemble working team
4	Prepare high level activities
5	**Confirm requirements**
6	Interview clients
7	Interview management
8	**Prepare Request for Information (RFI)**
9	Release RFI
10	**Prepare Request for Proposal**
11	Release Request for Proposal
12	**Hold Vendor Briefing**
13	**Prepare evaluation Parameters**
14	Prepare evaluation spreadsheet
15	Assign weights to criterion's
16	Prepare evaluation workplan
17	Assign tasks to workteam
18	Prepare test environment
19	**Evaluate product**
20	Make recommendation to mgt
21	Prepare cost structure
22	Design implementation plan
23	Select product
24	Update Standard catalog
25	Product Selection Complete...mod

Appendix A.1
Reviewing a DBMS Product

Task
Progress
Milestone

Summary
Rolled Up Task
Rolled Up Milestone

Rolled Up Progress

Page 1

328

uct. This design has both hardware and software components. Also, a systems development lifecycle is evident in the larger phases identified.

Focusing on the resources, the reader will notice the following skillset:

□ Project Manager
□ Technical Analyst
□ Business Analyst (B_Analyst)
□ Systems Analyst
□ Programmer
□ Marketing
□ Boardshop (designs circuit board)
□ Manufacturing

Most software development efforts will utilize the above resources identified (except maybe for the last two).

If the attached plan is to be used in an actual design, care should be exercised in adjusting the durations to fit the nature of the project.

DESIGNING A CLIENT/SERVER APPLICATION

The attached project plan provides the summary tasks for the design of a client/server application. This application essentially starts from the ground floor. If you follow the high-level summary tasks, you will see:

□ Tasks aimed at analyzing and designing an integrated development environment
□ Tasks for the selection and evaluation of the necessary development tools
□ Tasks for the design of a technology alternative based on the high-level requirements
□ Though not evident, this application replaces a legacy mainframe system

The general focus of this example are the tasks necessary to see this application through to implementation. The timing, durations, and relative relationships of the tasks will be dependent in part to your resource pool, funds availability, and so on.

330

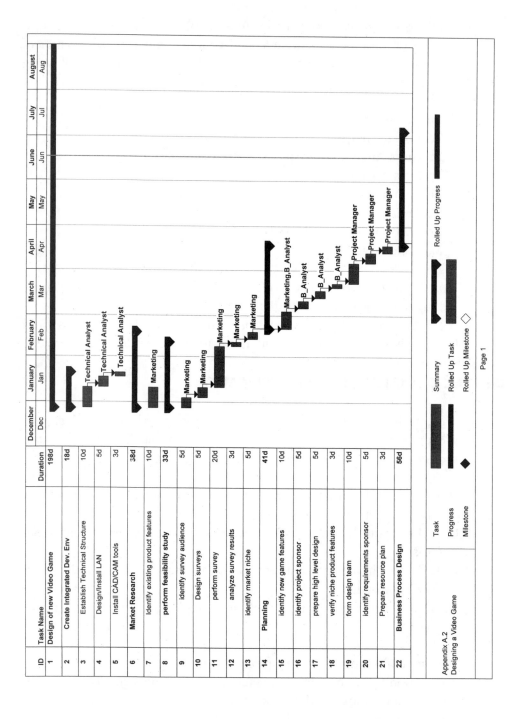

ID	Task Name	Duration
1	**Design of new Video Game**	**198d**
2	**Create Integrated Dev. Env**	**18d**
3	Establish Technical Structure	10d
4	Design/Install LAN	5d
5	Install CAD/CAM tools	3d
6	**Market Research**	**38d**
7	Identify existing product features	10d
8	**perform feasibility study**	**33d**
9	identify survey audience	5d
10	Design surveys	5d
11	perform survey	20d
12	analyze survey results	3d
13	identify market niche	5d
14	**Planning**	**41d**
15	identify new game features	10d
16	identify project sponsor	5d
17	prepare high level design	5d
18	verify niche product features	3d
19	form design team	10d
20	identify requirements sponsor	5d
21	Prepare resource plan	3d
22	**Business Process Design**	**56d**

Appendix A.2
Designing a Video Game

Page 1

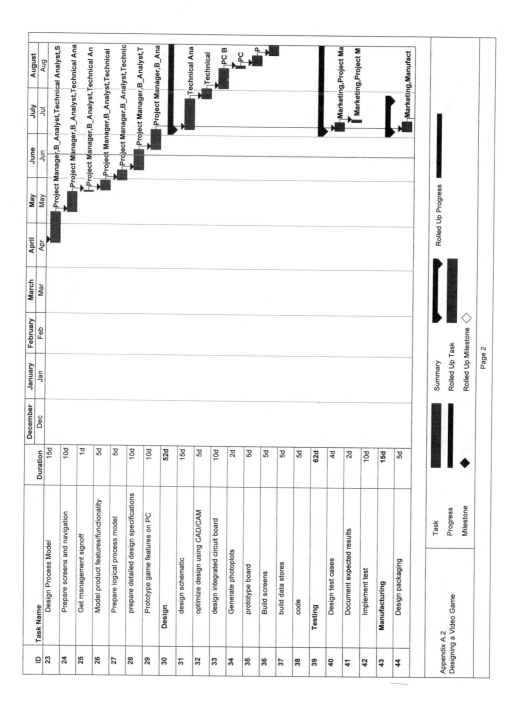

ID	Task Name	Duration
23	Design Process Model	15d
24	Prepare screens and navigation	10d
25	Get management signoff	1d
26	Model product features/functionality	5d
27	Prepare logical process model	5d
28	prepare detailed design specifications	10d
29	Prototype game features on PC	10d
30	Design	52d
31	design schematic	15d
32	optimize design using CAD/CAM	5d
33	design integrated circuit board	10d
34	Generate photoplots	2d
35	prototype board	5d
36	Build screens	5d
37	build data stores	5d
38	code	5d
39	Testing	62d
40	Design test cases	4d
41	Document expected results	2d
42	Implement test	10d
43	Manufacturing	15d
44	Design packaging	5d

Appendix A.2
Designing a Video Game

Task
Progress
Milestone

Summary
Rolled Up Task
Rolled Up Milestone

Rolled Up Progress

Page 2

331

ID	Task Name	Duration	December Dec	January Jan	February Feb	March Mar	April Apr	May May	June Jun	July Jul	August Aug
45	Design product housing	10d									
46	**Prepare promotional strategy**	**8d**									
47	promotional media	2d									
48	promotional timing	1d									
49	identify target audience	1d									
50	design release strategy	1d									
51	identify release forums	1d									
52	design inventory control	1d									
53	design support infrastructure	1d									
54	Release product to market	1d									Marketing,Man

Task		Summary	Rolled Up Progress
Progress		Rolled Up Task	
Milestone	◆	Rolled Up Milestone ◇	

Appendix A.2
Designing a Video Game

332

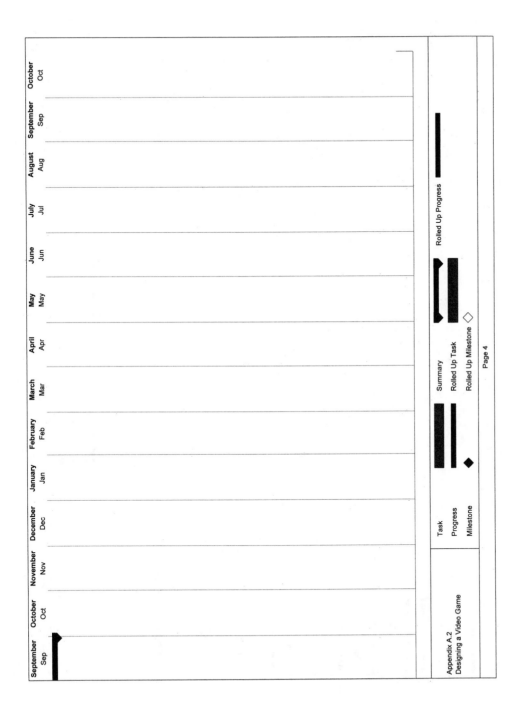

| September | October | November | December | January | February | March | April | May | June | July | August | September | October |
| Sep | Oct | Nov | Dec | Jan | Feb | Mar | Apr | May | Jun | Jul | Aug | Sep | Oct |

Appendix A.2
Designing a Video Game

Task	■■■	Summary	▼▼	Rolled Up Progress	■
Progress	■	Rolled Up Task	■		
Milestone	◆	Rolled Up Milestone	◇		

Page 4

333

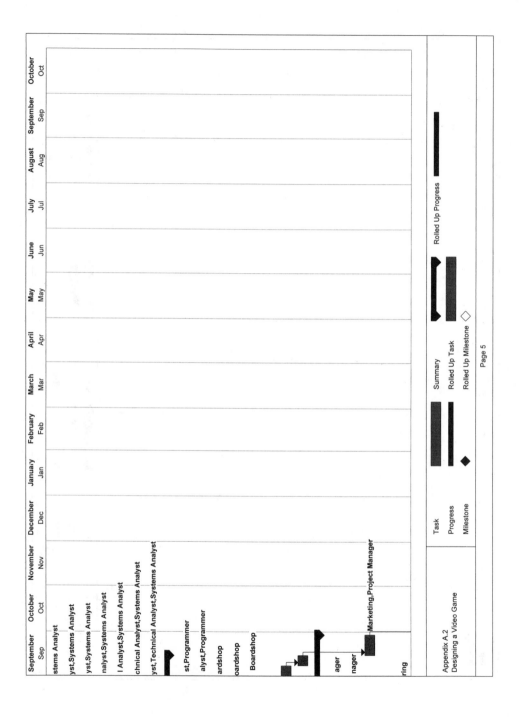

	September	October	November	December	January	February	March	April	May	June	July	August	September	October
	Sep	Oct	Nov	Dec	Jan	Feb	Mar	Apr	May	Jun	Jul	Aug	Sep	Oct

stems Analyst

yst,Systems Analyst

yst,Systems Analyst

nalyst,Systems Analyst

l Analyst,Systems Analyst

chnical Analyst,Systems Analyst

yst,Technical Analyst,Systems Analyst

st,Programmer

alyst,Programmer

oardshop

Boardshop

ager

nager

Marketing,Project Manager

ring

Task	▬	Summary	▬	Rolled Up Progress	▬
Progress	▬	Rolled Up Task	▬		
Milestone	◆	Rolled Up Milestone	◇		

Appendix A.2
Designing a Video Game

Page 5

September	October	November	December	January	February	March	April	May	June	July	August	September	October
Sep	Oct	Nov	Dec	Jan	Feb	Mar	Apr	May	Jun	Jul	Aug	Sep	Oct

facturing

9/29 ◆

Task	████	Summary	▐▌	Rolled Up Progress ▬
Progress	▐	Rolled Up Task	▐▌	
Milestone	◆	Rolled Up Milestone	◇	

Appendix A.2
Designing a Video Game

Appendix B

The Management Questionnaire

This management questionnaire was sent to over fifty managers and executives.

AN INTERVIEW GUIDE FOR PROJECT MANAGERS

Part I General Information

Name:

Organization:

Interview Date:

Title:

How long with the Organization:

Part II Project Management

1. Briefly describe typical projects managed in the past three years.
    a. Large projects (include project size in person-years, $)

Project   Size ($ & PYs)   Complexity   I.T. Environment

    b. Small Projects

2. How was the project initiated? (e.g., part of the I.T. strategic plan)
3. Was a business case prepared for the above projects?

Yes ____   No ____

   If yes, what were the key benefits identified as part of project justification.
4. Who were the stakeholders for the project?
5. Which application development tools were used?
6. How was the project managed?

   a. regular reporting to the steering committee (how frequently)
   b. project management tools used
   c. project management methodology used
   d. use of external resources to supplement project team
   e. exclusively external resources

7. How would you rate the success of this project?

____ Very successful ____ Moderately successful ____ Not successful

Explain:

8. Based on what you know now, how would you have managed the project?
9. Based on your experience in managing projects, would you manage small projects differently than large projects? Explain.
10. What are the five key attributes of successful project management?
11. What are five ingredients to watch for to ensure that projects do not fail?
12. A project manager should spend more time as a hands-on person and not planning and directing the project. Agree or disagree?
13. Any comments you wish to make about project management techniques or tools that could be of benefit to others?
14. Please rank the typical reasons for project failure in a descending order by placing a number at the right (we are interested in the top five):

Typical Reasons for Project Failure:

Reason	*Ranking*

1. Insufficient funding
2. Lack of technical skills
3. Insufficient time to complete the project
4. Lack of a project plan
5. Project team politics
6. Organizational politics
7. Lack of communications
8. Requirements not clearly understood
9. Lack of flexibility to accommodate changing requirements
10. Insufficient testing
11. Lack of post-implementation support
12. Technological limitations
13. Unrealistic expectations from stakeholders
14. Lack of project leadership and management
15. Other _____

_____

_____

Appendix

Management Survey Results—Why Projects Fail

O ver fifty managers were surveyed by the authors to build a broad base of project experiences. The survey gathered empirical information about reasons for project success, project failure, and other project issues. Responses to two questions on why projects fail are summarized in this section.

The following questions were included on the survey:

11. What are five ingredients to watch for to ensure that projects do not fail?
14. Please rank the typical reasons for project failure in a descending order by placing a number at the right (we are interested in the top five). [The complete list of possible reasons is shown in Table C.1.]

RESPONSES TO QUESTION 11

Because of the open-ended nature of the question, responses were diverse. A significant number of respondents felt that organizational and team politics were key contributors to project failure. Others felt that a lack of project direction—exemplified by a lack of executive commitment—fuzzy project deliverables, and poor project management were also key hindrances.

RESPONSES TO QUESTION 14

Table C.1 tabulates the number of respondents who selected a particular reason for project failure to be a top-five candidate:

The top five reasons for project failure selected by the respondents to this survey were:

TABLE C.1   Reasons for project failure

Typical Reasons for Project Failure	Rankings					
	1	2	3	4	5	SUM
1. Insufficient funding	4	2	2	3	5	16
2. Lack of technical skills	1	3	2	6	5	17
3. Insufficient time to complete the project			3	4	4	11
4. Lack of a project plan	9	2	6	7	5	29
5. Project team politics	2	5	1	2	1	11
6. Organizational politics	5	3	3	5	6	22
7. Lack of communication	6	11	2	5	6	30
8. Requirements not clearly understood	13	8	8	6	1	36
9. Lack of flexibility to accommodate changing requirements	1	7	1		4	13
10. Insufficient testing		2	2	1	1	6
11. Lack of post-implementation support	1		5			6
12. Technological limitations		1		2	3	6
13. Unrealistic expectations from stakeholders	2	5	9	5	7	28
14. Lack of project leadership and management	8	6	10	7	6	37
15. Insufficient commitment to project	2				1	3
16. Not learning from past experience	4	3	3	5	3	18
17. Insufficient scope control			1			1
Total Responses	58	58	58	58	58	290

1. Lack of project leadership and management (selected by 37 respondents)
2. Requirements not clearly understood (selected by 36 respondents)
3. Lack of communications (selected by 30 respondents)
4. Lack of a project plan (selected by 29 respondents)
5. Unrealistic expectations from stakeholders (selected by 28 respondents)

INTERPRETATION

Interestingly, a lack of technical skills was not selected enough times to appear in the top five, despite the fact that many employers spend a great deal of time asking prospective employees about their technical skills in painstaking detail. This observation is consistent with the successful projects discussed in Chapter 6, Why Projects Succeed—Case Studies, as projects using new technology succeeded with teams that needed to be trained on software/hardware after being hired.

Another observation is that organizational politics was selected in the top five 11 times, while project team politics was selected 22 times. Politics, on the whole, was selected 33 times. Had these two factors been combined on the survey, politics may have replaced unrealistic expectations from stakeholders in the top five. As mentioned in Chapter 4, Why Projects Fail, politics is a non–value-added activity that draws energy away from constructive project activities. Professionals who are preoccupied with trying to protect themselves, market their abilities, or play sparring matches with others are not focused on achieving a project deliverable. At a more insidious level, professionals who are engaged in playing the political game sometimes sabotage the project's potential for success if someone else appears to be getting the credit. After observing, and at times playing the political game, it seems that the game is difficult to eliminate entirely. There are not enough positions to go around, so team members will compete for advancement. Management at all levels should insist that this competition is played within some definite boundaries that will not allow the political game to degenerate into a free-for-all. All too often management does the opposite by rewarding those who play the game well, and by overlooking those who do not choose to participate. Is it any wonder that many projects are plagued by too much politics?

Another key area that was viewed as a major contributor toward project failure was "Requirements not clearly understood" and the related "Lack of flexibility to accommodate changing requirements." This is hardly surprising, considering some of the team dynamics at this particular phase of the project. Typically, IS has the skills and tools but not the business know-how, while the business community has the business knowledge but lacks the skill to pull this knowledge together to form a proper business requirements document. Also typical is the ongoing tension between the business and the IS communities. This gap is slowly closing as organizations evolve into operations where business planning skills are becoming embedded in the business environment and IT professionals provide services on an as-needed basis. This type of approach often results in a project that is managed jointly by IS and the business community. Though a bit awkward at first, this method of managing a project is quite successful, and a number of large organizations are evolving toward this mode of operation.

Table C.2 provides a cross reference of chapters the reader should consult in order to avoid each of the top five failure factors.

TABLE C.2 Top five failure factors

	Failure Factor	*Refer to Chapter(s)*
1	Lack of project leadership and management	1, 2, 5, 6, 7
2	Requirements not clearly understood	5, 6, 7
3	Lack of communication	5, 6
4	Lack of a project plan	4
5	Unrealistic expectations from stakeholders	3, 5, 6

Other chapters in the book deal with the other factors of failure that were identified in the management survey.

Appendix

Management Survey Results—Why Projects Succeed

The key ingredients for attaining project success as noted by the respondents to the management survey included having executive support, a good project plan, and good project management. Specific responses to the survey question are included in this section. These are grouped into categories to allow for easier comprehension.

SPECIFIC RESPONSES

Commitment

☐ Organizational support, executive support

Human Skills

☐ Skillsets, competent team, competent users
☐ Ability to identify problems quickly and resolve them
☐ Excellent facilitation/coordination
☐ Coaching ability
☐ Good communications
☐ Good interpersonal skills

□ Able and cooperative participation of project members and clients
□ Ensure scope is clear; get the right people involved/committed

Management

□ Project plan
□ Good project management
□ Expectation management
□ Conflict management
□ Monitor and following effectively through project lifecycle
□ Ability to separate funding from deliverables/resources
□ Accurate planning and budgeting
□ Full application of sufficient resources
□ Accurate tracking of progress

Requirements

□ Clear understanding of objectives
□ Full understanding of objectives

Planning

□ Agree on acceptance criteria
□ Contingency planning
□ Prioritization
□ Establish critical success factors

Resources

□ Adequate human and budget resources
□ Resource management

Standards

□ Ability to deliver quality

INTERPRETING SURVEY RESULTS

It has been said that the project manager is quite a unique individual. This person has to understand the technical intricacies of a project, have a keen understanding of human behavior, and be well organized. Not only is this person expected to deal with the daily gauntlet of project-related issues, he or she is expected to understand and provide encouragement to the staff whose personal problems have overflowed into the work environment. The results from the survey were not surprising and were consistent with the responses received for why projects fail. Projects succeed when:

☐ The project manager possesses superior management and human skills.
☐ The project manager takes the time to understand the dynamics of his or her working environment. This includes the players, their relationships, strengths, and weaknesses.
☐ The project manager takes the time to know his or her staff, and understand their individuality and orientation. This is crucial in motivating staff members.
☐ Project sponsorship is unequivocal.
☐ The project is funded adequately.

Of particular importance is that players get along, share a common goal, have talents and experience, and have a burning desire to succeed. Many successful projects also have a high-ranking champion who plays a pivotal role in ensuring that the project gets the attention and resources it needs. Such a champion is usually talented, has a mind for the big picture and details (where appropriate), and is highly regarded within the organization.

A clear understanding of a project's deliverables, how to reach them, and continuous monitoring are also strong contributors toward project success.

Appendix

E

Management Forms

This appendix contains sample forms that complement the material in Chapter 8, Project Resourcing—Roles, Responsibilities, and Monitoring.

Form 1 *MONTHLY STATUS REPORT*

A monthly status report is prepared by the project manager for the benefit of the project sponsor and the stakeholders. The monthly report will include the following:

Project Identification: This section will contain project identifying information including project name, project number (if applicable), project manager and names of the project team.

Project Summary: This section will include a brief summary of the project including scope.

Project Resources: This section includes project budget and actuals, planned project completion date, and percentage project completion. The dollar variance will also be included.

Accomplishments: This section includes key project accomplishments such as completion of a prototype, completion of logical design, and completion of integration testing.

Obstacles: This section includes any obstacles encountered by the project team, such as resignation of two programmer analysts, changed specifications, delay in the delivery of hardware, and so on.

Objectives for the Next Period: This section includes objectives for the next month, such as completion of physical design, completion of acceptance testing, and installation of software.

Form 2 ESTIMATING PROJECT COSTS

Project Name:

Project Number:

Project Sponsor:

Project Manager:

Project Cost Summary

1. People costs.

Position	Person-days	Cost/Day	Total Cost
Project Manager			
Data Analyst			
Business Analysts			
Systems Analysts			
Programmers			
Testers			
Documentation specialist			
Total			

2. Equipment costs (expressed monthly over the duration of the project).

Type	Cost
Hardware	
Software	
Communications	
Maintenance	
Total	

3. Travel and other costs (expressed monthly over the duration of the project).

Total People, Equipment, Travel and Other Costs

Form 3 PROJECT COST REPORT—DELIVERABLES BASED

Deliverable	Target Date	Actual Date	Planned Budget ($)	Actual Budget ($)	Variance ($)	Rem.
1) Data Collection						
2) Data Analysis						
3) Logical Design						
4) Functional Specs						

FORM 4   Project Cost Report—Resources

Time and Cost Analysis

	Report for the month of:		December, 199x	
	Plan	*Actual*	*Variance*	*Totals to Date*
(a) Resources (Hours)				
1) Programmer				
2) Programmer Analyst				
3) Systems Analyst				
4) Data Analyst				
5) Project Manager				
(b) Resources ($)				
1) Programmer				
2) Programmer Analyst				
3) Systems Analyst				
4) Data Analyst				
5) Project Manager				

FORM 5 MONTHLY TIMESHEET

Organization:

Project Name:

Project Number:

Team Member's Name: _____

Key Project Activities: _____

_____

Regular Hours Worked

	Monday	*Tuesday*	*Wednesday*	*Thursday*	*Friday*	*Overtime*	*Total*
Week 1:							
Week 2:							
Week 3:							
Week 4:							
Week 5:							
Total							

Remarks: _____

_____

Team Member's Signature   Authorized Signature

FORM 6   PROBLEM REPORT

Organization:

Project Name:

Project Number:

Client Contact:

Problem Number:

Problem Reported by:

Problem Description (provide relevant supporting documentation):

Problem Resolution:

Date Problem Reported:	Date Problem Resolved:
Resolved by:	Latest Status:

FORM 7   PROJECT CHANGE REQUEST FORM

Organization:

Project Name:

Project Number:

Client Contact:

Description of the Proposed Change:

Reason for Change (provide supporting documentation):

Impact of Change:

      a) Cost impact:

      b) Time impact:

Type of Change Required:

__ Program Change   __ Report Change

__ Screen Design Change   __ Documentation Change

__ Other (explain)

_____   _____

Requested by: Approved by:

FORM 8 PROJECT DELIVERABLE—SAMPLE SIGN-OFF DOCUMENT

Organization:

Project Name:

Project Number:

Client Contact:

Project Manager:

Authorization is hereby given to proceed with the conversion and implementation activities for the project. We confirm that the specifications and details contained within this document meet all deliverables and requirements outlined for the system integration test phase.

_____   _____

Requested by: Approved by:

FORM 9   PROJECT ACCEPTANCE FORM

Organization:

Project Name:

Project Number:

Client Contact:

We have reviewed the project deliverables and agree that:

☐ The project meets the acceptance test previously set forth.

☐ The documentation meets the criteria previously set forth.

_____   _____

Reviewed by: Approved by:

A Generic Project Lifecycle

A typical project lifecycle consists of the following phases, roughly in the order shown.

1. Establish initial staffing (architect, manager, data modeler, business analyst, steering committee).
2. Conduct feasibility study to establish a business need. This includes a cost/benefit analysis.
3. Build the project team.
4. Capture business requirements.
5. Confirm business requirements.

   ☐ Prototype
   ☐ Documentation
   ☐ JAD sessions

6. Establish pilot project (requirements and functionality).
7. Establish/design technology infrastructure.
8. Expand project team.
9. Establish milestones and project plan.
10. Build pilot.
11. Iterative testing.
12. Confirm audit/control requirements.
13. Implementation.

14. Review of important lessons.
15. Design of support infrastructure.
16. Post-implementation review.
17. Expand scope of pilot to include other business functions.

Several phases can be conducted at the same time. For example, development is started before analysis is complete. If this is done, management must be handled skillfully to avoid missing business requirements or creating other types of chaos on a project.

Bibliography

Band, Williams A. (1991). *Creating Value for Customers*. New York: John Wiley & Sons.

Beer, Stafford. (1985). *Diagnosing the System*. New York: John Wiley & Sons.

Bender, Paul S. (1983). *Resource Management*. New York: John Wiley & Sons.

Carson, William M. (1994, Spring). "Strategic Planning and the Anatomy of Change," *Journal of Management Consulting*, 30–39.

Davenport, Thomas H. (1993). *Process Innovation, Reengineering Work through Information Technology*. Boston: Harvard Business School Press.

Jones, Capers. (1994). *Assessment and Control of Software Risks*. NJ: Yourdon Press.

Jaques, Elliot, & Clement, Stephen. (1991). *Executive Leadership, A Practical Guide to Managing Complexity*. MA: Cason Hall & Co.

Gibbs, W. Wayt. (1994, September). "Software's Chronic Crisis," *Scientific American*, 86–95.

Gilbreath, Robert D. (1986). *Winning at Project Management*. New York: John Wiley & Sons.

Hammer, Michael, & Champy, James. (1993). *Reengineering the Corporation, A Manifesto for Business Revolution*. New York: HarperCollins Books.

Microsoft Project 4.0 Product Documentation, Microsoft Corporation.

Reynolds, George W. (1992). *Information Systems for Managers*. New York: West Publishing Company.

Walton, Mary. (1990). *Deming Management at Work*. New York: G.P. Putnam's Sons.

Weinberg, Gerald M. (1985). *The Secrets of Consulting*. New York: Dorset House Publishing.

Index